Praise for the 1st Edition

"Nancy Napier is a very wise woman who writes with courage and deep insight. She shows us how to bring all we are into a whole, without which life remains incomplete."

—Larry Dossey, M.D., author of *Prayer is Good Medicine*, *Healing Words*, and *Recovering the Soul*; executive editor, *Alternative Therapies*

"In this simple, elegant offering, Nancy Napier has distilled the spiritual teachings of the world's great wisdom traditions into a practical treasure chest of meditations and methods for living with joy, compassion, creativity and an awareness of the Sacred."

—Joan Borysenko, author of *Fire in the Soul: A New Psychology of Spiritual Optimism* and *Guilt Is the Teacher, Love Is the Lesson*

SECOND EDITION

Sacred Practices

FOR CONSCIOUS LIVING

SECOND EDITION

Sacred Practices

FOR CONSCIOUS LIVING

NANCY J. NAPIER

LOTUS BLOSSOM PRESS

© Nancy J. Napier, 2016

All rights reserved. This book, or parts thereof, may not be reproduced in any form without permission from the author.

ISBN-13: 978-0-9658191-4-5
LCCN: 2016911398

Lotus Blotssom Press
301 E. 79th Street, #10F
New York, NY 10075

Distributed by Itasca Books

Design by C. Tramell

Printed in the United States of America

Acknowledgments

TO THE SECOND EDITION

In the original edition of this book, I had many acknowledgments, which follow below. For this edition, I acknowledge some of the same people again, with special thanks. First, I want to express my deep gratitude to my sister, Carol Napier, for the journey we have taken together over these years. Consistently, our time together is nourishing, inspiring, and filled with laughter, and I so appreciate our friendship. I also want to again thank Carolyn Tricomi, my sacred sister in Spirit, for all the support and inspiration we have shared over so many years. As life takes us on our individual journeys, there is forever the thread of connection that guides us consistently back "home", where we share what we have learned along the way. To Dorothy Pietracatella, how to give adequate thanks for magnificent explorations of embodied presence? I have learned so much and feel so much more grounded because of all we've done. To Terra Tirapelli, my thanks are boundless for the years in which she has shared her wisdom and friendship with me. Again and again, she has been a source of inspiration, healing, and just plain relief to my whole body-mind being. To Diane Poole Heller, I offer so much gratitude for her faith in me and her steadfast friendship and support. She is a marvel of healing creativity and skill and I am privileged to know her and to be her friend. To Karen Peoples, Maxine Stein, and Christine Comstock, more thanks for continuing to hang in all these years, and for holding a space where I can continue to be me—a work in progress. I also want to express my gratitude to Jen Silacci for the enormous gifts she brought to my mother at a most important time in my mother's life, and for her contributions and participation as an honorary member of the family. And, there are the many friends and colleagues—sacred sisters and brothers—whose wisdom and presence have filled my life in recent years. For each and every one of you, I am profoundly grateful. I am not the same person I was when I wrote the first edition of this book because of the deep and meaningful times we have all spent together, and because of the constant cross-fertilization we share as we explore our experiences while helping others—and ourselves—to become more than we ever imagined.

Acknowledgments

TO THE FIRST EDITION

For a book such as this, which reflects thoughts, approaches, and experiences gathered over a lifetime, it is a challenge to know where to start to thank those who have played a meaningful role in its creation. Many teachers, authors, workshop leaders, and other wise people have influenced my thinking over the years. I have listed many of them under Recommended Readings. Even so, I am certain I have inadvertently omitted other important sources of inspiration and I apologize for that.

On a personal level, there are many people to whom thanks are due. First is to my grandmother, Ellen Hickman, for offering me a perspective on reality that continues to influence my experience of the world. To Pat Jobling, I can't give enough thanks. As with my previous books, her editorial input has been invaluable; I especially appreciate her incisive mind and her willingness to challenge my thinking, plus the time and effort she put into helping me meet deadlines and give input whenever I asked for it.

To Beverly Decker, Al Higgins, Suzanne Iasenza, and Carolyn Tricomi, I offer my deepest gratitude. Within this group of friends and colleagues, I have found a level of mutual respect and acceptance unparalleled in my experience. I thank them for the journeys we have shared together and their presence in my life as sacred sisters and brother who have offered, by their very presence, a continuing training ground for interpersonal and transpersonal deepening.

Special thanks go also to my sister, Carol Napier, who has become a closer friend, confidante, and playmate than I ever imagined possible; to Maxine Stein, who continues to be a source of challenging questions and inquiries that invite me to dig deeper into myself; to Karen Peoples, who is my spiritual sister and whose life journey constantly nourishes and supports my own next steps; to Maria Teresa Velez for always accepting what she fondly calls my "Martian" side; to Susan Benton, for her willingness to be available as both computer expert and friend; to Mikki Meyer, for her friendship, support, and all around "good sense"—and for suggesting from the beginning that this book reflect my own transpersonal process; to Virginia Goldner, for her wisdom and encouragement; to Christine Comstock, for many provocative and stimulating conversations and for her stabilizing presence; to Joe Adler and Lois Powers Adler for offering their love and centering presence during a particularly transformative time in my life; to Brooks Barton and Lorraine Weiss, for creating opportunities to deepen and expand my capacity to experience and imagine the shadow as well as the light; to Joan Pfitzenmaier, for what she has taught me about my body; to Debra Reiss, for a friendship begun at just the right time; to Rochelle Gordon, for inspiring discussions; to Sperry Andrews, for offering experiences of shared consciousness; and to my mother, Jean Hickman, for providing a context within which transpersonal realities have always been welcomed and supported.

To Susan Munro I offer special thanks for her continuing faith in me and her generous efforts on behalf of my

ACKNOWLEDGMENTS TO THE FIRST EDITION

work, to Margaret Ryan for editing this book with an open heart and focused mind—the book is better because of her comments and suggestions; to my agent, Jim Levine, for his support, and an extra thanks to Suzanne Iasenza for the title of the book.

Contents

Prologue: Fields, Visible and Invisible Worlds......I

Introduction to the Second Edition............III

Introduction to the First Edition.............IX

Chapter 1 **Fields Within Fields Within Fields**
Oceans of Consciousness 1

Chapter 2 **The Shadow**
An Invitation to Dynamic Wholeness..............7

Chapter 3 **Compassion and Lovingkindness**
Living with an Open Heart 41

Chapter 4 **Getting Grounded**
Nurturing Yourself as Bodymind 73

Chapter 5 **Practicing Mindfulness**
Living Consciously 107

Chapter 6 **Gratitude and Generosity**
Engaging a Prosperous Life 137

Chapter 7 **Oneness and Interconnection**
The Interplay of Collective Consciousness. 165

Chapter 8 **Creating Possibility**
The Dance of Intention and Synchronicity 195

Chapter 9 **Opening to Your Optimal Future**
Saying Yes to All You Can Be 227

Chapter 10 **Intuition and Well-Being**
Affirmation, Prayer, Guides, and
Other Nonlocal Phenomena 255

Chapter 11 **Living Consciously**
Putting It All Together 283

Recommended Readings. 315

Index . . . .

Prologue

TO THE SECOND EDITION

The Western perspective on reality has changed a good bit since I was a child. What began in public consciousness as a Newtonian world run by mechanistic, predictable rules has become, over these years, a quantum reality characterized by probabilities and the emerging notion of a *multiverse*. There is also a more dynamic relationship emerging between Western cosmologies and indigenous perspectives on nature and reality. Having grown up in a home where multidimensionality and interactions between visible and invisible realms of reality were taken for granted, my soul sings at the new openness to issues of non-rational ways of knowing, near-death experiences, life after death, the presence of nature spirits, and more.

This second edition of *Sacred Practices for Conscious Living* reflects changes in my thinking, and an increased willingness to express my inner experiences more openly and directly that has emerged in the years since the first edition was published. It also reflects the shifts in our culture at large, where people are now much more open to a multidimensional worldview than was the case when I originally wrote *Sacred Practices*.

Introduction

TO THE SECOND EDITION

As I sit down to finalize this new edition of *Sacred Practices for Conscious Living*, it is 2015 – fully 18 years since the original version of this book was published. At the time I first wrote it, *Sacred Practices* represented my deepest heart space, reflecting the aspects of my life I loved most, and continue to love even now. Since that time, this part of my life has remained the most central focus of how I move through each day and how I understand the world and my place in it.

When I was very young, my grandmother began to teach me her version of spirituality, reflecting the multidimensional world in which she lived. She taught me about reincarnation and karma, about different planes of existence, about healing and intuitive knowing. Her words were inspiring and sometimes frightening, as she shared stories of beings who live in non-physical realities, and who interact with us all the time. As a child, and then as an adolescent, I took in her words as truth, even as what she taught at times frightened me. Because of my own not-quite-conscious awareness of what was around me in the invisible realms, I sensed that there was much more to reality than my five senses registered. It wasn't until many years later that I realized how very different my fundamental assumptions about reality were, compared to the majority culture in which I lived. I realized, then, that my grandmother oriented me to a perspective of the world that is much closer to indigenous realities than it is to an everyday, Western understanding of how the world works and our relationship to it.

That early foundation shaped my development as a person and as a psychotherapist. I recall how, when I began to practice in New York City in the early to mid-80's, I began to get calls from people who wanted to be able to combine their psychotherapy experience with their spiritual lives. For me, there was never any question that spiritual experience and psychological experience were each their own valid source of information and inspiration, and it was natural for me to offer people an opportunity to explore both realms of consciousness equally. I recall the first time someone cried with relief that she was able to tell me about a spiritual experience and not have it interpreted as a delusion or as a misperception created by an underlying psychological issue.

I also remember when a close friend told me that I reminded her of a kite, flying way up in the sky with lots to share and yet no one had hold of the kite string down here on the ground. She made it her mission to help me find language to share my spiritual reality with people in a grounded and useful way, and I will always be grateful for that timely support. It coincided with my uncomfortable discovery that being from California and living in New York City meant I had to work very hard to be seriously accepted in my field. I hadn't known that there was a sense, for some East Coast people, that Californians are flaky. In response to this discovery, my spiritual life went underground publicly and only found its expression through the pathway of hypnotherapy, which thankfully gave me a language where I could speak about spiritual realities in non-threatening and more grounded ways.

Over all these years, I have become more able to translate and share my spiritual beliefs, practices, and experiences with others, and the publication of *Sacred Practices* was a major step in making that integration in my work real and tangible. This new edition of the book is another step, and includes even more of what has always been part of my spiritual world, but was not as overtly expressed in the first edition. I am grateful to have an opportunity to update the book, as the pieces that I've added are the glue that holds together, and makes comprehensible, my understanding and experience of my spiritual world.

In this new edition, I've added new content to existing chapters and begin with a new Chapter 1. What I add will reflect the deepening I have experienced over these years, along with a greater willingness to share my thoughts and experiences about two main themes that have shaped my world from the earliest time I can remember.

The first is that we live within fields of energy and information (language that wasn't available back then) that contain the wisdom of all humanity—all life, actually—over all time. These fields of information and energy are ever-present sources of support and inspiration, and are available in every moment. I call on these fields in my work and life every day. My awareness of them and belief in their existence shapes much of how I move through daily experiences. The work of Rupert Sheldrake, the British biologist, has been profoundly meaningful. His writings on *morphic resonance* and *morphic fields* offered me a way to speak about information fields in a coherent and understandable way.

The second theme is that our world is populated by countless intelligences and beings that inhabit frequencies of reality that are not visible in our usual, three-dimensional world and yet with whom we interact and collaborate all the time, usually without realizing it. Those who were fortunate enough to have been taught to follow a more indigenous-based perspective, where a world inhabited by non-physical beings is a given, have always had this rich and dynamic worldview. The particular paradigm I grew up learning, and which I still experience as my primary map of the world, emphasizes the presence of beings called "devas", along with a panoply of nature spirits and other non-physical beings. In Sanskrit, the word "deva" means *shining one* and can be translated as the word "angel." Other invisible beings might include deceased people, "ascended" spiritual beings and the like, although these are less part of my everyday experience.

The one request I make of you as you read the book is that you take all that I say as a metaphor, or a creative description of my particular experience, and let it touch you only in the ways that resonate with you. I have the deep feeling that reality is profoundly pliable, if I may put it that way, and that there very probably isn't actually a "right" or "correct" view or description of it. Whenever I teach a workshop, I generally end with suggestions to "allow everything that was said or experienced to find its place in the back of your mind, where the field of creative possibility receives the seeds of new ideas. Then, allow yourself to notice what finds its place because it resonates with you and your life experience, as you allow the rest to become compost." For me, it's essential that each of us engage our spiritual and daily lives as the unique beings we are. To live a life of kindness and not doing harm to others is, I believe, a universal invitation to all humanity. Beyond that, I believe there are no answers that are right for everyone, no one-size-fits-all approach to how to move through, or understand, life.

Nature thrives on diversity, and it's no different with our deeply intimate relationship with reality. I remember my grandmother saying to me that if someone someday were to tell me that it's impossible to perceive other dimensions, I might think of it as if someone who has no physical sight told me that there is no blue sky or clouds. The sky and clouds are outside their experience. I have always taken that to mean that some of us see things that others don't; and others of us hear, sense, or otherwise perceive things that may seem strange or impossible to most. For some people, multidimensional awareness is a given—it's as simple and obvious as being aware that there are white clouds in a blue sky. For others, the thought that other dimensions may be perceived is unappealing at best and crazy at worst.

For that reason, if you're uncomfortable with the idea of multidimensional awareness, or with perceptions that go beyond the five senses, this book probably isn't for you. On the other hand, if you're interested in what might be possible, or if you already perceive with more than your five senses, perhaps there will be information here that will be useful or inspiring for you.

It is, most of all, my deep pleasure to take this journey with you.

Nancy Napier
New York City, January 2016

Introduction

TO THE FIRST EDITION

It takes a lifetime to find our way home. We all suffer from homesickness, a longing to return to a cosmic household we have never left.

—Sam Keen

As this book took form, I realized it was going to require a level of personal sharing that I hadn't felt compelled to do in my previous writing. *Sacred Practices* draws on my own "journey home" to a more solid sense of self—a journey that has been colored, from the earliest time I can remember, by an awareness of spiritual realms.

The book could as easily have been called *Lessons My Grandmother Taught Me*, as it reflects many of the assumptions and themes I learned at my grandmother's knee. She was a rather proper, Victorian woman who also happened to be a healer, a clairvoyant, and a Theosophist, with a deep belief in, and experience of, multiple dimensions of reality.

Over the years, I have come to appreciate the impact my early experience has had on how I understand and function in the world. As a young adult, I turned my back on my grandmother's teachings, but I couldn't shut out my own perceptions and experiences of a world where visible and invisible dimensions constantly interact. Discovering books written for the public on the subject of quantum physics—with descriptions of a reality that reflected the one I inhabited as a child—began to give me a way to reconnect to, and translate, some of what my grandmother had taught me. This effort has culminated in a practical and evolving worldview focused on the marriage of spiritual and material realities.

My hunger for spiritual instruction has led me to read many books and explore many approaches to the sacred. All are reflected in these pages, but now they have become so intertwined—such a complex fabric of ideas and assumptions—that I no longer know what came from where. My background as a psychotherapist and hypnotherapist adds a perspective that supports a belief in change: that it is possible for all of us to move in new directions and to deepen the richness of daily experience.

Current brain research has validated this assumption. We now know that the brain is plastic, that it is open to change throughout life, and that it is capable of new learning and new connections in ways we never before would have imagined possible.

Fundamental to my worldview is a belief that reality is more fluid than we are able to perceive with our five senses, that there is a dynamic, creative interplay between seen and unseen dimensions of reality. Within this context, we are all *co-creators* of the life we experience.

Spiritual approaches around the world and throughout history have taught us how to enter unseen worlds and draw on them for inspiration and guidance. These traditions offer various means by which we may find a sense of meaning and purpose, regardless of which particular set of beliefs we follow. If the sacred practices you engage support and deepen your sense of wholeness and well-being, you have discovered a treasure beyond words. If these same practices allow you to contribute positively to your world, everyone benefits.

THEMES AND ASSUMPTIONS

In choosing which elements of my worldview to share on our journey together, I felt like a prospector panning for gold nuggets in a mountain of experiences and ideas. Eventually, I recognized a pattern of assumptions and repeating themes. Because these assumptions and themes weave their way throughout the book, I want to describe them here, to make what is invisible in my thinking visible and clearly defined in words.

Reality as an Art Form

Think of mud pies and finger painting and the pleasure you may have had as a child when you had permission to play in the goo, to make as big a mess as your creative impulses inspired. Then, imagine the primordial ooze from which life on this planet emerged—the slime and muck becoming a womb for unbridled creativity.

Basically, physical reality is an organic, messy, dynamic, and creative art form, comprised of unexpected shapes, sizes, and colors originating from an unseen and unknown source. At nonphysical levels of reality, human consciousness, too, has its own kind of messiness. It is filled with mixed feelings and beliefs: hopes and fears, love and hate, triumph and despair. It is also a wellspring of creativity, encompassing a variety and range of sentiency and thought. Consciousness also expresses its creativity within all the other species with whom we share the earth, increasing the complexity of elements in the constantly evolving art form that is our reality.

Is there an underlying intelligence behind all that emerges from the primal chaos? Who is the artist playing in all the goo? On a small scale, could it be that we humans, as individuals, somehow interact with each other and physical reality in ways that have an effect on what gets created in the world at large? This inquiry arises from one of the assumptions I bring to this journey, which is well captured in the familiar saying, "If you think you *can* do something—or you think you *can't*—you're right." This quotation encompasses my first assumption about reality: *We experience what we expect.*

Sometimes called self-fulfilling prophecies, these beliefs, fears, and assumptions about who we are and how the world operates combine to shape our perception of the quality and nature of our daily experience. In *Sacred Practices*, we will explore how we can become *conscious co-creators* of our reality, rather than remaining passive recipients of what our unexamined expectations reflect back to us.

It's important to know that there is a difference between seeing ourselves as co-creators and believing that we personally create every single thing that happens to us. Reality is too big and too complex for that. What we may be able to do, though, is learn to cooperate with the events, challenges, and experiences that come our way in a manner that enhances our quality of life. By looking at practices that deal with creating intentions, making conscious choices, living mindfully, and working with affirmations and rituals, we can create a storehouse of concrete tools with which to shape our expectations—and our personal reality.

My grandmother taught me many things about her perspective on reality and one of the things she talked about were group events—those larger contexts in which groups rather than individuals had experiences and outcomes that sometimes overrode individual intention. What this touches in me is how it resonates with our emerging understanding of the power of systems, and the impact of transgenerational trauma and healing, on the individuals connected to these systems.

In my work as a marriage and family therapist, as well as in my work with trauma, I have seen example after example of the power of family and societal systems to influence and impact individuals who are part of them. Even children who have been adopted, and who have no biological relationship with the transgenerational family system into which they are adopted, may develop illnesses and other physical conditions that are more characteristic of their adoptive family than of their biological family.

When I touch into my belief in collective consciousness, I am in awe when I think about all the ways in which we inevitably impact one another through the global information field that is collective human consciousness. It's one of the things that motivates me to be committed to kindness and compassion. Given that I believe that we each contribute to these larger collective fields in every moment, I want my contribution to be as positive and healing as possible. And so, when we explore the subject of living with intention and "reality as an art form", I want to make sure we keep the collective in mind, as well as our unfolding experience as individuals.

Life is Like a Kaleidoscope

My second assumption has been demonstrated by quantum physics and can be visualized as a kaleidoscope: no matter how fixed or unchanging the world may seem, *we actually live within a context of infinite probabilities*. We assume that reality is characterized by qualities of certainty and predictability but, in fact, it is more like a kaleidoscope which, when turned, shifts into new, unanticipated patterns. I use the image of the kaleidoscope from time to time because it so beautifully conveys in material form the tremendous array of possibilities that exist in what we imagine to be a fixed, predictable world.

With a kaleidoscope, there's no way to predict what pattern or colors will emerge next. There's just a turn of the tube and the surprising discovery of what has fallen into place.

What is exciting about the idea of probabilities and a fluid rather than fixed reality is that it means *we don't have to settle for how things are at present.* Instead, we have the power to turn the kaleidoscope of our lives by consciously making choices about the quality of life we want to have. In this way, we set in motion possibilities. We'll explore a number of ways to do just that in the chapters that follow.

Also, working with the metaphor of the kaleidoscope reminds us that wholeness is always present and that any shifts we experience represent elements of that wholeness moving from foreground to background. Throughout life, in any of the shifts and changes we experience, there is forever and always this underlying context of wholeness and, even in the presence of enormous change, nothing happens outside this fundamental reality. Aspects, qualities of ourselves, circumstances in which we live, all shift from foreground to background with nothing lost. Everything simply rearranges itself to allow new experience and may do so in totally unexpected and new ways.

We're All in This Together

One of the teachings of my grandmother's legacy is that each of us is but one cell in an unimaginably large organism. This early learning shapes a third basic assumption of mine: *each of us, as individuals, is part of One Life that expresses itself in an infinite variety of forms and consciousnesses.* Just as the individual cells in our bodies depend on the health and vitality of the overall organism, so do we, as individuals, depend on the well-being of our total organism—our species, every other life form, earth itself.

From this assumption emerges a companion idea that we each contribute to, and draw from, a collective consciousness comprised of the thoughts, feelings, expectations, impulses, beliefs, and wisdom of every one of us, past, present *and future*. To my delight, a number of years ago I discovered that there now is some research to support this idea, which we will explore in a later chapter.

I believe that we are never truly alone on our journey through life—however lonely we may feel at times—because we have constant access to the combined experience of our species throughout all time.

I would add, now, that we are also never alone because of all variety of intelligences and beings that journey with us in non-physical realms of reality. In my work as a psychotherapist, I have been comforted and held over all these years by the belief that I never work alone and that, in fact, it isn't I, as an individual self, who actually does the work. I experience myself as a violin, but not as the musician. I keep myself polished and well tuned and, in that way, I am able to be played creatively and well by the life that lives me.

There's More to Reality Than Meets the Eye

Because of my grandmother's emphasis on recognizing and interacting with invisible realms of reality, my world has always consisted of at least six senses. A pervasive assumption I bring to this book is one that I've already mentioned: *reality consists of both visible and invisible dimensions interacting in dynamic ways.*

Early on, I learned to be cautious about these "extra senses" when out in the world. My grandmother was concerned with what people would think, and she constantly warned me about the dangers of sharing with others what I learned from her. Were she alive today, I think she would be heartened by the emergence of popular books on spirituality, near-death experiences, miracles, and angels. She would discover first-hand that her experience of the world no longer needs to be hidden.

In later chapters we'll explore how to develop your "sixth sense" and look at the benefits and uses of intuition to enhance the quality of daily life. We will also look at how to access inspiration and a greater sense of connection with spiritual dimensions of experience.

Life Is Sacred and Has Meaning

There has not been a day in my life when I haven't felt a deep sense of meaning and purpose. For this reason, no matter how hard the struggle, how sharp the pain, how discouraging the moment may be, I have always had the belief that my life has meaning. This is the foundation to which I return, a place to lick my wounds, to rest and begin anew.

Experiencing a sense of purpose in life gives us a home base from which to draw nourishment, support, and encouragement and from which to venture forth. It is the place within which we connect to the *sacred*.

For me, what is sacred is that indescribable source of life and consciousness that cannot be named, and that pervades every particle of reality, visible and invisible. As we explore the sacred and the practices that acknowledge and honor it, allow yourself to make sense of this journey within the context of your own understanding. It is my belief that the diversity of religious and spiritual traditions emerges from the underlying impulse of the sacred in the first place, so whatever your tradition may be, you are celebrating the sacred in powerful and meaningful ways.

Also, this particular planet seems to thrive on diversity, as I mentioned earlier. Because of that, I believe that the sacred revels in the many paths humans taken to touch into it and, in a very real sense, the more approaches that emerge, the more Life seems to like it!

Life Is About Wholeness

As a psychotherapist, the theme of wholeness is important in my work with people. Wholeness—in a person or in the world at large—leaves out nothing. It encompasses light *and* shadow, that which is beautiful *and* that which is not, the sacred *and* the profane, the loved *and* the hated.

From studies on ecology, we know that we ignore the interconnectedness—the inherent wholeness—in the natural world at our own peril. This danger exists as well within individuals, communities, and cultures. To deny or disown any aspect of the whole of reality leads to the potential for destruction of the environment, the extinction of other species, wars, abuse, and social injustice on individual and collective levels. To affirm and embrace the existence and necessity of contrasting, even contradictory, elements in ourselves and our world leads to greater equilibrium and well-being.

The journey toward psychological wholeness is a deep, underlying urge to express the totality of our being. This is a theme we will return to again and again. When we can acknowledge our potential for both good *and* bad, we create the possibility of a greater degree of choice about how we want to be. By experiencing our whole selves, we not only promote a greater sense of self-acceptance and well-being, we also increase our capacity to tolerate and respect difference and diversity in others.

Living in the Present Moment Means Really Being Alive

A major theme that pervades just about every page of this book is the importance of learning to live in the present moment. Called *mindfulness* in Buddhist practice, being aware of what we are thinking, feeling, sensing, and doing right here, right now, offers us a means to be active participants in the reality we create.

If we are not awake, we cannot make choices. When our attention is anywhere and everywhere except on what we're doing and experiencing right now, we lose an opportunity to make moment-to-moment choices that create a life we enjoy living. Instead, we often end up immersed in frustration, boredom, or some other kind of discomfort. To become more mindful is one of the most valuable gifts you can give yourself in your journey toward greater psychological wholeness.

Suffering Is an Inevitable Part of Life

A final theme – and one that may at first sound more morbid than it actually is — involves the recognition that suffering is an inevitable part of *everyone's* life; it is impossible to escape experiencing some kind of suffering sometime in life. We share a capacity to suffer with all creatures. No sentient life form is exempt.

When we live consciously, we recognize that suffering isn't a signal that something is wrong, but rather a reminder to awaken to the source of the suffering and discover what may be done to ease it. When we can't ease it, suffering becomes a call to draw on practices that allow us to move through it with the least pain, the least wear and tear we can manage. We can at least be present with ourselves, experiencing what life demands in this moment.

Recognizing that suffering is part of life allows us to develop increasing compassion and lovingkindness toward ourselves and others. Whenever we suffer, we recognize that we participate in a universal experience. To embrace the reality of suffering allows us to stare it straight in the eye; we no longer have a need to fend it off or hide from it. Perhaps, because of this, we gain the freedom to choose to help ease suffering whenever and wherever we come upon it.

BRINGING IT DOWN TO EARTH

All the exciting possibilities inherent in a multidimensional, quantum view of the world won't mean much to us if they don't affect and improve the quality of daily life. To help ground these possibilities in everyday ways of being, each chapter contains numerous experiments—things you can do to translate new perspectives into action—and guided meditations that offer an opportunity to *embody* the possibilities.

The experiments are arranged in a way that builds and deepens awareness of the theme being explored. Some are quite simple, others more complex. With each, I invite you to engage in activities that will add directly to your understanding and experience. There is a power in *doing* that cannot be felt through words alone.

Some of the guided meditations are brief, while others are quite long. Whenever you feel it would help, you might record the meditations so you won't need to refer back to the written version during your experience. In each, draw on as many of your senses as you can engage comfortably. The more alive your experience, the more vivid your understanding will be of what the journey seeks to share.

Many of these experiments and guided meditations emerge from my own experience. Others are derived from a variety of spiritual and religious traditions. *All* are informed by the deep well of wisdom directly available to all of us, intuitively, from our collective consciousness.

First and foremost, these sacred practices are offered as *practical* ways of being and doing in the world today, right now. An added benefit is that they also enhance an underlying sense of aliveness, of spiritual and psychological vitality—the fruits of a life lived with greater awareness, ease, and equanimity.

Each chapter develops ideas that continue throughout. We begin where the world began—in the primordial muck and goo. For us humans, that means the realm of the disowned self. From there, we expand into an array of explorations, including the domain of our *bodymind* being, the power of gratitude and generosity, mindfulness practices, and so on, culminating with a review of rituals and practices that allow you to create sacred space wherever you find yourself. For this reason, I recommend that you first read the book from front to back; then, as you discover themes that resonate for you in the present moment, you can concentrate on the chapters and exercises that best support your current journey.

Most of the chapters contain examples of how people have applied these practices in their lives. All the examples, except my own, are composites and draw from the experiences and stories of relatives, friends, colleagues, clients, and workshop participants. Formulating composites is like writing a novel. It allows me creative license, even as it protects the privacy of people I care about. When my friends think they recognize themselves in what I know to be a composite example, I say, "Great!" The fact that the examples feel so familiar says something about the quality of our shared consciousness and universal experiences.

At the end of the book is a list of suggested readings for each chapter. You'll find some books listed for more than the one chapter; others will apply specifically to a given subject. As with all reading lists, this one will be limited and out of date by the time it appears in print! When choosing inspiration resources, perhaps the best method is to go to your favorite bookstore and notice what jumps off the shelf into your hands.

For those of us who are now so familiar with the Internet and all the resources to be found there, I would add the following: youtube and other resources on-line offer countless sources of inspiration and guidance for your spiritual journey. Just as books had a tendency to leap out at us when we had to go to bookstores all the time, I've found that links show up seemingly out of the blue to guide me to my next best resource. Also, given that it's been 18 years since the original reading list was created for the first edition of this book, there have been countless books and resources created since that time. They create a rich source of inspiration to support your journey.

AND SO WE BEGIN...

For the journey, I invite you to pack an open mind, a healthy dose of curiosity, and a willingness to suspend disbelief as we explore living consciously—what it encompasses and the unique gifts it holds for each of us—and allow the sacred to accompany you every step of the way. Even as you travel within the boundaries of your own psychological landscape, remember that you are never alone. Instead, at all times, we each journey alone *together*.

Chapter 1

FIELDS WITHIN FIELDS WITHIN FIELDS

Oceans of Consciousness

One of the things that has changed most for me in the past 18 years has been my willingness to share more openly how I experience and live in reality. Increasingly, I invite people in professional and public presentations to take time to attune to the field of information, wisdom, creativity, and experience that we generate whenever we come together in a group. I also invite people to pay attention to other fields of collective energy and information they swim in all the time—to actively hold the awareness that all of us constantly and inevitably contribute to and draw from these fields.

Along with an increasing emphasis on attending to and consciously invoking these fields, I also focus, increasingly, on inviting people to sense into their own presence, as well as the presence of any group in which they participate. Presence is that quality we radiate all the time, wherever we are, whatever we're doing. It's our "tone", our "color", the "flavor of us" that naturally emerges from us no matter where we are, no matter what we may be doing.

For example, take a moment now to find the place inside you that you identify as your *home base* or your *landing place*, your *core presence* when you settle into yourself. In a very real sense, this is a place in you that has never been hurt, that is like the deep currents in the ocean that are undisturbed by what goes on up on the surface.

Then, sense into the quality and tone you radiate into the world from the inside out. What kind of energy do you emanate? What qualities coming from you reach out and touch the people you interact with along the way? Does your presence bring calm, or does it elicit agitation in others? In every moment, we radiate our fundamental energy presence and this has an impact on everything around us.

Later in this chapter, we'll explore an exercise and guided meditation you can do to connect with your own presence and to sense the presence of any group to which you may belong. This includes any learning context—a class, a workshop, an ongoing study group—your church, synagogue, mosque, temple. Any group you encounter has its own unique presence, just as every person you encounter has his or her unique presence.

There are also global sources of presence, fields of information and energy within which we participate with people we will never know and who will never know us. For example, those of us involved in healing practices generate a field that I call our *global healing presence*. It touches every single person all the time and is comprised of all the men and women, all over the planet, in every human community, who work with healing practices of every kind on behalf of every conceivable life form, across all time. For me, it is a dynamic presence that I have come to count on throughout my workday.

In the chapter on Oneness and Interconnection, I write about *nonlocal* reality and *morphic fields*. Here, I'd like to focus on some of the current explorations that have emerged in recent years to support the idea of information and energy fields. It's a fundamental shift in thinking, and takes us naturally and inevitably into a more indigenous worldview.

For example, in the documentary, *The Living Matrix*, various scientists, teachers, healers, and lay people share their experiences and speak of the emerging idea that our bodies organize themselves around the *information* they receive, rather than just responding to medications we might take. These stories offer inspiration and support to the many people who have experienced spontaneous healings within non-traditional contexts, or as a result of prayer or sacred ceremonies.

In his experiments with *morphic fields*, Rupert Sheldrake demonstrates that we constantly participate in collective information fields that impact us all the time. One of his experiments involved the London Times crossword puzzle. He tracked the speed and correct answers in those who did the crossword puzzle on Saturday evening compared to those who did it on Monday morning. Essentially, he found that by Monday morning people completed the puzzle much more quickly and his hypothesis was that they had an easier time of it because the answers were now in the information field, put there by the people who worked the puzzle all weekend.

Information fields include many aspects of reality, some of which we Westerners have a hard time accepting or taking seriously. For example, the indigenous world embraces a much larger and dynamically interactive reality than does our Western point of view. For many indigenous peoples, the fact that we live in a larger context than what our five senses can perceive is a given. That there are non-visible beings who interact with us on a daily basis is also a given. We in the West have become accustomed to thinking of these kinds of assumptions about reality as naïve or based on fantasy. For people who live in societies that take these wider realities as a given, they are anything but fantasies.

For example, in some indigenous cultures, the experience of spirit guides and power animals are part of coming into one's own as a spiritual being. Rituals, prayers, blessings, and other activities that honor non-visible helpers, ancestors, and other sources of support along the way are part of the fabric of daily life. Honoring them is as natural as honoring the living. One of the things that has touched my daily life powerfully is the inclusion of rituals to honor my home and all the visible and non-visible beings who are part of my home environment. Whether or not what I believe and experience constitutes an "actual" reality, my sense of living within a dynamic context of non-visible support nourishes my quality of life and deepens my sense of ongoing gratitude.

I have lived within the concept of collective consciousness for most of my adult life and, even more clearly now, of the presence of different *frequencies* of reality. I am keenly aware of, and interested in, the subject of frequencies as they represent differing aspects and qualities of consciousness and reality. In a forthcoming book, *Living Paradox*, I talk a lot about how we can attune ourselves to particular frequencies depending on what quality of experience we want to have. Within collective consciousness, I believe that we can attune ourselves to frequencies that put us into a dynamic relationship with fields of, say, kindness, compassion, nature's intelligence, and guidance from various non-physical sources, and more.

As a reminder, just as we have access to deep sources of wisdom within our collective consciousness, we also have the capacity to resonate with collective fear, anger, hatred, animosity—with *any* kind of feeling of which humans are capable. For this reason, it is useful to develop a habit of noticing where you resonate emotionally and mentally in any given moment, as the focus of your attention will also point to the collective frequency with which you resonate in that moment, the frequency that automatically amplifies your personal experience.

So, as we go forward with this journey into sacred practices, I invite you to keep in mind that we travel within fields of consciousness that we contribute to and draw from all the time—most often unconsciously. These fields of consciousness may be sources of inspiration and guidance, as when we attune ourselves to Nature's Intelligence and open to what Nature wants to teach us about how to live with her. Or, when we choose consciously attune to the field of information that enfolds the human experience of healing the body and open ourselves to what might impact our understanding or unexpectedly inspire us, we are able to draw on that collective wisdom.

The key here is that we constantly participate in fields of information that are well beyond our individual awareness and knowledge. These fields of awareness contain collective wisdom, experience, and creativity upon which we can't help but draw all the time. They also contain collective fears, animosities, historical antagonisms which we may not want to magnify in our personal lives. As we move through this book together, remember that everything we explore has its place as both individual awareness/wisdom and as collective fields of immense and expansive wisdom from human experience over all time.

Chapter 2

THE SHADOW

An Invitation to Dynamic Wholeness

> *To honor and accept one's shadow is a profound spiritual discipline. It is whole-making and the most important experience of a lifetime.*
> —*Robert A. Johnson*

One of the most powerful journeys we can take together is through a land of shadows wherein lurk the disowned, unacceptable parts of ourselves. This landscape can be a frightening place to visit, or it can become a source of discovery and deepening into greater psychological wholeness and vitality—and a more skillful capacity to live consciously. It's up to each person: if we allow ourselves to become willing explorers of the terrain of human fallibility, we can experience a rich and satisfying journey. If we are attached to an image of ourselves that allows no faults to show, looking at our shadow side can be a distinctly uncomfortable experience.

I would add, now, that the journey into wholeness not only offers us an opportunity to feel more empowered and able to be present, but it also invites us into an expression of authenticity that nourishes us in the presence of others. To trust oneself to be able to express wholeness, to be fully human, generates a sense of safety with other people that is impossible to experience when we have parts of ourselves we need to hide. The flow of self-expression and presence emerges spontaneously and easily when we so deeply embrace our wholeness that our authenticity becomes the only natural place from which to live.

For me, the content of this chapter is both the most exhilarating and the most challenging to convey. It is difficult and uncomfortable, in many ways, to look at disowned parts of ourselves. But such a process provides a powerful means of achieving a greater sense of wholeness and self-acceptance. I can only tell you that it has been one of the most profound parts of my own journey.

Here, we ask ourselves to tolerate our own "messiness", to become comfortable with the knowledge that we are inherently imperfect beings, that we are frail, greedy, selfish creatures—even as we are magnificent and beautiful expressions of the sacred in action. Repeatedly, I have observed people—myself included—blossom as they develop a lighter, more forgiving relationship with their own fallibility. Somehow, it seems, our willingness to know ourselves as whole people, warts and all, stimulates a capacity to be more comfortable in our own skin and to express ourselves more openly, spontaneously, and congruently.

And so, we begin our journey by deepening our awareness of the most hidden aspects of ourselves that comprise our *shadow*. For each of us, the shadow consists of disowned and unexpressed aspects of our personalities—positive as well as negative—that had to be hidden when we were young; those elements of our natural self-expression that were disapproved of, punished, humiliated, or otherwise judged as unacceptable by the important people in our lives.

Disowning parts of the self is an unconscious, self-protective mechanism that allows us to fit in as we grow up. The shadow doesn't exist only for people who come from troubled families or for individuals with particular kinds of psychological problems. The psychological dynamics that create the shadow provide a necessary and inevitable adaptation to our interpersonal world. We *all* participate in creating shadow selves that contain whatever qualities we were not allowed to express openly.

When we don't acknowledge our own wholeness — when we continue to push away parts of ourselves that are a source of shame, fear, or anger — these parts erupt unexpectedly and create all manner of difficulty. For example, we may unconsciously make enemies of those who act as the representatives of the very characteristics we can't tolerate in ourselves. We create a world of "us versus them", in which we spend an inordinate amount of time trying to get *other* people to change. In fact, if we would only stop and look in a mirror, we would discover the source of much of our discomfort and displeasure staring back at us.

The shadow is not just a garbage can filled with ugliness and unsavory characteristics, however. *It also contains all manner of human potential and creativity* — for both good and ill. It's a treasure chest filled with aspects of personal power, talent, resourcefulness, and other useful and positive attributes that, for whatever reason, were not tolerated or celebrated when we were young.

The shadow also contains *more than* disowned attributes, be they positive or negative. It holds all the known elements of our personalities that are outside conscious awareness most of the time. Think of the movement of sunlight around the planet. In the same way that it can't be daytime all around the world at the same moment, we can't be totally self-aware at any given time. Half the world is in darkness when the other half is in daylight, just as some parts of ourselves are in shadow while others are in conscious awareness. What counts is that we develop the capacity to allow our awareness to move as naturally as sunlight, to illuminate and acknowledge any aspect of us that may rise to the surface.

Since much of the shadow is unlovely, when I work with people to uncover disowned aspects of themselves, many initially find the work unsettling. Even so, what excites and inspires me about the process are those times when I experience these same people coming alive with an increased sense of self-acceptance and personal power. For this reason, even though the shadow contains elements that may be downright undesirable or unfriendly, acknowledging and accepting them as part of our inevitable wholeness is profoundly liberating.

There are important reasons for connecting with the shadow side of ourselves before moving on to explore "lighter" and more expansive attributes of the spiritual side of being. It's been my experience that burrowing down into the shadow offers a natural, spontaneous way to move into a more expansive, lighter sense of self, just as an inherent urge for equilibrium constantly moves us toward wholeness. It's as though the deeper we go, the more open and transparent we become.

On the other hand, when we seek expansive states without including our shadow aspects, an equal tendency toward internal balance plunges us spontaneously into the muck and mire to bring us back into wholeness. By beginning with the shadow, we consciously *choose* when and how we want to engage aspects of ourselves that are a source of discomfort, even as we open to more expansive, compassionate, and accepting states of being.

I have a deeply personal reason for honoring shadow work. My experience of my grandmother was that she sought the light at the expense of acknowledging the darker aspects of her being. As a result, her need to control and overpower those around her often was acted out on me and other family members. My grandmother had no conscious notion that she could act as a tyrant. Her self-image allowed awareness of only those aspects of her personality that reflected her role as healer and spiritual teacher.

In these past 15 years and more, I have deepened my understanding of my grandmother's place in my life. I understand, in clearer ways now, how the shadow side of her expression served to offer me a way to keep my own rudder moving in a direction of wholeness. So often, the very people who challenge us also serve us. They become our most potent teachers, and my grandmother was one of these people for me on so many levels, in so many ways.

The Beauty of Light and Shadow Combined

Wholeness requires us to discover the contribution and value of *both* light and shadow. Everywhere we turn, we find evidence of the constructive and creative interplay of these two elements. When the artist draws or paints, she uses shading to create depth and complexity. The writer depends on the conflict between good and evil, or suffering and joy, to drive his stories. In a concrete and tangible way, without the presence of both light and shadow, we couldn't read the words on this page.

In nature, sunlight without shade can burn us; shade with no sunlight can create a chill. Light plays in the shadows of a forest, dappling the ground and bringing tree trunks, branches, and leaves into bold relief against the darker background of the shade created by the trees. The serene, often dramatic, beauty of a forest emerges in the play of light and shadow. With only light, a forest would appear flat, like the artist's drawing without shading. With only shadow, there wouldn't be much to see.

In human experience, we learn the delicious gift of happiness even more powerfully when we have also tasted sorrow. Eating a beautiful meal is even more satisfying when we come to it hungry. Friendship becomes more precious when we can recall times we've been alone. As these examples demonstrate, all light or all dark, all one thing or the other, reveals only half a picture. To be whole means, of necessity, to embrace *both*.

The Power of Projection

The shadow becomes dangerous—within and between individuals, and collectively in society—when we insist on pushing out of conscious awareness those aspects of ourselves we just can't bear to own. When this happens, the disowned contents travel in one of two possible directions. We run the risk of expressing disowned parts of ourselves unconsciously and indirectly—as my grandmother did—when we say something cruel without realizing it, or when we deny we're angry and, say, eat instead of acknowledging our true feelings. The second, and potentially more destructive, possibility is one I mentioned earlier and it bears repeating: *when we project our disowned parts onto others and make them into the enemy, we assign to them what we refuse to see in ourselves.*

Projection operates in interpersonal relationships, at work and, on a larger scale, within communities and between groups and nations. When we can't bear to know that we feel vulnerable or helpless about a situation, for example, we run the risk of projecting that intolerable feeling of helplessness onto others and then vilifying or attacking them. At unconscious levels, the attack is an attempt to destroy *in them* the very thing we can't acknowledge or experience *in ourselves*.

Think of a co-worker or friend who drives you up a wall. Your reaction may stem from the fact that you think she dresses inappropriately. With a feeling of righteous indignation, you want to tell her to get her act together and dress in a more subdued or business-like manner. After doing some shadow work on your feelings, you may discover that your co-worker or friend mirrors a daily battle you had with your parents about how you had to dress before you were allowed to go to school. Rather than being fully aware of how humiliated or angry you felt when they wouldn't let you wear what was in style, you may have pushed those feelings into the shadow. Now, decades later, you are activated by this person's ability to wear the kinds of clothes you wanted to wear but couldn't.

On a collective level, people of color are often the recipients of shadow projections. Due to a history of slavery and the presence of shadow dynamics, many white people experience an underlying fear of people of color. These reactions reflect a discomfort with difference that arises, in part, from unintegrated aspects of the self, and in reality have nothing to do with people who are perceived as a dangerous "other".

The pay-off for projecting shadow parts is that, if we succeed in assigning negative traits and characteristics to someone else, we feel more comfortable in two ways: we access a soothing feeling of self-righteousness—we're better than someone else, and we don't have to think about how *we* might possess the hated characteristics as part of our own inevitably-flawed human makeup.

Someone once said that whatever any human being is capable of being or doing is also within the capacity of each and every one of us to be and do. This is a discomfiting thought for a lot of people, because most of us don't want to know that we have the capacity to hate, kill, rape, torture, or steal. Take a moment to think about the vilest, most despicable behavior you can imagine. What's it like to know that the capacity to behave in that way exists in you, too—that it is part and parcel of being human? When you move into an experience of psychological wholeness, you can tolerate knowing this about yourself because you also know that you have the choice as to whether you would ever *act* on this inherent human potential.

The same is true on the positive side of things. Think of a person you admire in a heartfelt way, someone you feel is the kind of person you'd like to be. It's important to know that you also have, as your own potential, the capacity to actualize the qualities you so admire in the other. You just haven't allowed these qualities to come alive in yourself yet.

There are real benefits in discovering your own projections. If, for example, you are someone who has had to disown your desire to be first in line, the first person served, the most important person at a meeting, owning this part might help you overcome an inappropriate tendency to put yourself last, even as you resent doing so. Acknowledging your wish to be first allows you to have the choice to ask for what you want, rather than forcing you to be indignant when other people get what *they* want instead.

Or, if you can acknowledge your disowned fear, for example, rather than projecting it onto others by getting angry at people who are afraid to try new things, you create an opportunity to learn how to manage your own fear more effectively. As long as the fear is *out there*, in the other, you are helpless to deal with how the unconscious power of your projection shapes the quality and tone of your daily life.

The other side of projection is "god-making"—idealization. In addition to projecting negative qualities onto people, each of us also has the capacity to see in another the disowned power, love, and talent we cannot own in ourselves. For example, I recall a friend's description of an affair she had that began as if it were a dream come true and ultimately ended up a bitter disappointment. When she met the man in question, my friend experienced him as someone who was strong and reliable, a person she could turn to for love, comfort, and security. She assumed he had plenty of money and that he was a "solid citizen." Much to her dismay, she eventually discovered that he was quite irresponsible and that he turned to her to get *his* needs met without giving much in return. As she explored what had attracted her to this man, my friend realized that she had projected her own strength, reliability, and competency onto him. She didn't know she could experience in herself the very qualities she believed she could get only from a man.

My friend's experience isn't at all unusual. Many of us project positive disowned parts of ourselves onto other people and then think it is only through being connected to them that we can have good feelings. We hand over power to people without realizing that the power resides in us, as well. We lose ourselves through this kind of projection and never recognize, let alone actualize, our own deep potential.

Discovering Aspects of Your Own Shadow

It's not too hard to discover telltale signs of your shadow, once you get the hang of it. Shadow projections elicit powerfully intense reactions, usually accompanied by a strong feeling of self-righteousness or justification for how you feel.

When I was younger—thank goodness it was many years ago now—I always had at least one friend whom no one else could stand. This person was invariably difficult to get along with, had an abrasive personality, and was generally unlikeable. People often asked me why I was friendly with these kinds of people, and I had no good answer. It was only as I began to explore my disowned self that I discovered the service these friends provided as they expressed the disowned nastiness and unfriendliness that lived in me as part of my shadow.

Having grown up in a family where being good was a prerequisite to being safe, I learned early on to hide angry and "unreasonable" responses, even from myself. As I matured and went through therapy, I became increasingly able to tolerate and value these parts of me. Slowly, over time, they were transformed into adult resources, which automatically became the ability to stand up for myself and to disagree with people in more open, direct ways. Now I no longer need friends who express in themselves what is disowned in me. Not only am I more comfortable in my own skin, but I also feel more at ease with other people.

A friend of mine discovered a disowned part of herself in relation to her work. Coming from a family that had strongly valued education, my friend was told from the earliest time she can remember that she would grow up and go to college. All through school, she took college preparatory courses and set her mind on a career as a professional. She followed through and succeeded. She got a job at a good school and began to climb the professional ladder towards tenure and a full professorship.

Throughout her schooling, and then in her academic position, my friend experienced a particular kind of impatience with students and colleagues who took time off to, as she called it, "play". She realized that her reaction was irrational, but it was also powerful and felt completely real and justified. Simply put, she felt that she was better than these people because she worked all the time. She was at school early and stayed late. She published. She went to conferences. She read journals.

What she didn't realize was that the students and colleagues who knew how to take some time off and enjoy life mirrored a disowned part of herself that she couldn't bear to acknowledge. If she had consciously felt how much she longed to be an artist, and how much she liked to be outdoors in nature, she would never have been able to fulfill her family's expectations.

As she connected with the disowned artist in herself, my friend began to shift her emphasis at work. Even with the sadness she felt at the lost years spending time doing something she didn't actually care about, she experienced an underlying excitement and energy around reclaiming a part of herself that yearned for expression. She didn't leave her work. She was so well established at this point that her profession provided a regular and reliable source of income. Instead, she created more time off and used it to develop her artistic skills. If she hadn't discovered her disowned artist, she would have continued to drive herself mercilessly in a job that didn't fully express her creative urges, and she would have continued to experience contempt for those who honored their true needs.

The shadow has so much power only because it is completely outside conscious awareness. Because of this, it gets "its way"—until we take the time to pay attention to it. In fact, its sole "job" is to remain outside conscious awareness. In the exercises and guided meditations that follow, you are invited to access different aspects of your shadow. First, you'll have an opportunity to explore parts of yourself that most people would consider unacceptable, unsavory, or undesirable. You'll identify these parts in several ways. In the experiment, I invite you to look for qualities, reactions, thoughts, and feelings that represent aspects of your shadow. In the guided meditation, you'll then have a chance to experience these aspects symbolically, represented as objects, people, animals, colors, or a "felt-sense".

As you move through the experiment and guided meditation, give yourself permission to be curious and open-minded about what you discover. Keep in mind that the more you know about your whole self—the more you acknowledge and accept the totality of your entire range of being—the more comfortable you will be in the world and the safer you are for others to be around. It is the unacknowledged and unconscious aspects of the shadow that slip out sideways and cause unexpected and unwanted problems with others. Becoming conscious of the disowned parts of yourself allows you a greater choice in how you want to *be*.

In the second set of exercises, you'll explore your "golden shadow", that realm of disowned resources, talents, power, and abilities that you had to push out of awareness, for whatever reasons. It may surprise you to discover that it is often more difficult to reclaim your golden shadow parts than it is to acknowledge your unsavory characteristics. This is because your family, school, peer group, or religion probably didn't celebrate or approve of your particular talent. When you explore the golden shadow, allow yourself to bring the same curiosity, open-mindedness, and willingness to be whole that you bring to your work with the darker side of yourself.

I recall a workshop participant who discovered a golden shadow part that represented a degree of competence she hadn't previously imagined she had available. When she first experienced this part of herself, she was exhilarated. Soon, though, mixed feelings arose. As she explored her discomfort, she realized that to become more competent in managing her daily life she would have to shift her relationship with her father. No longer would she be his "little girl." She hadn't realized that she was worried about taking this part of herself away from him. As she explored her response further, she realized that it didn't have anything to do with the present day. It was an old, unexamined response that no longer had meaning for her.

For a friend of mine, connecting with the golden shadow was an equally powerful experience. At first, he thought he had revealed a negative part of himself, because the qualities conveyed a sense of disowned entitlement. This was a person who always presented the image of being a "nice guy", someone who accommodated others and rarely stood up for himself. Represented symbolically as a Zorro figure, this emerging part knew exactly what he wanted. My friend's mixed feelings ranged from excitement to a fearful conviction that no one would like him if he became more assertive. As part of the journey of integrating a conscious awareness of his natural feelings of entitlement, my friend also had to resolve his insecurities around not being liked. This turned out to be a rich and satisfying journey for him, which is a response many people have when they discover previously disowned aspects of their golden shadow.

As you identify shadow parts and get to know them consciously, it is useful to track the shifting body states that accompany the process. For example, if you were to become aware of a previously unacknowledged part of you that was deeply suspicious, you might notice a sudden tension throughout your body that wasn't present before. Connecting with disowned feelings of playfulness, on the other hand, might be accompanied by a feeling of expansion in your chest or excitement in your stomach. Sadness might bring a sensation of heaviness in your heart, whereas anger or fear might create a gripping sensation in your gut.

These physical responses are different for each of us. Tracking them as they come and go offers yet one more way to become familiar with the qualities and responses in those parts of ourselves we have pushed outside conscious awareness.

Also, attending to our physical sensations allows us to integrate awareness more powerfully. As you explore the disowned self, your shadow side, the more you can bring the experience into your body, the more fully you'll be able to integrate these aspects of your wholeness. And, the more whole you feel, the more authentic you'll be able to be in the world, the more comfortable with yourself you'll be able to be.

Whichever aspects of the disowned self you address, the important thing to be aware of is that your goal is not to bring *all* the qualities in your shadow into active expression in your life. Rather, it is to experience psychological wholeness and self-acceptance in a real and dynamic sense. It is also important to stress that the point of reclaiming aspects of your disowned self isn't to extend carte blanche acceptance to everyone or to behaviors that truly are destructive and unacceptable to you. In reality, there *are* people who do things that hurt others, that aren't helpful, that are what we might call "evil". There really *are* characteristics that you will not want to express or support in the world. Instead, as I mentioned above, an important outcome of doing shadow work is developing a greater ability to *choose*, moment to moment, how and who you want to be, and be with.

MAKE IT REAL
EXPERIMENT #1:
Identifying Disowned Parts

This experiment invites you to dive right in and begin to become increasingly conscious of the shadow parts of yourself.

- Make a list of people you absolutely cannot stand. They may be family members, friends, neighbors, people at work, famous people—anyone who causes a strong, knee-jerk reaction in you.

- Now, list the qualities you dislike in them. You may describe them as evil, greedy, insensitive, lazy, dishonest, or whatever it is about them that sends you up a wall. Also note what it is about the *quality* of what they express that is so upsetting to you. Take some time to describe it.

- For the guided meditation that follows, choose one quality you would like to explore, and imagine that the quality describes something about *you*. Notice how you feel about it. If you're like most people, your first response is likely to be, *"I'm not like that!"*

- Let yourself become aware of the judgments you have about this quality and notice the strength of your need to convince yourself it couldn't possibly illustrate something about *you*. Wonder a bit about how you would feel if it *were* possible that this quality describes a part of yourself. Be honest with yourself. This exercise is just between you and you. There is nothing to lose. What you have to gain is a dynamic wholeness that brings a greater sense of self-acceptance and well-being.

- Finally, wonder how this quality, once accepted and understood, might be transformed into an unexpected and *valuable* resource, or into a greater awareness of impulses and responses you want to *know about* but not *express*.

GUIDED MEDITATION #1:
Discovering Disowned Parts

To begin this meditative journey, settle yourself comfortably and be sure to invite mixed feelings to come along. It's natural to have them when dealing with shadow aspects, and you don't want to leave out any part of yourself. As you settle in, give yourself a few moments to focus on your breathing. Pay particular attention to the ways in which your body settles even more when you follow your exhalation all the way to the bottom of the breath.

Allow yourself to become aware of the still point that exists between one breath and the next. There is no need for strain or struggle. Just notice the still point without demanding that it be either expansive or brief.

Now allow your body to continue to find its own level of comfort as your mind moves into your shadow journey. Imagine that you are walking along a path in a landscape that feels safe and supportive to you. It is a place where the sounds, smells, colors, and shapes all come together to convey a sense of being in the right place at this moment in time. If no imagery comes to mind, ask yourself what you would sense if you could be aware of moving along a path. There's no need to see where you are; it's enough to sense it.

Up ahead is one of the cages in which you have stored disowned parts of yourself. In this particular cage, there is a symbolic representation of the shadow aspect you've chosen to explore. It may appear as an object, a person, an animal, another kind of creature, anything at all. Be sure to allow yourself simply to discover what is in the cage, without any preconceptions or demands that it be this or that. If you happen to find that the cage is empty, emptiness itself is a quality and can represent an aspect of your shadow self.

What are your first impressions of the shadow part in the cage? Notice the shape, color, and qualities that come into your awareness, without editing or pushing away anything that comes spontaneously. Trust your unconscious to give you whatever impressions you need this time. Notice your reactions and responses to this part of yourself. Be sure to allow any mixed feelings you might have. Is curiosity one of the feelings you discover?

For just a moment, allow yourself to blend with the part of you that is in the cage, so that you can experience it from the inside. As this part, what is the first thing you notice about yourself? How do you feel about what you discover? What's it like to experience this part of yourself? Spend a few minutes exploring your awareness as this part.

Now move outside the cage. What do you feel? Can you imagine the resource that this shadow part might hold for you? What if it were to provide you with the opposite quality of what you experienced when you first discovered it? For example, if it represented fear, might it become a source of courage?

Take a few moments to review your experience. You may want to think about what it would be like if you were to unlock the cage, if you haven't already, and allow yourself to get to know this part better over time. Remember, there's no rush. If you want to keep the cage locked, that's fine, too. Just keep in mind that whatever has been locked away in the cage is part of your being, that you are less than whole—and have less than your full energy available— as long as it is disowned.

When you're ready, begin to come back, knowing that you can return as many times as you'd like to get to know this part better. You may be surprised to discover that, even after one visit, a new and positive energy or capacity related to this part becomes more available to you, or that you feel more open, or stronger, in some new way.

Once you've reoriented to the here and now, take a few moments to wiggle your fingers and toes, to make sure you're all the way back. Then allow yourself some time to write down your experience.

EXPERIMENT #2
Identifying Golden Shadow Parts

This experiment builds on the one you did on the darker side of the shadow by asking you to explore the disowned parts of yourself that are desirable qualities and talents.

- Take a few moments to think of people you really admire. List their qualities, what it is about them that moves you the most. Now consider that these qualities may actually reflect disowned parts of you.

- Once you have identified these golden shadow qualities, ask yourself what family rules you will break as you bring these qualities more actively into your life. Notice, especially, any fears you have about the reaction of people close to you if you were to actualize these golden shadow qualities.

GUIDED MEDITATION #2
Accessing Your Golden Shadow

Follow the same format as the meditation for the darker side of the shadow, only this time choose a golden shadow quality you have projected onto someone. Allow the cage to contain whatever quality arises as you search for something that you know is a positive aspect of your being. Pay particular attention to what you experience in your body as you blend with this part of yourself. Notice, as well, the quality of your thoughts and emotions as you experience yourself from the perspective of this golden shadow part. Take time to imagine how your life might be changed by consciously embracing the qualities and abilities that become available within this part of you.

Shadowboxing: Projecting Disowned Parts into Partners

Projection of disowned shadow parts really gets cooking in intimate relationships and family interactions. The people with whom we are most closely connected often receive our most powerful projections. In working with couples, I repeatedly see the ways in which disowned parts of the self are put into the other person—at which point the unconscious goal of the relationship becomes an ongoing effort to change the other by exorcising and eliminating the characteristics partners can't own in themselves.

A classic example of how projection works in an intimate relationship was provided by a couple who had been together for only a short time. They had gotten married after a brief courtship and hadn't really had an opportunity to get to know each other very well before they began living together. Early on, the husband discovered that his wife was more timid than he had realized. He found that, whenever wanted to take her on a skiing trip, or scuba diving, she didn't show the kind of enthusiasm he wanted her to have. Instead she often expressed fear and hesitation about going on the excursions he so enthusiastically planned.

Initially he allowed her the benefit of the doubt. Love conquers all, and his rose-colored glasses allowed him to overlook his growing irritation at her lack of delight at his recreational suggestions. Eventually, though, he grew increasingly angry at what he called her "unreasonable fear." He experienced her as a "wimp" and just wanted her to get her act together and come with him without comment.

It was only as he got in touch with his own disallowed fear that his reaction began to clarify. It turned out that, as a child, he had fallen into a lake and nearly drowned. Because of his father's attitude about the accident – that it wasn't any big deal and he should jump right in again and ignore his fear—my client's initial response of terror got shoved into his shadow self. From that time on, whenever he met someone who expressed fear, he felt impatient with the other person—just as his father had with him. He couldn't understand their fear and, more importantly, didn't want to be around it.

After working on reclaiming his natural reaction to almost drowning, his irritation with his wife lessened and, eventually, he stopped pressuring her. Between them, they worked out vacations that allowed him to do the things he loved and gave her the option to participate or not, depending on how she felt at any given time. He no longer had to push her fear away because he didn't have to push away his own. In addition, he began to acknowledge and experience more of his own fear and, over time, became less enamored of some of the riskier activities he had so hotly pursued early in his marriage.

MAKE IT REAL
EXPERIMENT #3:
Identifying Disowned Parts Projected into Loved Ones

In this experiment, allow yourself to review your relationships with family members, your significant other, and close friends.

- To begin, look for areas where you find yourself reacting intensely to any of these loved ones. Identify what it is they do that elicits your impatience, contempt, anger, hatred, fear, or sense of helplessness. Ask yourself the following question: If only they would change _____ or become _____ [*fill in the blanks yourself*], then I—or the situation—would be fine.

- Reflect on the descriptions you put in the blanks and then do the guided meditation on discovering disowned parts to find out if you have projected part of yourself into the other person. Chances are that *any quality that evokes an intense reaction in you points to a reflection of a disowned part of yourself.*

Shadowboxing in the Community

We seek to kill off in the other what we cannot acknowledge in ourselves. The potential destructiveness of unconscious shadow projections operating on the collective level of communities and nations is truly stunning. Even a cursory look at the condition of world politics at this point in human history is enough to take my breath away when I pay attention to how many people are fighting one another over political ideologies, borders, ethnic differences, and religious beliefs, and how many people around the world are homeless and starving. I can't help thinking that the human species as a whole is having a shadow crisis, a veritable orgy of projection of disowned parts.

As hard as it may be to do, it is important for each of us to ask what part we play, as individuals, in this collective need to blame others for being different from ourselves. While there is no way one person can make a powerful impact on such a general and pervasive expression of human activity and consciousness, it *is* possible for each one of us to do our own work with the intention of taking at least some of the shadow pressure off the current world crisis.

In the experiment that follows, I invite you to become aware of your individual contribution to collective shadow-boxing and offer you an opportunity to explore how you might reclaim whatever part of yourself you have put into the fray.

It helps to remember that we project aspects of ourselves that we fear or intensely dislike. We also project negative aspects of ourselves onto others when we are afraid of the difference that people or groups who are unfamiliar to us may represent. We manage many of our insecurities through this process, so allow yourself to initially be willing to be uncomfortable as you engage this process of tracking your patterns of projection.

MAKE IT REAL
EXPERIMENT #4:
Reclaiming Generalized Shadow Projections

- In this experiment, think of groups of people you dislike or even detest. Identify their characteristics and what it is about them that makes you feel self-righteous, angry, afraid, jealous, indignant, contemptuous, or whatever. Then, take those characteristics, one by one, into guided meditation #1 or #2.

- Over time, as you work with these upsetting characteristics in the guided meditation, notice any parallel changes you become aware of in your real-life interactions with people from these groups. Pay particular attention to those times when you no longer find yourself experiencing the kind of discomfort, judgment, or other negative responses you might have had before you took a look at your own issues.

Experiencing Yourself as a Kaleidoscope

As I mentioned in the Introduction, one of my favorite metaphors for representing the intricacy of psychological wholeness is the kaleidoscope. The kaleidoscope I have in my office has many pieces of clear glass. Only now and then do a few pieces of bright purple, blue, or orange glass appear. As clients turn the tube, pattern after pattern emerges, each different from the one before. Once in a while, the purple or orange pieces appear and change the quality of the patterns altogether.

For me, the important meaning of the kaleidoscope as a metaphor for wholeness is that at no time are new pieces added. Every change in pattern and color happens as a result of a shift of pieces that already exist, that already are part of the whole. Pieces that were hidden suddenly come into view and add their quality to the overall pattern. When that happens, other pieces fade into the background, their qualities less distinctive, with less impact on the pattern that emerges.

It's the same with shadow work. As we allow ourselves to see the disowned parts of ourselves reflected in the kaleidoscope that is our being, we don't add anything that hasn't been part of us all along. All we do is shift what has been foreground and background. We bring characteristics and elements of our personalities that were in the background more directly into self-expression. Even when we choose not to act on aspects of our shadow self, our new *consciousness* of the qualities adds depth and character to our personality.

In the guided meditation that follows, you are invited to imagine yourself as a kaleidoscope and to acknowledge the fact that *all* the pieces of your whole self are required to create who you are at any given moment. Simply because some of them don't show doesn't mean they don't add their part to your self-expression, if only behind the scenes.

MAKE IT REAL
GUIDED MEDITATION #3:
On Being a Kaleidoscope

For this meditation, if you have access to an actual kaleidoscope, take a few minutes to look at it. Turn the tube and notice the shifting patterns that arise from exactly the same pieces of glass as they are rearranged over and over again. You will experience the metaphor more powerfully if it's real to you.

Take a few moments to settle yourself comfortably in a place where you will be undisturbed for about ten minutes or so. Focus your attention on the still point between one breath and the next, on the gap between your last exhalation and the next inhalation. There's nothing else to do. Simply invite your awareness to notice the gap and explore what it's like to linger there.

Next, bring to mind a kaleidoscope you've seen, or one that comes into your imagination now. Simply allow it to come to mind. If an image doesn't appear, notice what you sense, what comes if you ask yourself, "If I could be aware of a kaleidoscope right now, what would I notice?"

Put the eyepiece to your inner eye and notice the pattern inside the kaleidoscope. Simply become aware of the pattern you dis-

cover there. In your imagination, turn the kaleidoscope now and notice how the pattern changes. Keep turning it and notice the ever-changing patterns as the pieces of glass shift.

Remind yourself that nothing new is added when you change the pattern. All the pieces of glass remain the same - they just change position.

Bring to mind your own complex self—all the parts of yourself that constantly shift and change as life presents you with opportunities and challenges. As you acknowledge and reclaim your disowned self, you don't add anything new. You simply become aware of what has been there all along.

Take a moment to remind yourself that an experience of psychological wholeness simply means that you allow yourself to be aware of all your characteristics and qualities. It doesn't mean you have to express them or show them to everyone. Recall that the kaleidoscope draws on all the pieces as the pattern shifts and changes. Take a moment to ponder what it means to you to allow all the aspects of your being to be available to you, all the time, whenever you need to access them.

When you're ready, reorient yourself to the outer world, to your everyday consciousness. Bring with you whatever sense you may have of the importance that each part within you plays in creating an experience of wholeness and connection with yourself.

The Shadow Side of Spirituality

In a world characterized by wholeness, *every* aspect of life has its hidden side. Spirituality is no exception. I recall a Buddhist meditation teacher who, after many years of meditation practice, discovered the benefits of psychotherapy. He talked about the tremendous help he received when he combined the two approaches as part of an overall process of centering and deepening his consciousness. What he learned was the undeniable fact that to enhance a sense of wholeness, every aspect of our experience needs to be included.

For many of us, spiritual beliefs and practices enhance a daily sense of connection to something larger than ourselves. Whether we believe in an organized religion, find our place within a biological whole, or create our own spiritual approach, spirituality can be a powerful source of comfort.

Unfortunately—and not surprisingly—it also can become a hiding place. Shadow issues emerge in our spiritual lives in a number of powerful ways. For example, we may use our spiritual beliefs to entrench or justify a sense of "us versus them", whereby we project our disowned self onto others with the added element of religious or spiritual conviction. If your belief system promotes an idea of "us versus them," it is worth asking yourself how you can increase your awareness of the ways in which you may be using your beliefs to hide from aspects of your own shadow self.

Some of us find deep solace in our spiritual beliefs and practices, and this is a beneficial and life-enhancing experience. The shadow side of seeking solace, though, emerges when we refuse to deal with discomfort or conflict and escape instead into a "spiritual outlook." For example, in my work with couples, I occasionally find someone who retreats into religion or spirituality when there has been an argument. People have different ways of expressing this kind of protective response, and one of the most common is by going off to meditate or pray, or by refusing to talk about difficult or charged issues and putting on a cheerful face instead. This kind of response allows the person to avoid the sometimes painful process of working through disagreements, which not only leaves the partner hanging but also prevents communication and intimacy.

You can tell the shadow is present when you use this kind of strategy and have the experience of feeling perfectly justified—in fact, self-righteous—about your actions. You really believe it is beneath you to get angry or to express "negative" feelings. As was true with my grandmother, chances are that your unconscious goal is to push out of awareness any anger, fear, or other intense emotion in order to maintain a state of calm. The problem is that this strategy is like trying to put the lid back on the proverbial can of worms.

The stillness and calm of meditation offer a respite, a place to settle and just *be* for a while. But meditation, too, has a shadow side when it is used as a way to hide from the tasks and responsibilities of daily life. In fact, expanded states of consciousness of all kinds can become hiding places—or the compulsive focus of an addictive response. I have known people who tend toward addictive behaviors—overeating, compulsive shopping, overworking—who create a meditation practice that takes over their lives. They overdo it, sitting for hours at a time. That's fine when they're at a retreat. It's a problem when the rest of their life suffers because they spend every spare moment in an altered state of consciousness.

The sense of connection that emerges when we tap into expansive states of consciousness offers a profoundly nourishing experience that is further enhanced when we have a sense of receiving spiritual inspiration or divine guidance. These experiences can convey a feeling of never truly being alone, of having somewhere to turn when we are in need. The shadow side—a and there's a powerful one here—is the belief of being special, superior to other people, because of the guidance or inspiration that is received.

When we fall into this trap, which actually is a natural development as we mature spiritually, we are usually unaware of the humbling fact that expanded states of consciousness bring a *universal* experience of being special, loved, and valued. Instead of understanding that we have personally experienced a universally available state, we draw on the feeling of being special to add further fuel to a sense of "us versus them." Now, *we* can be the good, worthy, valued one and, conveniently enough, the others—the recipients of our shadow projections—can be unworthy.

Another area where the shadow emerges with potentially disastrous results is in the special relationship that arises with spiritual teachers or religious leaders and those who follow them. Under normal circumstances, these relationships offer invaluable support and guidance. When disowned aspects of the golden shadow relate to our own sense of personal power, though, we may find a feeling of empowerment and security *only* in relation to someone else. Our association with the spiritual teacher or religious figure then becomes the source of feelings of power and connection. It is all too easy to relinquish good judgment when we disown our own sense of personal power. One of the worst examples of what can happen when people project their disowned power onto another person is Jonestown, Guyana, where 900 people died at Jim Jones's command.

I recall a workshop participant who had a spiritual teacher whom she deeply loved. It was only in the presence of her teacher that this woman found comfort and any sense of wholeness at all. During one of the exercises on reclaiming the disowned self, she found a part of herself that seemed to overflow with feelings of love. As the exercise progressed, she discovered that she could experience, in herself, some of the feelings she had thought possible only in relation to her teacher.

It is equally important to keep in mind that *shadow parts can become resources once they are brought into conscious awareness.* For example, spiritual pride—acting out a sense of superiority over others—has the potential to become a healthy sense of spiritual empowerment.

A relative of mine had a long history of following spiritual teachers. He experienced fervent devotion with each, only to become disillusioned and disappointed when each teacher revealed inevitable flaws. Over time, the spiritual pride that my relative had invested in his teachers became conscious. He realized he was seeking in them a sense of empowerment and connection that he didn't believe he could attain on his own. Once this awareness was available to him, he began to explore his own spiritual power and capacities. Eventually, he found within himself the sense of belonging he had always sought from others.

Have you noticed that there is simply no place you can go without bringing your shadow along? That's why the goal isn't to get rid of it. What you do want to achieve is the ability to recognize and acknowledge it, knowing that the awareness you develop means you don't have to *live* in your shadow.

MAKE IT REAL
EXPERIMENT #5:
Identifying Disowned Aspects of Your Spiritual Self

This experiment draws on the others that have invited you to identify disowned aspects of yourself.

- To begin, identify spiritual leaders you have known or read about who have a particularly powerful impact on you, whether positive or negative. You may also want to include friends or co-workers who express their spirituality in a way that has a notable impact on you.

- Pay attention to those people whom you feel have qualities you believe you could never experience in yourself and explore the possibility that they reflect a disowned part of yourself. Ask yourself if there were any childhood experiences or unspoken family "rules" that conveyed disapproval of these qualities.

- Then ask yourself what it would be like to express those qualities in your own life. You might want to return to the *Golden Shadow Meditation* with this issue in mind.

Whatever you choose to do, remember that the journey into wholeness invites you into a level of self-acceptance that is transforming. When you know and embrace your whole self, both you and the world are safer for it. When you allow yourself to know your spiritual strengths as well as your vulnerabilities, the journey becomes more comfortable for you and those who travel with you.

GUIDED MEDITATION #4:
The Spiritual Shadow

Settle in comfortably now before taking a journey into the shadow realm of spirituality. Spend a few moments simply noticing your breathing. Give yourself permission to travel with each exhalation to the bottom of the breath. Spend a few moments there, at the bottom of the breath, connecting with "home base."

Now, take a moment to imagine that you are on a journey in a beautiful place. It may be an actual place you've seen before, or a place in your imagination that is beautiful in some way that has particular meaning to you right now. Notice that, somewhere in this beautiful place, you discover a mirror. It is a special mirror, focused on your spiritual development. It has the capacity to reflect two sides of you. On one side of the mirror is the aspect of yourself that is giving, loving, nurturing—all the positive qualities you can imagine about yourself. On the other side of the mirror are reflections of your spiritual pride, feelings of separateness or being better than other people—or any of the other potentially negative aspects of the shadow side of spirituality.

Allow the mirror to turn so that the reflection of the shadow side of your spirituality is facing you. Simply be open and aware. There is nothing to do, nothing to change. Just notice what you discover reflected in the mirror. The reflection may be a symbol, an image, a word, a color, a person, an animal, or anything at all that has meaning for you.

- *What is your first reaction to what is reflected in the mirror? Just notice whatever comes.*

- *What qualities are predominant in the reflection?*

- *What associations, thoughts, feelings, or sensations do you have in response to what is reflected there?*

Give yourself a moment now to become the reflection in the mirror so that you can experience it from the inside. There is a part of your mind that knows how to do this automatically and perfectly. Just move your awareness inside the reflection now and notice what comes to you.

- *What is your first impression?*

- *Does any part of your body draw your attention through either discomfort, comfort, or some other sensation?*

- *Notice any sensations in your body that weren't there a moment ago. Are you calmer or more centered? Do you hold your body in a new way?*

- *What feelings, thoughts, state of mind, or perspective accompany your experience of being the reflection?*

Take a few moments now just to be with your experience. Remember that you are bringing part of yourself into conscious awareness. It is part of your wholeness and you need to know about it. Be sure to allow yourself to be fully aware of any mixed feelings you may have.

Imagine that this shadow aspect of you has qualities that would make it a useful resource. You may not even be able to imagine, just now, what those might be. Just let yourself remain open to the possibility.

Now allow the mirror to turn to the positive side and experience the resource that is reflected there, the translation of the shadow part into something useful.

- *What is your first impression?*

- *What feelings, thoughts, state of mind, or perspective accompany your experience of being this resourceful reflection?*

- *What sensations do you notice? Are you calmer? Do you feel steadier or more solidly centered in your body? Do you feel more expansive or powerful?*

Spend a few moments exploring whatever has come into your experience. Be sure to allow mixed feelings and curiosity to accompany you every step of the way. Now, go back to the shadow side of the reflections and notice that you may be able to hold both reflections in your mind at once: the shadow side and the resource side. There is nothing else to do at this point. Just allow yourself to return to that beautiful place where you began.

- *Take a few moments to review your experience of the two reflections and how you felt about each.*

- *How might your life and relationships be different if you were to shift from shadow to resource?*

- *What might you have to lose if you were to transform this shadow part?*

Remember that you can return to this journey any time to look at as many shadow aspects of your spiritual journey as you want to discover and resolve. And, most important of all, remember that the journey into wholeness invites you into awarenesses that can make it safer for you to be in the world and that empower you to feel more centered and grounded.

Our Collective Shadow

One more aspect of the shadow requires our attention: the aspect of consciousness that is *collective* in nature. In the realm of collective consciousness, where we are both an individual and part of a larger whole, at some level we participate in everything that happens in our world. When we, as a species, refuse to look at our individual and collective shadow issues, they break through on a large scale and affect us in powerful ways.

For example, notice how many wars are waged on the planet at any given time. Skirmishes and conflicts abound around the entire globe so that, as a war is resolved in one part of the world, another begins somewhere else. It's worth pondering what is going on in human consciousness that seems to require conflict to erupt *somewhere* all the time.

There are some people who say that we, as a species, unconsciously enlist individuals to express our collective shadow issues for us. If this were true, then those people who cause injury to others, who act in antisocial ways, who spearhead movements or activities that pit one group against another, may actually function in service to the rest of us by expressing aspects of the shadow we refuse to acknowledge in ourselves.

This notion may sound crazy, but imagine what would happen if you believed it were true. What would it be like for you if the person who robs you, or the serial killer who threatens whole communities, were viewed as an expression of your own disowned rage and sadism? What would you experience if you thought that the person who asks you to dislike another group of people because they are "inferior," "less intelligent," "aggressive," or any other description, were viewed as representing a part of *your own* fears of difference?

A terribly traumatic story comes to mind of a man who viciously attacked a woman in Central Park in broad daylight. He went on to kill another woman and seriously injure two more before he was stopped. The reason he gave for his behavior was that his girlfriend had left him and he hated women.

I remember thinking at the time how this man represented, for me, an externalization of an unacknowledged vulnerability and rage that exists in many of us. His actions both frightened and saddened me. As a woman, I was reminded how precarious my lot can be in the face of a man's uncontrolled rage. As an individual within a collective context, my conviction was reinforced that this man's behavior reflected something present in both men *and* women whose pain and vulnerability have been disowned, pushed into the shadow, and then projected onto others who are less powerful. Seeking to destroy their own vulnerability, these wounded people vent their rage against the very same helplessness they cannot face in themselves. Even as I write, I know that "these people" are all of us—"they" are you and I, as well.

To recognize how an individual may express our personal shadow issues in these collective ways doesn't take away that individual's responsibility for his or her actions, nor does it lessen the outrage we feel in the presence of inhumane behavior. The point of this perspective is to emphasize the hard-to-grasp truth that doing our own individual shadow work has profound implications that extend far beyond our field of personal vision. For this reason, it seems to me that, as individuals, we *must* reclaim our whole selves in order to help heal our world, our relationships with our own species, and with other forms of life that share our planet with us. As each of us becomes whole and is willing to experience both light and shadow, our collective humanity may have less need to express the shadow on a mass scale.

And so . . .

At the beginning of our exploration of the shadow, I mentioned the metaphor of how light and shadow give depth and beauty to nature. Always, it is the *combination* of both that creates a context of wholeness. Increasingly, you can notice the play of light and shadow in all arenas of life. For example, pay attention to the people you care about, to those with whom you spend time when at work. Become aware of those who remind you of light, those who remind you of shadow, and those in whom you notice some of both. Let these people become mirrors for you, even as you recognize that part of yourself will always be in the shadow and part in the light. Remember that there is no way to be fully conscious of your whole self at any one moment. The creative solution is to be able to move through both light and shadow with openness and a willingness to be self-aware on an ongoing basis.

Living consciously from an experience of wholeness leaves out nothing and invites every element to be present. Total shadow can be threatening and frightening, while total light can be overwhelming or downright uninteresting. In the blend of the two you discover something much richer.

Allowing yourself and your life to be as rich and deep as possible requires that you adopt an attitude of self-acceptance, a recognition of your inevitable frailty and imperfection, and that of others. In the next chapter, we'll explore natural companions to shadow work—compassion and lovingkindness.

Chapter 3

COMPASSION AND LOVINGKINDNESS

Living with an Open Heart

> *To be compassionate is to wish that a being or all beings be free from pain. To be compassionate is to sense from within what it must be like to experience someone else's experience.*
>
> —*Sharon Salzberg*

The journey into wholeness brings many unexpected gifts. One of these is compassion. This extraordinary state of being arises spontaneously when we allow ourselves to recognize that we have at least one thing in common with *all* beings: our capacity to suffer. This realization creates a bridge of understanding between others and ourselves.

As we become more whole and acknowledge the inevitability of our inherent imperfection, our capacity for compassion increases. As it does, a sense of connection with others deepens and expands. Within a context of compassion, we tap into a collective human experience and realize that we are not alone in our suffering. The world becomes populated with people we can relate to, even if we've never met them—people whose deepest yearnings for love, comfort, and security aren't so very different from our own. For this reason, even as the sources of our suffering may differ, depending on our culture and life circumstances, we are alike when it comes to the inevitable fact that we all can be touched by feelings and experiences that cause distress.

Compassion becomes a way of being. As it develops in your experience, it shifts and shapes your view of the world. It is hard to recognize other people's pain unless you have experienced something similar—unless you've "walked a mile in their shoes." In this chapter you'll find lots of experiments and guided meditations geared to foster the response of compassion within you. Then the next time you have an experience that challenges, upsets, or stretches you in some way, ask yourself how you can use it to help develop a capacity to respond to others with more compassion.

Examples abound. In New York City, for instance, it's not uncommon to be without heat or hot water for varying periods of time. Such a mundane experience offers an opportunity to recognize that the situation may be a temporary inconvenience for you, while for others, being without heat or comforting shelter is a way of life. There may be times when you can't eat as soon as you'd like, and you register the gnawing pangs of hunger. You can extend this common experience to include a compassionate awareness of those who literally are starving. When you lose someone you care about a great deal, you have an opportunity to acknowledge the pain of others who suffer similar losses.

The Gifts of Compassion

Learning to allow the daily bumps and bruises of life to extend your awareness to include the suffering we all share brings with it many gifts. While it might seem that increased compassion would become a source of discomfort, it is actually soothing, like the soft ripples of current created when you drop a pebble into a lake. Ever-widening, the ripples steadily become larger circles, expanding until the energy from them disperses. Eventually, the movement that began in response to the pebble appears as water lapping on some distant shore. Compassion has a similar capacity: it expands as far as we are willing to allow it, creating ever-widening circles of awareness within and between individuals.

To foster compassion within ourselves also fosters tolerance—the recognition and acceptance of our inability to control all that life brings our way. When we understand that feeling pain, sorrow, loss, disappointment, greed, anger, envy, and fear are inevitable elements of human experience, it is easier to be in the presence of these feelings without criticizing those— including ourselves—who express them.

For some people, opening themselves to compassionate responses initially creates its own kind of pain. When we recognize that all people— actually, *all beings*—are capable of suffering, our relationship to others changes. As the ripples of compassion move out beyond the circumference of our own suffering or that of our loved ones and friends, we may find it increasingly impossible to ignore the plight of people we've never met. At first, this can be a difficult experience, as we may discover that we can't ignore homeless people quite as easily as we did before. Their situation and their capacity to suffer become piercingly real.

When we have a personal connection to another person's suffering, our level of compassion becomes even more powerful and tangible. I remember a client who had always enjoyed good physical health and then was stricken with a life-threatening illness. His recovery was long and arduous, filled with endless doctor visits and tests that were punctuated by uncertain outcomes. The experience of negotiating the medical world rocked him as severely as the illness itself. As a result, he gives freely of his time and energy to help people undergoing similar experiences. He understands their suffering more deeply now, the ripples of his compassion have expanded to encompass a whole new group of people.

For a friend of mine, the experience of awakening compassion first broke her heart, then melted it. The pebble that created the ripples of her expanding compassion was a news report of a massacre of civilians in a war-torn country. Even though these were people with whom she had no overt connection—they weren't relatives or friends of friends—something in their experience of helplessness and despair touched her deeply. Suddenly, she felt, and could no longer ignore, the fact that there was terrible suffering in the world. The news report stirred an awareness of her own experiences of helplessness and shifted her experience of these people she had never met. Their suffering no longer was a vague or abstract idea, it was real to her.

At first she cried often, as feelings about the magnitude of suffering these people endured, and her inability to prevent it, washed through her. Eventually, her pain turned into a deepening commitment to live more compassionately in her daily life. She began to look for ways she could help others. Her experience of feeling connected expanded and she began to feel that she was never alone. All around her, in her everyday life, were countless others sharing a most fundamental commonality: their ability to suffer and feel pain.

What One Person Can Do: The Practice of Compassionate Action

For many people, the process of awakening to a greater sense of compassion initially feels overwhelming. A question many ask is, "What can I, one person, do in the face of so much suffering?" The answer is, perhaps surprisingly, *quite a lot*. For example, you can make a commitment to engage in the practice of *compassionate action*. Doing so does not require you to undertake any specific activities, or extend dramatic efforts, to make a difference. Compassionate action is a state of mind that is focused on relieving suffering when and where you can, within the context of your life situation and circumstances.

Compassionate action can be as basic as giving coins to the homeless or holding open a door for people who are physically unable to do so for themselves. Small, moment-to-moment actions arising from compassion add up. Something as simple as smiling becomes a practice of compassionate action, as potentially powerful as anything else you might do.

Sometimes your experience of personal suffering—or that of others—may prompt you to act on a larger scale. For example, if you have experienced oppression of any kind, you might find yourself drawn to volunteer for an organization that promotes civil rights. If the suffering of animals touches you, your practice of compassionate action might include offering time or money to an animal shelter. There are organizations and community activities that encompass almost any area of interest, with many levels of involvement possible.

For example, a friend described to me her decision to volunteer with an organization that feeds the homeless in her community. Having been unemployed for a time opened her awareness to the uncertainty and fear of becoming homeless. Because of her experience, homelessness was no longer something that touched only people she didn't know. She recognized herself in others, and her compassion opened her heart to the plight of the unemployed in a new way. No longer did she view homeless people as solely responsible for their situation. Instead, she found herself feeling, *"There but for the grace of God, go I."* By offering her services as a volunteer, she put her compassion and new understanding into action.

A colleague took a different approach to compassionate action. Aware of the many young people who can't go to college because of a lack of money or adult support, he committed to helping one person at a time achieve his or her educational dream. With some, he offers money. With others, he becomes a mentor. Sometimes he does both. Over the years he has helped a number of young people whose life circumstances surely would have derailed their best efforts get all the way through school.

Does my colleague wish he could help more people? Certainly. What he has come to understand, though, is that part of engaging in compassionate action is to recognize that no one person can do it all. The need is too great, the suffering too widespread. Instead, he allows himself to focus on what he *can* do, as his compassion continues to fuel his commitment to those he is able to help.

As I wrote this chapter, I asked friends for examples of suffering they recognized and yet felt they couldn't alleviate directly. One friend told me of the young girls in Thailand who are forced into prostitution. Another mentioned the children of Bosnia and her agony at the powerful losses they have had to bear. Yet another friend talked about elephants and other animals routinely decimated by poachers.

Each person I talked to described a different example. I was struck by the fact that all the responses had one thing in common: both a feeling of helplessness *and* a determination to continue to be aware of, and to act to ease, suffering in whatever ways possible. For some, this meant sending money to organizations. For others, compassionate action consisted of writing letters to government agencies. For still others, daily prayers for those who suffer seemed the most appropriate response.

As you explore your experience of compassion and your feelings about the practice of compassionate action, it is important to know that there are times when there is nothing you can do to relieve suffering in any direct way. When this happens, what you do have to offer is your willingness to be present in your awareness without withdrawing into apathy or a self-protective detachment.

MAKE IT REAL
EXPERIMENT #1:
Bringing Compassion Alive in Yourself

The next time you are around people—walking down the street, in a meeting, out with friends or family—allow the following thought to run through your mind:

I am you and you are me.

I heard this particular phrase many years ago, as part of a song created by someone visiting the ashram of Bede Griffiths in India. Overlooking the grammar glitch, with the statement ending in "me" rather than "I", it has become a constant companion in my daily life.

There is nothing else to do with this thought. Just allow it to be present, and when you realize that you have forgotten it, bring it to mind again.

- Notice any changes in your awareness after a couple of hours of reminding yourself that *I am you and you are me*, whether you are thinking of a person, an animal, a plant, or some other living being. Notice what happens when you sustain this awareness for a few days. The more you know that *I am you and you are me*, the more your heart will open with compassion for others. It's just the way that energy of compassion works. When you realize your connection with others, an automatic response of compassion enfolds them in a sense of shared identity, caring, and connection.

- When you see someone who is suffering, whether it is a child crying or someone who is homeless, notice your initial response. Ask yourself:
    - Do I recoil, turn my back, or want to withdraw?
    - Do I wish I had been somewhere else so I wouldn't have had to be aware of the plight of the other person?
    - Do I experience irritation, anger, or any other emotion that serves to distance me from the other person?
    - Do I want to reach out and relieve the suffering?

There is nothing else to do but notice the ways in which you distance yourself from the suffering of others. This is the first step in opening yourself to compassion.

- The next step in this experiment is to allow yourself to wonder how it feels to be the one who suffers. Ask yourself:
    - What would my life be like if I were that person?
    - How would I feel if I were that person?

- Bring mindfulness to this exercise. All you need to do is *notice*. Through noticing your responses and reactions, you increase your capacity to be aware. That's all you need to do for now. Just be aware. Be awake to the fact that *I am you and you are me*, and that you can notice your responses when you are aware of the suffering in others.

- Finally, ask yourself what healing needs to happen in you that might allow you to feel more comfortable in the presence of suffering—your own and that of others.

EXPERIMENT #2:
Exploring Compassion Toward Yourself

This experiment is basically the same as the first, except that that object of your attention is *you*. This time, focus on what you discover when you interact compassionately with yourself. When something bad happens—perhaps you make a mistake or do something that leaves you feeling ashamed—you have an opportunity to respond to yourself with compassion.

- Begin with an awareness of your initial uncensored responses to yourself. Notice and acknowledge any negative feelings that may arise. Then take a moment to imagine you are feeling these things about someone else. Give yourself whatever help you need to in order to access an experience of compassion and then direct it toward yourself.

- To have compassion for yourself is a way to honor that which is sacred in you. You acknowledge that you are as valuable and precious as any other being, and that you, too, are worthy of compassion and understanding. Sometimes the most difficult thing of all is to be as generous and forgiving with ourselves as we are with others.

As you may have noticed in these exercises, sometimes it is difficult to move beyond negative feelings toward yourself. Many of us struggle with what to do with mixed feelings. As you continue to move through the exercises and meditations, recognize that mixed feelings about yourself are inevitable. There will surely be times when to have compassion for yourself is simply too big a step to take all at once. At these times, allow yourself at least to recognize that your struggle is a natural outgrowth of stretching your experience of yourself beyond where it has been.

Lovingkindness

Lovingkindness, called *metta* in Sanskrit, is the state of mind and being from which compassion emerges naturally. When we practice lovingkindness, we truly enter a realm in which we recognize that *all* beings—including ourselves, our loved ones, and our enemies—seek to be happy and free from suffering. We not only recognize and empathize with the suffering of others, as we do when we experience compassion, we also *actively wish for all beings to be free from suffering and to find happiness.*

Imagine what would shift in the quality of your daily interactions with yourself and others if you hold to the thought, *May I be happy today. May all beings be happy.* For example, instead of stewing in resentment or bitterness toward someone who has hurt you, lovingkindness invites you to wish the other person freedom from suffering, even as you may disapprove of his or her actions against you and do what is appropriate to take care of yourself.

The most powerful example of lovingkindness for me is provided by the Dalai Lama and his relationship to the Chinese nation. While they have virtually ravaged Tibet, the Dalai Lama insists on wishing the Chinese people well, even as he acknowledges their wrongdoing. He recognizes that they, too, suffer and wish to be happy. When someone once asked him if he were angry with the Chinese nation for what they have done to his people and his country, he said that, of course, he was. He went on to say that they should stop and that he would do everything within his power to restore what had been taken. Throughout the discussion, he commented on his wish that they not suffer, that they be happy, even as he also insisted they go home. His example has been a consistent beacon for many who seek to bring sacred practices such as lovingkindness into action.

I remember when I first experienced a lovingkindness meditation. Initially, I resisted it. While it wasn't so hard to wish myself happiness, to do so with people with whom I was angry felt like letting them off the hook. It was as if I were overlooking what they had done. I found it hard to acknowledge my anger *and* experience my kinship with them as people who also sought to be free from suffering. Justifying my position seemed more important.

With practice, I discovered something that surprised me. Wishing myself and others well being reduced the distress and tension that had marked some of my close relationships. Most importantly, it gave me someplace new to go with my upset, an internal state of openness instead of constriction, of letting go instead of becoming mired in irritation or frustration. I've heard this from others as well. Clients and friends describe how the practice of lovingkindness shifts their responses to themselves and others. This doesn't mean there are no more negative feelings or critical thoughts. It does mean that these reactions lose some of their punch when they emerge from a well of lovingkindness.

I recall a friend's description of a powerful shift that occurred spontaneously when she focused her lovingkindness meditation on a cousin with whom she had been engaged in a longstanding battle. The conflict centered around some furniture that had been in the family for years. She felt her cousin had unjustifiably taken the lion's share of desirable items. It grated on her not because she needed the furniture but because she felt her cousin was selfishly disregarding the nostalgic importance of the furniture to other members of the family.

After she learned to practice lovingkindness, my friend found that her reaction to her cousin began to shift. While she continued to feel he was wrong for refusing to share the furniture, she also *sincerely* wished him well. It surprised her that her good wishes for him felt so genuine.

Focusing lovingkindness on ourselves sometimes creates unexpected mixed feelings. I remember a client who had learned as a child to put his energy and attention into fulfilling the needs of others at all cost. Because of this, he had grown into a responsible, competent man who took good care of his family. The problem was that he didn't take good care of himself. When he began to wish himself well, he found that he felt profoundly uncomfortable. Initially, he protested against the possibility that he could be happy. In his mind, happiness was an unattainable fantasy, especially for him. He scoffed at the notion that, deep inside, he really wanted to be happy. Over time, his heart melted a bit and he began to permit himself to feel his wish to be happy. He also discovered that he was deeply moved by his wish to be free from suffering.

In her book, *Lovingkindness*, Sharon Salzberg describes how, in this practice, we develop the capacity to become a true friend to ourselves and others. This means we can move through the ups and downs of our interpersonal journeys with others and maintain a sense of connection and kinship. Something shifts when we add lovingkindness to our lives. A quality of wholeness spontaneously and naturally enters our experience. Rather than judging people to be *all good* or *all bad*, wishing them freedom from suffering even when we disagree with them or don't like them expands our sense of who they are as *whole* people. Imagine how family, community, and political life might change if we interacted with each other from a perspective of lovingkindness. What kind of revolution might ensue if we truly wished each other well, even as we went about our daily business of resolving conflict and addressing differing needs?

An update to this particular aspect of wishing others well brings in the importance of talks by Charles Eisenstein, the author and speaker on issues around ecology, interbeing, "sacred economics", and other collective concerns. In these talks, Charles emphasizes how important it is to consider that people's actions emerge from the contexts in which they live, as well as from their personal beliefs and values. He invites us to imagine ourselves living within our life circumstance and acting from the beliefs related to that particular perspective. He proposes that we would understand—if not agree with—the actions of others if we could truly experience the worldview that they live.

This focus reminds me of a lovingkindness practice, where we assume that all people also seek to be free from suffering and to be safe and happy, just as we do. I find that his thoughts and talks reinforce my commitment to hold an attitude of lovingkindness in a world that has many things happening with which I don't agree.

As a psychotherapist, I initially worried that practicing lovingkindness could lead to denial or passivity in relationships with others. Many of us want to rush into forgiveness before truly acknowledging and resolving the conflicted and negative feelings we have about others. The surprise to me was that mixed feelings have a home in lovingkindness, and wishing others well in no way diminishes awareness of the consequences of their actions.

I discovered that in my personal life my capacity to assert myself effectively actually increased after I began to practice lovingkindness. My understanding of this shift is that I am less defensive now and constantly remember that I share an inescapable bond with everyone, even my supposed enemies.

When you first begin to practice lovingkindness, you may have to engage it "as if" you wish happiness and freedom from suffering for yourself and others. If this is the case, I encourage you to be willing to experiment with the following meditations, and give yourself an opportunity to discover the surprising power of lovingkindness as it develops into an experience that is alive and real for you.

MAKE IT REAL
GUIDED MEDITATION #1:
Wishing Yourself Freedom from Suffering

It is said that we cannot truly love anyone else until we have the capacity to love ourselves, so the exploration of lovingkindness practice begins with a focus on yourself:

Find a place to sit comfortably and quietly for ten or fifteen minutes. Settle in with your spine comfortably erect, your body at ease. Spend a few moments focusing your attention on your breathing, especially in the gap—the still point—between one breath and the next.

Now, shift your awareness into your heart. Imagine your heart opening to yourself, as a flower opens and offers itself to the world. Mentally say to yourself the following words:

- *"May I be free from the causes of suffering."*
- *"May I live with compassion for myself."*
- *"May I be happy."*

Repeat these phrases several times and notice how you feel. Be sure to allow mixed feelings and, if any do arise, simply become aware of them.

Focus again on your heart now and notice how it feels to wish yourself well. Repeat the words again and notice how you feel this time. Be aware of the lingering tone of your experience as you would the lingering tone of a bell just rung.

Bring yourself back whenever you're ready and jot down any part of your experience you'd like to record.

GUIDED MEDITATION #2:
Expanding Lovingkindness

In this meditation, you have an opportunity to extend your experience of lovingkindness to include others.

Take a few moments to settle in, to discover a position for your body where your mind can stay alert and aware, even as the sensation of comfort deepens throughout. Begin by focusing your attention on the bottom of the breath; with each exhalation, allow yourself to travel all the way to the bottom of the breath and settle into the still point that exists between this breath and the next. There is nothing to do in the still point. Just notice it. Sometimes it is expansive and lasts for several moments. At other times, you may not even notice the still point, but it is there nonetheless.

Now, become aware of your chest, the area around your heart. Focus your attention on your "inner" heart, your spiritual heart. You may imagine that your inner heart appears as a light, or an inner chamber of some kind, or a certain feeling or sensation. Settle yourself in the very center of your inner heart, perhaps imagining that you sit in a beautiful chair that supports you completely.

From your place within the center of your heart, become aware of all the people, animals, and other life forms that live within your home and the surrounding area. Then expand your awareness to your neighborhood . . . then your community . . . then your entire State or province . . . your whole country . . . neighboring countries . . . and, finally, the entire globe . . . all beings living in all the seas, lakes, streams, rivers . . . in the sky . . . on all the continents and islands, on all the land masses around the entire globe. Invite your awareness to encompass all the other beings in the world, creatures and life forms of every kind. Feel your heart expand to include all of them. Then remind yourself that all of these beings are part of you and you are part of them. There is no separation. I am you and you are me.

Now take a few moments just to sit with this awareness. When your mind wanders, gently invite it back to the experience of your connection with all living things. Add to your awareness that all living things are capable of suffering and that you share this capacity with them. We all understand what it means to suffer. No one is exempt.

After a few minutes of sitting with this awareness and noticing what it elicits in you, mentally say to yourself something along the lines of the following, being sure to let yourself create a statement that is personally meaningful to you:

- "May all beings be free from suffering."
- "May all beings be happy."

Be sure to allow phrases to emerge that move you, that you can say with full conviction. The important focus is that you give yourself a chance to experience these statements as something meaningful and true.

When they arise, notice any mixed feelings, allow them, and then return to your meditation on lovingkindness. There is no need to struggle. Acknowledge your mixed feelings as evidence of your wholeness and your willingness to engage the practice of lovingkindness with full awareness.

When you are ready to come back, take a few moments to return to the bottom of the breath. Just remember to travel with your exhalations down to the still point in-between breaths. Then, when you feel ready, take a moment to review your experience, open your eyes, and come back to your everyday awareness. Wiggle your fingers and toes to bring yourself all the way back. You might want to make some notes if something came to mind that you'd like to explore more deeply later.

Living with an Open Heart

A closed heart creates a barrier between heart and mind that allows us to tell ourselves that we are all separate and different, rather than feeling the pain of how much we share similar hurts and yearnings. To experience compassion and lovingkindness as integral parts of daily life means to allow our hearts to open and let in the reality that we all have the capacity to feel rejection, humiliation, fear, rage, love, desire, hunger, and joy.

In my workshops, I offer exercises that invite participants to open their hearts, usually beginning with focusing on themselves. People often report feeling actual chest pains after experiencing their hearts opening to themselves. As we expand the open heart to include others, some participants feel unable to contain an awareness of the suffering of so many people. What these experiences reveal is that it can be quite painful to open your heart, and to do so requires that you be willing to acknowledge and feel both love and suffering.

Fortunately, there is a comforting paradox at work here: the more you open your heart, the more flexible and resilient you become in the face of life's daily challenges and unexpected demands. What develops is similar to the difference between a tree that is stiff and brittle and one that is supple and able to bend. The first tree is at risk for injury in high winds and storms; the second has a much better chance of surviving intact.

Most of us know more about living with a closed heart than we would like. As a psychotherapist, I see people everyday whose hearts are shut tight for a variety of reasons. At the top of the list is fear: fear of helplessness, abandonment, change. Closing our hearts, we fend off the natural flow and progression of experience from that which is familiar to that which is new, from the habitual and predictable to the unexpected.

A colleague who occasionally consults with me described how her experience of sitting in her office with clients has shifted as she has learned to open her heart to feelings of helplessness. Where she used to feel compelled to jump in and try to "fix" people, now she can sit with her clients in a state of "compassionate curiosity," her heart open and willing to be present with whatever the session may bring. When her heart was closed, she wasn't nearly as available or truly present to the healing journey of her clients.

I recall a relative telling me about a time he and his wife were struggling with an issue they could not resolve. They did some couples' counseling and were stunned to discover the degree to which they *both* closed their hearts whenever they tapped into the unacknowledged power struggle between them. Once they learned how to open their hearts to the issue *and* to their own vulnerabilities, they were able to listen to one another in a whole new way. They found that communicating with an open heart created a foundation of good will and connection from which they experienced a new interest in each other's position.

A closed heart is brittle and may shatter when confronted by a crisis. An open heart is soft and supple, drawing from a strength that makes room for what life brings its way. It is as though, in opening our hearts, we create all the internal space we need to allow awareness and feelings to move through us, as the wind moves through the space between the branches of a tree, or between the leaves on the branches. The more open our hearts, the more room we have inside to meet ourselves and others with a willingness to connect and be aware. The love that is generated spontaneously by an open heart pours into our experience even as it flows out to others.

The challenge is that, even as living with an open heart in the face of suffering creates a deeper sense of connection, it also requires that we deal with possible feelings of helplessness. For example, in New York City—as in most major urban centers—it is nearly impossible to ignore suffering. Homeless people are everywhere, untreated people with profound psychological problems wander the streets, children are dying on drugs in schools and in random shootings in the streets, racial tension erupts from time to time, and the stark distinction between "have's" and "have-not's" are hard to ignore. All in all, it would seem that to have an open heart here would be just too painful to endure.

The fact is, though, attempting to *cut off* awareness of all this is far more distressing than meeting it with an open heart. When we attempt to close our hearts to these realities, we add an internal struggle to the distress we perceive in others. By acknowledging the pain of others with compassion and lovingkindness, our awareness can arise and move through us and we don't waste time and energy struggling with what is.

Another gift that emerges naturally from living with an open heart is that of becoming increasingly aware of the quality of our ongoing experiences. For example, when you are familiar with how relaxed your chest feels when your heart is open—and how tight and clenched it feels when you close your heart—you have a reliable barometer available for measuring your responses to any situation or person. If you become aware that your chest is tight, you can ask yourself what's going on and notice what you feel if you open your heart and allow whatever is happening to move through you.

For example, after returning from a conference, I received a hotel bill with an inaccurate charge that had been added after I checked out. I telephoned the hotel's accounting office to question the charge and the conversation quickly deteriorated into an argument. When I became aware of how short of breath I was and how tight my chest felt, I recognized that I wasn't being very "supple." I realized that this "wind" was going to blow me down if I didn't open up to the experience. I calmed myself and even though miracles didn't ensue, I did get through the rest of the conversation with a greater sense of connection to the other person and a less antagonistic stance. In the long run, I saved myself and the other person some wear and tear. I still disagreed with the added charge, but the negotiations took on a different tone and weren't nearly as arduous. In fact, with an open heart, I felt able to protest more firmly, free from the stress I had felt when my heart was clamped down around the feeling that I was out of control of the situation. I was able to remember that the other person was just doing her job and that we were connected at a heart level.

Opening your heart to people doesn't mean you have to like them, agree with them, or be friends with them. *It simply means that you recognize your shared human experience and acknowledge that even people you dislike have the same capacity to suffer as you have.*

Yet another unexpected gift of living with an open heart is the increased capacity for joy and delight that emerges spontaneously. When you open your heart to all beings and to your whole environment, you begin to notice the magical moments and small surprises that are present all around you. I have a friend who takes regular walks in Central Park, as I do. Often, she leaves messages on my voicemail about what she discovered that day. One of her favorite activities is to choose a new tree each visit and take time to get to know it. She and I share a love of trees, and she describes her experiences in some detail: how she touches the bark, the branches, the leaves, and how she always hugs the tree before leaving. It may sound silly, but hugging trees is a terrific way to express the delight of an open heart. It requires nothing back and is a moment of simply being present to an experience we generally take for granted: an appreciation of the existence of trees.

I met a colleague on the street one day and he related a story of having watched a puppy playing with a larger dog in a dog park. Initially, he had gone to the park because he needed to clear his mind after a quarrel with his boyfriend. Feeling irritated, it took him awhile to shift gears. Eventually, he noticed these two particular dogs. The unbridled enthusiasm of the puppy's play reached into his heart and touched him with a sudden feeling of delight. Because his heart was open, he experienced some of the puppy's energy inside himself as he resonated with the play going on between the two dogs.

Another time I was with a friend and her husband at their country house for the weekend. In the back of the house, they had created a meditation space, in the center of which was a small statue of a sitting Buddha. One morning, we looked outside and saw a small chipmunk curled up on the statue's head in such a way that it looked like Daniel Boone's coon-skin cap. We were so amused that we took most of the morning doing nothing much but watching the chipmunk sleep. We laughed many times that day, and it still causes me to chuckle every time I recall the chipmunk curled up on top of the bald head of the Buddha statue. In addition, a cow from a neighboring farm came up onto the porch that day and settled in on the doormat, as if she were the dog of the house. Delight after delight, as our hearts opened to what nature had to share with us that day. Taking it all in just increased the expansiveness we already felt.

I have noticed that laughter tends to bubble up from an open heart. For whatever reasons, this more flexible, supple way of being allows us to connect more deeply with a healthy sense of humor—with the capacity to laugh at ourselves and at the play of life going on all around us. The open heart recognizes the *whole* picture—the delight as well as the suffering.

MAKE IT REAL
EXPERIMENT #3:
Connecting Heart-to-Heart with Others

- When you interact with others, or even just think about them, imagine that you are linked to them with a line of light, heart-to-heart. Know that the link represents the truth that *I am you and you are me*, and say these words in your mind as you did with the exercise on developing compassion.

- As part of the experiment, imagine yourself *opening your face*, along with your heart. When you do this, it means you look at other people softly, openly, your gaze uncluttered by judgments. Imagine that your facial expression sends friendliness and good will toward them, rather than viewing them through the lens of your needs and expectations.

This doesn't mean you actually have to approach someone else or reach out overtly in any way. Simply open yourself to someone, to the fact that you are connected and that your heart is open to send a line of light from you to other beings. Then simply notice what happens over time, in terms of how you feel about yourself and the quality of your interactions in general.

GUIDED MEDITATION #3:
Opening Your Heart

Begin by becoming aware of your chest in the area of your heart. Notice whether your chest feels at ease and open or tight and closed. Are your shoulders comfortably back so that your chest is open? Or are your shoulders hunched forward, causing your chest to cave in? Just notice the position of your body naturally settles into without changing anything right now.

When your heart is open, your chest will be open as well. You can breathe more freely, from deep in your belly. When you are frightened or your heart is constricted for some other reason, you may feel a tension in your chest and your breathing may be shallow. Notice your breath. Are you breathing from your belly or your chest? If you discover that your chest is tense or your breathing shallow, take a few moments now to acknowledge that awareness. There is no need to struggle to relax or to be any different from how you are right at this moment. Just be with yourself as you are.

Next, imagine a beautiful light of a color that is deeply comforting to you. Imagine that the light fills the area of your heart and permeates all the muscles in your shoulders, arms, back, and chest. This is a healing, nurturing light that supports you in your willingness to live with an open heart. Allow the light to convey its quality to you in a way that relaxes your chest and shoulders. Even if your heart doesn't open right away, allow yourself to explore whatever degree of tension or relaxation you may feel. As you heighten your awareness of when your heart is open and when it is closed, you can become more conscious of the situations that cause you to protect yourself by closing your heart. You also can become more familiar with those circumstances in which you feel safe enough to open up to the world.

Now imagine yourself in a situation where you normally tense up and, in effect, close your heart. Start with one that's not too challenging (perhaps, waiting in a bank or market line). Imagine you are there, in the midst of that situation, with the light in your chest. Explore what it would be like for you if you could connect a little more fully with the situation: with yourself as well as others who may be involved, and make all the room you need to allow the experience to move through you, as a breeze blows through the space between the branches of a tree.

As you make room, imagine how you might handle the situation differently. Would you leave more quickly? Would you speak, act, or feel differently? What new or unexpected awareness or solution might spring to mind?

There is nothing else to do here. Simply explore how it feels to engage your experiences with your heart a bit more open. You can carry the light with you wherever you go. Give yourself permission to become aware of those times when you close your heart. These are important moments. They tell you where healing is needed.

When you feel ready, come back to your everyday state of mind and notice how it feels to keep the light in your heart as you go about your next activity.

GUIDED MEDITATION #4:
Opening Your Heart to Yourself

To begin this journey, become aware of your breathing without attempting to control it in any way. Simply notice the natural in and out of the breath. Follow the next exhalation all the way to the bottom of the breath and rest there for a moment.

Now become aware of your chest. It is at ease and open, or tight and closed? Simply bring awareness to your chest without doing anything to change it.

Imagine that you are in a beautiful place that conveys a sense of safety. In this place is a special full-length mirror. It has a magical quality that helps you connect to yourself, heart-to-heart.

Find the mirror and sense your reflection in it. If the mirror appears to be blank, ask yourself what your reflection would be like if you could be aware of it. Notice how it feels to connect with yourself. Do you feel love? Compassion? Shame? Discomfort? Pleasure? Whatever arises, notice it and pay attention to how your heart responds.

Become aware of a healing light in your chest. It may be the same color as before, or a new color may appear. Imagine that you are sending a line of light from your heart to the heart of your reflection in the mirror. This is a lifeline, a line of communication and connection. Send it gently and notice how it feels to connect, heart-to-heart, with yourself.

As you open your heart to yourself, do you sense the deep love that is possible in this connection? If not, that's fine. It takes time to discover the compassion and love for ourselves that are so much part of an open heart. Remember to notice and allow any mixed feelings. Keep in mind that, over time, your heart will open to your reflection more deeply and more fully, with greater self-acceptance and lovingkindness than you may feel right now.

EXPERIMENT #4:
Looking for Laughter

The more you focus on particular qualities in daily life, the more these qualities seem to multiply or intensify. For this reason, the following exercise asks you to focus on whatever occurs in your life that evokes a sense of delight, that creates an opportunity for you to laugh and smile. Allow yourself to discover that the more you focus on laughter, the more it will become an everyday companion.

At least once a day, find one thing that delights you, that causes you to smirk, chuckle, guffaw, belly laugh, or simply smile with pleasure. It doesn't have to be anything dramatic or hilarious, just something that touches the place of delight in you.

If you find that the day has passed and you haven't had a delightful moment, take the time to think of something that always brings a smile: some memory, anecdote, or joke that inevitably touches your funny bone or tickles you in some way. Then notice how you increasingly tend to become aware of those small moments that are the messengers of delight throughout any given day.

GUIDED MEDITATION #5:
Opening Your Heart to Laughter and Delight

This meditation invites you to discover the play that constantly punctuates daily experience when you take the time to notice it.

Begin by settling inside, focusing your attention on the space between breaths. Become aware of your heart. Imagine it as a flower that is opening, blossoming, revealing its beauty and fragrance to the world.

Recall the last time you experienced something that delighted or amused you. Remember what it felt like to laugh. Open your heart to the laughter and allow it to intensify in your experience. Recall what it feels like to have a real belly laugh. Your whole body responds, your immune system benefits, your sense of well-being increases.

Take a moment now to rest in your open heart and invite more laughter into your life. There is nothing else to do. Simply allow yourself to remember that one of the gifts of an open heart is an increasing number of delightful moments in the course of daily life.

When you're ready, come back, continuing to imagine your heart as open. Welcoming whatever laughter or delight may surprise you today.

Taking a Bodhisattva Vow

If you have discovered any of the material on "random acts of kindness," you have come upon a Western version of a reverend Buddhist tradition. In Buddhism one of the most powerful expressions of compassion in action are those of a *bodhisattva*. This is a person who has dedicated his or her life to the service of others, to easing suffering whenever and wherever possible.

In weeklong conferences that emphasize living in a context of compassion and lovingkindness, the Dalai Lama has offered people around the world an opportunity to take a *bodhisattva* vow. These events are attended by thousands of people, all intent on being of service to the world. Taking a *bodhisattva* vow doesn't mean you have to spend every moment in selfless service to others. It *does* mean that you make a vow to offer assistance, open your heart, share a smile, or ease suffering in whatever ways may be possible whenever the opportunity arises.

For example, on what may seem the smallest scale possible, you might choose to take insects outdoors when you find them inside, instead of arbitrarily killing them. You might give your seat to someone else on the bus, or let the driver next to you pull in front of your car, even when your initial urge is to speed up and cut him or her off. You might decide to lend a hand to someone struggling to cross the street, or pick up a piece of paper lying in the hallway of your office building, even though it isn't yours.

Grander acts abound as well. You might choose a charity and offer your services, or money, on a regular basis. You might visit a shut-in person or deliver food to the elderly. You might offer to help an overwhelmed mother with some of her chores, or babysit for her so that she can take some time for herself.

It is a powerful experience to observe the effects of random acts of kindness on people you know. A friend called and excitedly told me about how she had been at the florist buying special, and expensive, flowers for her sister's birthday party. When she mentioned this to the salesperson helping her, he put in an extra bouquet of tulips without charging her as his way of adding to the abundance and beauty of the floral arrangement. It delighted my friend to receive the extra, unexpected flowers, but most of all she was delighted by her interaction with the salesperson and pleased to be able to give her sister even more than she had planned.

What moved me was the effect this unexpected moment had on my friend. It came on the heels of a notably difficult day and was just what she needed to bolster her flagging belief in the basic goodness of people

Another friend makes it a practice to look for opportunities to commit random acts of kindness as often as possible. Usually these are small acts, as in the many times she opens doors for people or lets them go in front of her in lines at the grocery store. Sometimes, though, she outdoes herself. One time she learned that a friend's wife faced a difficult job interview. Because my friend is a psychotherapist, she offered to coach her friend's wife in preparation for the interview.

There are countless ways to serve and countless random acts of kindness to commit. The main point is to offer yourself when and where needed. But taking a *bodhisattva* bow doesn't mean serving others to the extent that you overlook your own needs and pleasures. You, too, deserve care, rest, and nourishment. As with all aspects of psychological wholeness, creating a balance between serving others and serving yourself is usually a safe, effective foundation on which to base your choices.

MAKE IT REAL
EXPERIMENT #5:
Committing Random Acts of Kindness

- In the coming week, perform one small act of service each day—something that may have come to mind in the past but didn't get done. It can be anything, large or small, that constitutes a service to any life form—an insect, a stray cat, a person, your community, an organization, or any other context you choose or that presents itself.

- While you can't control the ultimate outcome of the situations you seek to serve, you can allow yourself to notice how it feels to respond to need, to ease suffering, to bring delight. Often, there is just a sense of rightness about helping others and sometimes a certain kind of satisfaction. Notice how it feels to begin to develop a habit of responding to the moment of opportunity when you can choose to act—or not. Over time, become aware of how your perception of the presence of opportunities to serve others increases spontaneously.

Be sure to include yourself, too, in your willingness to respond to need, share delight, and ease suffering.

Living in a World of Compassion and Lovingkindness

It is an understatement to say that we live in a world that is quite a bit less than ideal. There are many circumstances and events we can't change, even if we want to do so. The most important thing is to allow our hearts to open and learn to love ourselves and others more freely and fully. The more we are able to experience compassion and lovingkindness toward ourselves, the more we will expand this capacity to include others as well.

In the meditation that follows, allow yourself to imagine what your life would be like if you could remember, at all times, that there is never a moment, not a flicker of a nanosecond, when you are not completely and inescapably connected with every living being on this planet.

MAKE IT REAL
GUIDED MEDITATION #6:
Expanding Your Sense of Connection

The following meditation promotes and supports an experience of connection within the greater context of the world at large and your place in it. As you go through the meditation, allow yourself to notice whatever feelings or thoughts arise, and be sure to allow yourself to be aware of any mixed feelings you might have. In a world of compassion and lovingkindness, there is plenty of room for a full range of responses.

Close your eyes and settle in for an inner journey. Begin by becoming aware of "home base" at the bottom of your breath. Just settle there.

Now become aware of your surroundings. Notice where you are and simply take in the shapes, colors, and textures around you. Notice the temperature of the air on your skin. In fact, notice the air itself—that wherever you are, at some point space surrounds you, as it does every other solid object in your vicinity.

Now imagine that the space that surrounds you and everything else is quite substantial in its own way. Rather than representing emptiness, *it has a certain "somethingness" to it. This invisible* something *actually connects you, right now, with everything around you. It enfolds you and everything else within itself.*

Notice what you discover if you expand your awareness of space to include the environment that extends beyond the room or place where you are right now. Include the area around the trees, houses, buildings, roads, lakes, mountains, or any other natural or constructed phenomena that are part of your extended environment. Continue to expand your awareness until you include your entire neighborhood and community, then your city, state, and country. Eventually, let your mind wander around the entire globe, imagining the ever-present space that connects everything on the planet with everything else.

Consider the fact that the very substance of space touches you and everything else in a continuous, unbroken connection. *Within this connection, nothing is separate from anything else. Reflect on how compassion and lovingkindness are means to make this awareness real in your everyday life.*

When you offer your life to serve the whole, within which you are one part, you honor the fact that every move you make is felt within the whole of space that connects you with everything else.

In the same way, every move made by every other life form touches you in some way, even if you are completely unaware of it.

Take a few moments now simply to notice what this meditation has brought into your experience . . . whatever thoughts, feelings, sensations, or other awarenesses have come to you. Recall how the space that seemingly separates you from everything else actually creates an inescapable interconnection within which you participate, whether you are aware of it or not.

When you are ready, wiggle your fingers and toes and bring your attention back to your body, to the space around you. As you come back, give yourself a moment to notice your heart and reaffirm your openness to the space around you, to the connection that surrounds you at every turn.

A New World

Imagine a world in which great numbers of people experience compassion and lovingkindness as fundamental responses when dealing with others in all manner of relationships. In my imaginings about this, I envision a world that is quite different from the one we experience today. In this new world, each of us would naturally and automatically act to ease one small portion of our collective pain, as well as to add to our collective laughter and delight.

Revolutionary as it would be, such a change happens one person at a time, as each of us brings into our daily life a conscious willingness and ability to make a difference, no matter how small, one act at a time. To do this safely, from a position of personal integrity, you need to be grounded in your body and aware of yourself as part of your physical world. In the next chapter, we will explore how to strengthen and enrich your connection to your own *bodymind*.

Chapter 4

GETTING GROUNDED

Nurturing Yourself as *Bodymind*

Instead of abandoning ourselves, we can learn to inhabit ourselves. The body is tremendously homesick for us, and it waits patiently for our return.
—*Denise Taylor*

Wise people have long said that the body is the temple of the soul. It is also the medium through which we express in physical form the deepest qualities and intentions we carry inside. In a world of wholeness, a vast array of issues, states of mind, and feelings manifest in and through our bodies. Compassion, lovingkindness, an open heart, disowned feelings, tension, and stress all shape our physical experience as if we were clay in a sculptor's hands—and we are the sculptors.

Stories told throughout time by healers from all parts of the world, as well as findings in modern-day research in psychoneuroimmunology, speak of an intelligence that operates in our bodies and responds exquisitely to our mental and emotional experiences. Spontaneous and miraculous healings, such as the immediate disappearance of tumors or illness, magnificent and seemingly impossible physical feats, such as a parent lifting a car off a trapped child; and, unexpected achievements, such as physically disabled artists who pain with their mouths or toes, all stand as vivid evidence that our bodies are living miracles of complex processes that strive toward expressions of creativity and adaptability.

We are accustomed to thinking of the body and the mind as separate phenomena, but the inescapable interplay between psychological and physical states suggests a profound unity—a *bodymind.* If you believe that consciousness exists separately from the body, or that there is a continuity of consciousness after death, you may wonder how to reconcile these beliefs with the idea of a *bodymind*. Whatever your beliefs about whether or not consciousness continues after death, while we are live, *all our perceptions and experiences are filtered through our brains and bodies.* This even applies to out-of-body experiences and mystical states. As *bodyminds*, our thoughts and feelings constantly affect the health of our bodies and how they function. This is no great piece of news. We know, all too well, how feeling nervous or frightened can cause nausea, lightheadedness, or sweaty palms. In the same way, our bodies intimately affect our state of mind: when sick with flu, or recuperating from surgery, nothing holds our attention in the usual ways.

The Power of the Breath

We begin our exploration of the *bodymind* experience with the breath. It is through the breath that the body and mind find their most intimate and immediate connection. According to many sacred traditions, the breath is the source of energy and life for both body and psyche. Through ancient breathing practices, yogis change their metabolism, slowing their physical functions so profoundly that they seem to take no breaths at all. Other kinds of breathing exercises create transcendent states and allow access to sources of powerful energy and vitality.

As odd as this may seem, *learning to breathe* is an essential part of becoming grounded in your physical experience. To be able to breathe fully is natural to children, but it is a skill many of us have lost. As we grow up, we shut down our natural ability to breathe deeply and well. When we feel anxious or afraid, we often hold our breath, which "helps" us to stop feeling, sensing, and being aware of our bodies. Most of us breathe up in our chests, creating shallow breaths that barely nourish our bodies. Few of us naturally breathe from the belly, which is the center of vital physical energy.

While we could delve deeply into the mysteries of the breath, here we'll keep it simple. The exercises that follow show you how to use the breath as a way to ground yourself in your body *and* as a means of recentering yourself when you get caught up in life's busyness. We will also touch on ways to use the breath to create a meditative, quiet state of mind.

MAKE IT REAL
GUIDED MEDITATION #1:
Breathing from Your Belly

This meditation is a familiar and popular one, practiced by many traditions around the world. Its basic focus is to help you breathe from your belly rather than from your chest.

To begin, find a place where you can settle in for about ten minutes without being disturbed. Lie down so that you are flat on the floor or on a surface that supports you comfortably. If you have a physical condition that does not allow you to do this, find whatever position creates the greatest space and freedom in your solar plexus and chest.

Allow your body to settle and then become aware of the natural rhythm and quality of your breathing. There is nothing else to do but notice. Don't change anything. Just notice how you breathe naturally. Pay particular attention to whether your breath comes into your chest, so that your shoulders rise slightly when you breathe, or if it travels deeper into your abdomen, where the only movement with each breath is the gentle rise and fall of your belly.

Now place your hand on your belly in the area of your navel. On the next breath, inhale in such a way that your belly rises. Feel the movement with your hand. Then exhale in a way that causes your belly to fall. Follow that movement with your hand.

If you find that your breath is shallow and located up in your chest, spend a few moments experimenting with what happens when you concentrate on taking the breath in so that the hand resting on your belly feels an upward movement as you inhale. Give yourself permission to play with this. There is no need to struggle, nothing to force. Simply focusing your attention on the breath in this way invites your body to remember how it used to breathe naturally and fully when you were young.

GUIDED MEDITATION #2:
Inhaling through Alternate Nostrils

This is another well-known meditation. In its simplest form, it goes like this:

Settle yourself in a seated position in which your spine is comfortably erect. Again, if you have a physical condition that prohibits this, find whatever position works for you.

Place the index finger of your right hand over your right nostril. On the next inhalation, count to four as you inhale through your left nostril. Hold your breath to a count of seven, then exhale to a count of eight.

Change hands and place the index finger of your left hand over your left nostril and repeat the process, inhaling and exhaling through your right nostril.

You can repeat the alternating nostril breathing as many times as you'd like. You can also do this same meditation without alternating nostrils, where the focus of the meditation is on the slow, rhythmic counting that accompanies each inhalation and exhalation.

I urge you to look up some of the many fine books on breathing techniques that are available online, or at your local bookstore, some of which are listed in the recommended readings for this chapter. Learning to breathe properly, and then expanding your knowledge to include breathing practices that extend your awareness, is a powerful gift to yourself. Breathing properly contributes to a clear mind and a vibrant and energized body.

The Importance of Being Grounded

Because of the intricate interplay between the psychological and physical aspects of ourselves, it is important to be fully grounded in both the psyche and the body. At a practical, mundane level, when you are grounded in your body, you know whether you are hungry or full. Walking down a street, you know whether you feel safe, or if you need to pay more attention to where you are putting your feet. At a psychological level, it is useful to be able to recognize that the flutter in your stomach or the weakness in your knees may have more to do with fear than the onset of an illness.

How we relate to pain and other kinds of physical discomfort has a lot to do with our state of mind. Those of us who use hypnosis to teach pain management have observed countless incidents of individuals changing their level of pain, and their relationship to it, through the use of imagery and by developing a new level of awareness of their physical experience. Even if you are coping with intractable discomfort, you might discover that, by focusing your attention on the qualities and characteristics of the sensations in your body, something shifts in your perception of what, before, you characterized as pain.

Because learning about the body is accomplished more effectively through *experience* than discussion, there are many experiments and guided meditations throughout this chapter. In them, I invite you to explore the relationship you can have with your body and to discover the experience of yourself as a *bodymind*. As you work with these exercises, allow yourself to notice which approaches are useful and which don't hold any energy for you. What feels alive and right for one person may be flat or offensive to another, so allow yourself to be present with your experience and sense which of these exercises works for you. You may find that exercises that don't appeal to you this week feel on target next week. Making these subtle discernments is part of the process of becoming grounded in your body.

MAKE IT REAL
GUIDED MEDITATION #3:
Exploring Ways of Grounding Yourself

In this meditation, you will have an opportunity to shift your awareness to different places in your body. Find a place that's comfortable to sit, where your spine is erect and you are supported. If you have a physical disability or condition that prevents you from sitting, find a position that is comfortable for you and imagine the following journey in whatever way makes it real and alive for you. For each step in this meditation, pause and take as much or as little time as you need to explore your experience fully.

During the meditation, you will focus on two aspects of your physical being: the material body of muscles, bones, skin, and other components; the electromagnetic *energy* body that interpenetrates and extends beyond your skin.

Begin by reconnecting with the way in which you automatically settle into yourself. Settle in and take a few minutes to focus your attention in the space between one breath and the next. Just notice and enjoy the stillness that emerges when you allow your awareness to enter the quiet there.

If your consciousness is not focused in your head already, take a moment to do so now. Locate your awareness where you imagine the center of your brain to be, at the level of your forehead. Recall how your spine goes all the way from the base of your skull to the tip of your tailbone. Take a few moments to sense, feel, or imagine your spine.

Imagine now that energy runs up and down your spine. This is your "energy spine" and it continues up the back of your head and above you for about three feet. Follow it with your awareness and allow yourself to imagine what it's like to move up your energy spine beyond your head.

Next, allow your awareness to travel down your energy spine to the tip of your tailbone. Continue to follow your energy spine down three feet or so beneath you. Imagine that your energy spine runs several feet down, into the earth. Spend a few moments exploring what it is like to be connected to the earth in this way. What is it like for you to experience your self securely grounded in this way?

If you are in a building high above the ground, imagine that the energy of your spine continues to move down until it goes into the earth.

Recall the complete flow of your energy spine, from above your head down into the ground. As you do this, pay attention to your physical responses. Do you begin to feel more solidly planted in some way? Do you experience any sensations that convey to you a feeling of having more stability in the bottom portion of your body? Do you notice any sense of stretching in your back and neck, perhaps a sense of sitting taller?

Shift your attention away from your spine, now, and into your throat. Become aware of settling into your throat and notice how it feels to do so. Do you experience any sensations of dropping down into yourself a bit more?

Now, shift your attention farther down into your body, into your chest this time, in the area of your heart. Is your chest loose or tight? If you imagine your chest opening like a flower, what happens? Does your body settle even more? Do your shoulders drop a bit as you open your chest? Do you notice the increased sense of balance that accompanies an open, relaxed chest? Be sure to pay attention to any thoughts or emotional responses that may arise. Remember to invite mixed feelings and notice any areas of tension they may create.

Next, shift the focus of your awareness down to your solar plexus, just above your navel. Do you sense a greater degree of settling, as if you were moving more directly into your body a section at a time? Do you discover any flutters, or is there a feeling of solidity?

Notice what it is like to imagine inhabiting the top half of your body with more awareness than you may have given it a few moments ago. Pay particular attention to sensations of being more deeply embodied within yourself. As always, track any mixed feelings you may have. Just notice them and then return to the meditation.

Now bring your attention into your belly, just below the navel. Imagine that your belly is a bowl; pour your awareness into it and allow yourself to settle there. If you have difficulty actually experiencing your belly, imagine what it would be like if you could focus there. Do you notice that when you attain a belly focus, your mind may spontaneously quiet down and become still? What happens when you also recall how your energy spine grounds you into the earth itself? When awareness is so fully grounded in the body, your mind can rest comfortably in an experience of being securely housed. Be sure to allow any mixed feelings that may arise as you explore the sensation of being grounded in your belly.

Another way to imagine this is to place your awareness and the bowl in your belly on your pelvic floor, at the bottom of your pelvis.

Next, gently move your attention to your tailbone at the base of your spine. Stay there a moment, feeling the connection along your spine from head to tailbone. Now, notice what you experience when you focus on your legs and the bottoms of your feet. You can always ground yourself all the way into your body by moving your awareness into your legs and feet.

Then, return to your belly, refocusing there, and recall your energy spine running up and down your entire body, rising above and descending below the physical boundaries of your head and tailbone. Spend a few moments with your sensations, thoughts, and feelings.

When you're ready, refocus your attention on the external environment around you. Become aware of the sights, sounds, and smells that connect you with your environment, even as you stay grounded in your body.

When you feel ready, slowly open your eyes, wiggle your fingers and toes, and write down any impressions you have of your experience. If you choose, you can use this meditation as a way of grounding yourself before you begin your day.

Dealing with Mixed Feelings about Your Body

In the meditation, did you notice any places where you had mixed feelings about being in touch with your body? If you did, your response is not unusual. As we deepen our exploration of what it means to live as a *bodymind*, it's essential to take some time to consider the many ways in which most of us have mixed feelings about our bodies. If you are someone who lives with a physical disability or a condition that causes chronic pain or difficulty, your feelings about your body may be different from someone who has few physical complaints. If you are overweight and don't want to be, or consider yourself unattractive in some way, you probably have mixed feelings about that, too. If you are someone whom everyone else considers beautiful, you may have mixed feelings, especially if your psychological sense of yourself is at odds with your physical appearance, or if you feel inadequate or not beautiful enough.

Lots of mixed feelings may arise if you have suffered from a disease or an unexpected illness. For example, living with cancer, multiple sclerosis, or another challenging physical condition may leave you feeling betrayed by your body. It is important to realize that these mixed feelings are a perfectly natural response.

Some people blame their bodies or themselves for the illnesses or accidents that befall them. Unfortunately, some authors have suggested that we create our physical experiences as a result of unresolved or unconscious feelings and wishes. While there is no doubt that psychological factors play a significant role in disease processes, they are not the only factor involved. In a world where environmental and social stresses increase yearly, our bodies have to struggle to operate at optimal levels.

The bottom line is: it's not useful to blame your body for painful or unfortunate experiences you have had. It's also not helpful to blame yourself for not doing more to prevent whatever you experienced. Blaming your body, or yourself, implies that you should be able to stop suffering, to keep yourself from having painful or unpleasant experiences. This is a familiar feeling to most of us, and it's one of the ways we reinforce the illusion of having more control than is possible on a day-to-day basis. If you truly feel that other behaviors or attitudes would have made a difference, you can use that awareness to initiate those new responses now. Sometimes, though, there is nothing that can prevent a disease or keep you from having experiences in which you are truly helpless and out of control. Even when there are behaviors or states of mind that might help keep you safe or prevent certain physical conditions, self-blame diverts your capacity to deal with your body in a constructive way.

It may seem infuriatingly optimistic to suggest that physical difficulties can become opportunities for transformation, and I wouldn't presume to suggest that this is the initial response most of us have to unexpected changes in our physical well-being. The fact is, though, that stories abound about people who have had cancer or other illnesses and disabilities, reporting that these experiences have changed their lives for the better. Within the crisis, it seems, are possibilities for learning new coping mechanisms, for tapping into hidden resources, and eliciting new talents and capabilities that previously were not needed.

MAKE IT REAL EXPERIMENT #1:
Your Body as Your Friend

If you blame yourself or your body for some physical condition, or if you struggle with physical challenges, explore what it's like to set aside old, familiar responses for the moment and allow yourself to try on some other possibilities.

- Say to yourself, *My body is my friend*, and notice what responses first arise in your awareness. Be sure to leave room for mixed feelings – for both positive and negative signals.

- If you find you have negative feelings about your body, allow them to come forward into your conscious awareness and open yourself fully to them.

- In answering the following questions, just overlook those that aren't relevant to your particular situation:
    - If you blame your body for an illness or some other source of discomfort, are there other ways you can look at your experience? Are there any responses other than blame available to you?

- Was there something you could have done to prevent it?
- Was it just one of those things that happens and that nothing could have prevented?
- What are the learnings or opportunities inherent in your physical experience?

MAKE IT REAL
GUIDED MEDITATION #4:
Exploring Acceptance of Your Body

The next time you find yourself responding negatively or self-destructively to your body, take a moment to remember that you are a *body-mind*, that your body is part of the totality of your consciousness and being, and that it is not separate from you. Then bring your experience into the following meditation.

With the thought in mind that you are a totality of bodymind, take a few moments to settle into your breathing. If you are in physical discomfort, allow that to be present as fully as it needs to be. Do this meditation without struggle by allowing whatever is in your awareness simply to be present and move along naturally.

Take a few moments to move into the part of your body that has caused you discomfort or that has been the source of pain, anger, or other suffering. Simply be there with your heart open and your awareness willing to commune with this part of your body. There is nothing else to do, nothing to change right now. You are just being present, noticing whatever responses arise as you remain connected to yourself.

Take a moment to realize that there may be things you can do to help your body, and there also may not be. If there is something you can do, allow yourself to mentally rehearse what it would be like to take that action. How does your body respond? Send some heart energy to this part of your body and notice how that feels.

Be sure to allow any mixed feelings to come forward. There is nothing to do; just notice them.

Now notice what it would feel like to imagine a more positive and loving relationship with this aspect of your body. There is no rush to arrive at this place. Just try on the possibility.

Now refocus your attention in your heart and spend a few moments being present with your body, sensing it, accepting it just as it is. When you feel ready, bring yourself back to your surroundings by wiggling your fingers and toes.

Communing with Your Body

This temple that is your body, which blends so completely with your mind and feelings, is your best friend, even if your relationship with it is conflicted. Because you need your body in order to live, it matters a great deal whether you listen to, and take care of, its needs. It also matters that you are aware of the quality of your thoughts and feelings as they move through, and live in, your body.

Becoming more grounded, more whole as a *bodymind*, requires taking time to commune with your body. Your sense of wholeness is enhanced if you take some time each day, or once a week, to talk to your body and listen to what it has to convey to you. Just *residing* in your body isn't enough. The quality of your relationship with this miracle that gives you physical life is a powerful element in creating a sense of either psychological wholeness or alienation.

A close friend began a regimen of regular exercise after learning to commune with her body. For a few minutes at the end of her meditation each day she asked her body, *What do you need from me?* At first, she didn't receive a direct response, but she just kept asking anyway. Over a period of several weeks, she began to notice the presence of a recurring thought: *I ought to exercise.* Eventually, she responded to this inner prompting and feels better now than she did ten years ago.

A client took up yoga after learning to commune with his body. The more he asked his body what it needed from him, the more he felt compelled to stretch and limber up. He also noticed that he was not craving meat as he had for most of his life. Naturally, and without any struggle, he slowly shifted to a more vegetarian diet and, as is true with so many people who learn to listen to their bodies' needs, he felt better than he had in many years, if ever.

As the above examples indicate, communing with your body means asking it what it needs from you in order for it to be physically healthy and strong. The process also involves learning to notice areas of stored tension and then finding ways to release them. One way is to get massages or do bodywork of some kind. Another is to move your consciousness into the tension and have a dialogue with it.

For example, through a series of sessions with a Feldenkrais practitioner—Feldenkrais is a highly focused form of bodywork that allows the body to function much more comfortably and efficiently—I became aware of how I store tension in my jaw, something I had been completely unaware of until then. Once I was able to experience the tension, I did two things. First, I entered the tension in my imagination and asked it what it was about. The response was that there were times I needed to speak up, or at least to notice something I needed to say *to myself*. Once I was able to listen to the tension, I could recognize what I was holding back and then choose whether to say anything out loud. At the very least, I was aware of what was going on within myself and no longer needed to carry the tension in my jaw. Second, I imagined clouds floating between my teeth, which taught me to relax my jaw. I discovered that releasing this tension affected the comfort and posture of the rest of my body.

Because there is a constant flow of communication between body and psyche, whether or not we are aware of it, taking time to commune with the body creates a two-way channel of awareness to receive and transmit the messages. In this way, you can train yourself to pay attention to the small physical messages that you might otherwise overlook. In the exercises that follow, you have an opportunity to practice communing with your body to enhance the flow of communication with yourself as *bodymind*.

MAKE IT REAL EXPERIMENT #2:
Affirming Your Body's Importance

Using affirmations as a means of communing with your body can be a powerful and effective way to enhance the relationship between body and psyche. What follows are a few examples of affirmations you might use. Change their wording, if you need to, until they feel relevant and achievable to you. Affirmations lose their effectiveness if they are too difficult for you to believe or if they feel rote or mechanical.

- The most basic affirmation to give yourself about your body is:

    I need my body to live.

    Notice whatever thoughts, feelings, reactions, or responses arise when you say this affirmation out loud or repeat it mentally. Allow mixed feelings and give yourself permission to explore further whatever emerges in your awareness. You may find that you have negative or limiting beliefs about your body that you hadn't recognized before. Or you may discover a deep love and respect for your body that had not been in your conscious awareness until now.

- Another basic affirmation is:

    My body is a miracle.

    Again, simply notice your response to this affirmation as you say it. Do you find yourself arguing with the idea that your body is a miracle? Or do you find yourself feeling even more attuned to the fact that your body functions in ways that are hard to imagine, that it keeps itself working without any conscious input from you whatsoever? Just be aware of whatever feelings emerge as you work with the affirmation.

- The following affirmations explore the dynamic quality of your relationship to your body:
    - *My body is my friend.*
    - *I am learning to listen to my body more deeply than ever before.*
    - *My conscious awareness lives in my body and my body's awareness lives in me.*

As you work with these affirmations, and/or others you create for yourself, simply notice any shifts that occur in how you feel about your body. Over time, replace affirmations that have become second nature to you with new ideas that deepen your sense of connection to, and appreciation for, your body.

(From the perspective of self-hypnosis, affirmations are a form of self-talk, a form of self-hypnosis. When we become more aware of the kinds of suggestions we give ourselves through our self-talk, we engage a deep potential for healing as we "update" our internal conversation with positive affirmations, positive self-hypnosis.)

GUIDED MEDITATION #5:
Communing with Your Body

In this meditation you have an opportunity to spend some time listening to your body. There is nothing you have to do. The meditation simply offers an invitation to be present.

Sitting or lying down, take some time to focus your attention in your body. Begin with an awareness of your breathing, without changing its natural flow in and out of your nose, in and out of your lungs.

Allow your awareness to begin to move, gently and slowly, from the top of your head all the way down your body to the tips of your toes. Pretend you are taking a leisurely journey, stopping for a moment at your fingers or lingering in your belly. Follow your awareness through your body in whatever depth or detail you would like. Give yourself whatever time you need to become thoroughly aware of your body. Be sure to include any discomfort and/or pleasurable sensations you may discover.

When you feel satisfied that you have explored your body as fully as you want to this time, focus your attention in your heart. Give yourself the suggestion that you will open your heart to your body, that you will make room in your heart for a deeply felt sense of relationship between your psyche and your body.

From this point of awareness, repeat one or more affirmations about your body. For example, you might say to yourself mentally, My body is a miracle and I need it to live, while you experience your heart extending a welcoming energy throughout your body.

If mixed feelings arise, include them in your experience. They are a natural part of your relationship with your body.

Allow yourself to spend a few moments listening to your

body, opening yourself to whatever it may want to share with you right now. Ask your body, What do you need? Again, there is nothing to strive for here. Simply allow yourself to be open to whatever impressions emerge as you commune with your body. Your body may offer you a sensation of comfort, or it may bring your attention to some discomfort you hadn't noticed before. An idea may drop into your awareness that develops over time, or perhaps nothing will come. The important thing is to allow yourself to focus for a few moments, without preconceptions, on whatever your body may want to communicate to you.

When you're ready, shift your focus back to your heart and take a moment to be there, reviewing whatever this experience has given you. Then, wiggle your fingers and toes and come all the way back to your surroundings.

Honoring Your Body

There's no getting around it: we are in this life with the bodies we've got, and we're in it for life. Whatever the strengths, potentials, shortcomings, and weaknesses of our bodies, there is no escape from them. If we want to thrive psychologically and experience a state of wholeness, we need to learn to honor our bodies.

It is all too easy to take the body for granted. We feed it, wash it, move around in the world in it. It works or it doesn't. Unless we experience physical distress or limitations, many of us don't pay much attention to our bodies. Instead we live mostly in our thoughts and feelings.

I recall all the years I spent wishing my eyes hadn't been crossed as a child and the countless times I hid from cameras and mirrors. In a slow process of healing and acceptance, I have come to terms with my eyes and even feel some affection for the slightly different cast they have, even now. I am much more able to honor the fact that I have sight, even as I acknowledge the visual limitations resulting from my eyes not being completely aligned in childhood.

The importance of honoring the body we have been given was driven home to me during a consultation with someone who came to me specifically to work on a physical disability with which she had struggled all her life. We did a guided meditation into the future and she was surprised by a deep agitation resulting from the fact that she experienced her *future self* as able-bodied. The body that came into her imaginal experience was so different from the one she knew on a day-to-day basis that it didn't feel normal to her. Her self-identity had always included her physical disability and she felt she would dishonor the body she had if she accepted the image that came up spontaneously during her guided meditation journey. I suggested that she focus on the *qualities* of the able body and discover how these could be useful to her in the present. She was relieved to realize that this was an empowering and useful option for her.

A friend of mine underwent treatment for breast cancer a number of years ago. Rather than struggle with and rail against her condition, she chose a different attitude: to give her body her full attention and commitment during this important time. As a way of honoring her body, she conscientiously used self-hypnosis, physical therapy, medical treatments, and good nutrition to support her body's healing process, as well as to honor its value to her.

Another friend discovered sacred approaches that honor women's bodies. The *yoni*, a Sanskrit word for the female genitalia, represents the creative power of the vulva, vagina, and uterus. As a result of reading about images of the *yoni* found in natural formations such as caverns, rocks, deep holes in tree trunks, as well as in ancient statues that emphasize female genitals, my friend learned to more deeply appreciate the mystery, beauty, and power of her *woman's* body. As she described it, she was amazed at how many *yoni* images had been present all around her and yet completely outside her conscious awareness.

As you work with the following exercises, give yourself permission to discover ways in which you can acknowledge and honor your body. Keep an open mind and be sure to invite mixed feelings. As you become aware of those ways in which you dishonor your body through mistreatment—not getting enough sleep, eating poorly, using drugs, overworking, exercising too strenuously—allow yourself to experiment with the idea of taking better care of yourself. If disgust or anger emerge, pay attention to your feelings and seek help, if necessary, to work them through so that you can discover the enhanced sense of wholeness that emerges naturally when you honor your body.

MAKE IT REAL EXPERIMENT #3:
Uncovering Ways You Dishonor Your Body

In this experiment you have an opportunity to explore how you may dishonor your body without realizing it. Once you are aware of any mixed or negative feelings you may have about your body, it will be easier to remember to honor yourself.

- Make a list of the things about your body that disgust you, are a source of shame, pain, or other discomfort, or that you wish were different. There is nothing to do with these responses just now. Simply note them.

- Next, acknowledge and honor the fact that you have struggled with these aspects of your physical self. The mixed feelings are part of your wholeness and have a place in your awareness.

- Focus on a specific complaint you have about your body. Explore it as fully as you want to, bringing into your explorations an awareness of all the reasons why this aspect of your physical self bothers you, how that makes you feel, what you imagine others think about this part of your body, and any other elements of the complaint you wish to examine more closely. Then take some time to consider how this aspect of your body also serves you, as I did with my eyes. Find the value *in spite* of the problem.

- Ask yourself how you can *both* acknowledge a physical limitation or difficulty *and* recognize the service that part of your body provides. Take some time to honor that part of your body by acknowledging that it is an aspect of who you are and has a place in your self-identity.

- Over time, notice if consciously honoring your body in this way helps you shift from what may have been a conflicted relationship into one that is more settled and accepting.

EXPERIMENT #4:
Honoring Your Body

- At least once a week, perform some activity with the specific intention of honoring and nurturing your body. For example, you might take a warm bath with special oils or other preparations that leave you feeling relaxed and rejuvenated. Another possibility is some kind of exercise or activity that is energizing and that promotes a feeling of health and well-being, such as yoga or walking. Notice that the activity may be something "routine," which you now change into something special by means of the intention you bring to it.

- Whatever you decide to do to honor your body, do it with full awareness that the activity you have chosen is an expression of gratitude for your body's service to you. Eventually, you may discover that you have an urge to do something good for your body on an ongoing basis, if you don't do so already. If this happens, simply notice it and remember to open your heart to your body and allow the gratitude you feel to flow through it.

EXPERIMENT #5:
Honoring Your Sensuality and Sexuality

Not only does your body offer you a means of being in the world, it is also a source of deep pleasure. In this next experiment you have an opportunity to explore your relationship with your sensual/sexual self and enrich your capacity to experience these aspects of your body.

As you do this exercise, pay attention to your tactile awareness *and* to how your body responds to being touched. Notice whatever sensations arise and whether or not they are accompanied by mixed feelings, unexpected thoughts, or other responses. Consider the experience a journey of exploration and discovery.

- Begin by focusing your awareness in your fingertips as you run them across a piece of fabric. Notice the sensations you experience. Then run your fingertips across a hard surface, such as a kitchen sink, or a tile floor. Next, put your fingers under cool running water, then warm running water. There is nothing to do but notice the sensations in your fingertips as you come in contact with these different textures and temperatures.

- Take a few moments now to run your hands down the front of your thighs. You may do this wearing clothes if you are uncomfortable being naked.

- Next, run your hands up and down your arms. Do so gently and yet be strongly present as you focus your awareness in the palms of your hands and your fingers. Really *feel* the sensations of moving your hands up and down your arms.

- Now touch your face with your fingertips, feeling all the surfaces of your forehead, eyebrows, eyes, nose, cheeks, mouth, jaw. Again, simply notice how it feels to be conscious of experiencing your sensations.

- You can extend this experiment by focusing on other sensory modalities. For example, you might center the experiment around tasting different foods, smelling a variety of fragrances, or listening to music and other sounds with your full awareness.

- If it is comfortable for you, extend the experiment even further and allow yourself sessions where you explore your sexual senses. For example, if you already have a favorite form of masturbation, engage it with an increased sense of touch, focusing your awareness fully in whatever parts of your body are involved. Allow your fingertips to explore the parts of your body that are particularly erotic, taking the time to notice *all* the different sensations that accompany your sexual pleasure.

    The goal of this experiment is to help you reconnect with the richness and variety of the kind of enlivened sensuality that children experience naturally. Being present in your body and noticing your senses add to your feeling of being alive.

Dealing with Physical Distress

Since most of us have to deal with physical difficulties at some point in our lives, I want to include some exercises you can do when your body is in distress. These exercises are based on well-known and much-used hypnotic approaches for dealing with physical pain, disease, and preparation for surgery and other medical procedures. As with all other exercises of this kind, allow yourself to be creative and change what is offered here in ways that make the approaches more dynamic and powerful for you.

As I mentioned earlier, it is very important to allow yourself to be present with any discomfort you may feel. Experience has shown repeatedly that inviting pain or distress *into* awareness, rather than attempting to push it away, tends to lessen its intensity. Allow yourself to experiment with this process. Deliberately struggle with your discomfort and notice whether or not it gets worse. Then relax around it, hold it in your awareness *softly*, and see what happens. Focus on the sensations that accompany it and describe them to yourself: are they sharp, dull, textured, smooth, prickly, throbbing? As you practice softening around discomfort and simply noticing it, it often eases more quickly.

It is possible to become even more consciously aware of the elements involved in physical distress by allowing sensations and conditions to develop into images. These symbolic representations can be anything that spontaneously comes to mind—colors, shapes, creatures, objects, people—anything that your deeper wisdom chooses to convey the quality and message of the physical distress.

For example, one woman came to see me to work on severe back pain. The image that emerged in her mind's eye to represent the pain was a complicated knot. Through a process of imagining that the knot loosened and began to untangle, this woman was able to ease her pain to a noticeable degree. Another person experienced a sharp pain in her neck as the talons of a large bird digging into her flesh. As she talked with the bird, she learned that it represented old grief she had stored in her muscles. Through a process of getting in touch with the feelings, the bird slowly released its grip and her muscle pain eased.

As the above example illustrates, it is also useful to remember that many kinds of physical distress are psychological in origin. Because so many of us translate our emotional and mental pain and conflict into physical difficulties, we will also explore how to translate psychological states back into their appropriate language—the language of thoughts and feelings.

MAKE IT REAL
EXPERIMENT #6:
Physical and Psychological Pain Control

The form of this exercise is a little different. Based on a common hypnotic approach to easing physical pain, it can be conceived in any way that makes sense to you each time you use it. For example, it may be used to diminish physical pain or, equally powerfully, it can translate physical pain into psychological awareness.

Even as you strive to achieve greater physical comfort, it is important to know that a certain amount of pain is beneficial. People who don't feel any physical pain are at great risk because they can develop life-threatening infections without realizing it and incur debilitating injuries without knowing they have hurt themselves. For this reason, I encourage you always to have a little pain, a little discomfort. It is an important early-warning system.

One woman came to see me to work on alleviating her knee pain. In her imagination the pain appeared as a large black circle. By visualizing the circle shrinking to a small dot, a little bit at a time, the pain in her knee diminished noticeably. She was left with a sensation that was perfectly manageable and that allowed her to remain aware of her knee so she wouldn't hurt it further.

Another individual came to work with me on his chronic shoulder tension. In letting the sensation form into an image, he discovered a large fist gripping his muscles. He gave the fist a voice and listened to what it had to say to him. The message revealed feelings he hadn't brought into conscious awareness. As he allowed himself to acknowledge his anger toward a co-worker, and then to experience and describe these feelings. As he did so, the fist relaxed and the shoulder muscles became more comfortable. From then on, he knew how to give his body a respite from holding his psychological distress by listening to the gripping feelings he had translated into muscle tension.

- Begin by identifying a physical condition you'd like to work on and move into the sensations that accompany the condition. Allow yourself to be fully present with whatever sensations come to the forefront of your awareness.

- Without conscious preconception, allow an image that represents the sensation to drop into your awareness. Let the image develop and notice its dominant characteristics, such as the *gripping* in the above example.

- Once you have a vivid awareness of the image, decide whether you need to have a dialogue with it. If you think your physical distress has psychological origins, take some time to talk with the image and find out what it has to say.

- Next, discover what will help shift the image and reduce its intensity.

    - What will it look like when it no longer causes you noticeable physical distress?

    - Would it help for you to imagine the changes that need to occur in the image?

- Does it need to fade? Shrink? Change form entirely?

- Take whatever time you need to work with the imagery. Allow the image to evolve, shift, change in whatever ways support the outcome you seek. If the image shows no change right now, continue to imagine what it will look like when it *does* change and send that message to your body.

  - As the image changes, notice any shifts in the sensations in your body. When these shifts are in a more comfortable direction, give yourself a bit of time simply to experience them.

- When you feel finished, give yourself a few moments to refocus your attention on your surroundings, so that you come all the way back into your present-moment focus.

GUIDED MEDITATION #6:
Relieving Stress, Tension, and Fatigue

This meditation can be used whenever you need to reduce stress, tension, and fatigue or diffuse the effects of powerful emotional states or disease processes. Its main focus is to create an experience in which your body fills with warm, clean, clear, and heavy sand that absorbs all fatigue, discomfort, or anything else you want to release. For some people, the idea of filling up with sand is uncomfortable. If this is true for you, substitute the image of sand with one of warm, clear water, or a beautiful light of any color, or some other substance that brings to mind peaceful, soothing, settled, and comforting sensations in your body. This meditation may be done in whatever position affords you the most comfort.

Begin by settling in and taking a few moments to follow your exhalation down to the still point at the bottom of the breath, the gap between the outbreath and the inbreath.

Next, imagine that clear, clean warm sand begins to flow into your body through your shoulders. Allow the flow to be gentle and easy, as it fills your entire body from your neck down to your toes. Some people like to fill up their heads as well. Just be aware of whatever pleasant sensations your body feels as it fills with warm, clean, clear sand.

Pay attention to the natural, delicious heaviness and internal warmth that develop as your arms, legs, torso, hands, and feet fill with the sand. Simply allow your body's response to emerge and then notice it. There is nothing else you have to do beyond sensing the sand filling you.

Imagine the sand absorbing any fatigue, stress, pain, or anything else that you want to release now. Give yourself some moments to allow the sand to absorb whatever you want to release. Notice how your body responds as you allow the sand to do its work, relieving your body of the distress it has carried. Take however long you want to experience the sand and the comfort it brings.

Now, allow the sand to flow out through your hands and the bottoms of your feet, including your toes and fingers as well. Imagine that the sand flows down into the very core of the earth, where it is melted down and recycled. If you originally filled yourself with light, or some other substance, allow that to flow out of you now, leaving you cleansed and nourished.

Return to an awareness of your breath and allow the next inhalation to fill you with life giving oxygen. As you exhale, return to the still point, the gap between breaths, and spend a few moments in the silence that exists there.

Then, when you feel ready, bring yourself back to your surroundings by wiggling your fingers and toes.

Another Way of Being Grounded

Being grounded means more than being fully present in your physical body. It also means being fully connected to the context in which you live, able to move between the demands of the rational, everyday world and the non-rational needs and aspirations of your interior self, the part of you that seeks to experience the sacred.

When I was young, I was taught that the material world was inferior to spiritual realities. I was told to focus my attention on developing lofty morals, spiritual values, on helping others instead of myself. For my grandmother, living a spiritual life meant devaluing or "rising above" the body in favor of a more enlightened mind. For example, my grandmother was proud to tell us that she and my grandfather had engaged in sexual relations only to procreate—and she had only two children. For her, sexuality was to be "transmuted," its energy used instead for loftier acts of creativity.

This mind-body split never felt comfortable to me and, as I grew up, I found myself increasingly drawn to ideas that emphasized the *continuum* of spirit and matter—that matter is spirit in dense form and that spirit is matter at ever-higher vibratory frequencies. In this approach, one is not better than the other. Instead, each is an aspect of an integrated whole.

When we believe that spirit and matter are fundamentally different, we are as ungrounded as we are when we split body and mind. From an integrative spiritual perspective, you might consider yourself to be *spirit embodied*, just as you are a bodymind in the physical world. As *spirit embodied*, it is useful to be able to translate transcendent awareness and realities into everyday, physical terms.

As a young adult, I had many transcendent experiences involving perceptions and awarenesses that went beyond the boundaries of "normal" sensory experience. The problem was that, even with all my grandmother's teachings, I had no effective ways of grounding what I learned in my expanded states of consciousness into anything meaningful in my daily life. As I mentioned earlier, a friend once said I was like a kite flying high in the sky with no one on the ground holding onto my string. I found each new revelation or meditative experience to be profoundly moving, but I couldn't share these experiences with others; I didn't have a language that could describe them in practical terms.

In addition, I wasn't truly alive in my body. Though my journeys in consciousness took me to wondrous places, I wasn't really present in my daily activities. I certainly was not living a mindful life, despite all the meditating and transcendent explorations I did. To become psychologically whole, to live more consciously, I had to spend many years learning how to be present on all levels of awareness, from the most expanded to the most mundane, from lofty inspiration to a bellyache. I also had to learn to honor all these experiences equally, without judging some as more valuable than others because they were "spiritual."

Honoring both spiritual and physical awareness as equal parts of your whole self allows you to translate spiritual realizations into everyday activities. For example, a meditation that deepens your understanding of the spiritual truth that *the only moment you really have is the one that is happening now* might prompt you to complete a task today that, ordinarily, you would put off until some other time, to make a telephone call you have put off for weeks, or to clean up the mess you have learned to ignore by telling yourself you'll do it later.

Grounding spiritual experiences into everyday activities also gives you an opportunity to affect the *quality* you bring into daily living. You can do this by continuing to carry in your awareness any spiritual insight that may have emerged during periods of meditation. For example, you might tap into an experience of oneness with all life forms; grounding this awareness might involve more consciously honoring all the life around you. As I mentioned in an earlier chapter, you might explore what you would experience if you stopped an immediate impulse to kill a bug or spider, noticing instead what it feels like to honor that life by taking it outside where it can continue on its way unharmed. If you feel you must kill a bug or some other creature, perhaps your experience of oneness would allow you to do so with increased respect for the life you take.

The following exercises invite you to explore your experience as *spirit in action* and to be curious about the quality of yourself as a *bodymind* that functions in a physical world permeated by spiritual realities.

MAKE IT REAL
EXPERIMENT #7:
Grounding Spiritual Experiences

The next time you have a spiritual insight, ask yourself how your new awareness might enhance your connection with the sacred in everyday life, how you might apply it, or how it might change the way in which you think about or do something. If you have a meditation that is particularly powerful, or you find yourself contemplating a new understanding of a concept that is especially meaningful to you, in what ways might your daily life be informed or enhanced by this awareness?

- Pay attention to the *quality* you bring to your activities as you continue to carry in your awareness the spiritual insight that came to you in your meditation.

- As spiritual insights and realities become more integrated into your daily life and activities, notice how much more present you are for each task you undertake, however mundane.

- Explore freely how to bring into grounded physical expression your spiritual experiences and insights—the fruits of your journey into the sacred.

GUIDED MEDITATION #6:
Relieving Stress, Tension, and Fatigue

For this meditation, find a place where you can sit for a few minutes without being disturbed. Sit with your spine erect and your body comfortable. Once you are settled, take a few moments to be present with your breathing following the exhalations down to the bottom of the breath. Settle into "home base," in the very middle of yourself, and pay attention to the still point that exists between each exhalation and inhalation. Sometimes you won't even notice that the still point is present, but it is always there, inviting you to settle even more.

Next, allow yourself to imagine a stream of light that comes from the sun down through the top of your head. The light flows gently as it enters your body and continues down your neck, your spine, your legs, and out the bottoms of your feet, flowing down into the very center of the earth.

This stream of light from the sun is always present, always available, and always nourishing you. Notice how the sun's energy, as it flows down your spine, also flows into your body, nourishing every cell, every particle of your being. It also fills your thoughts and feelings, nourishing them as well.

Allow yourself to be like a sponge and soak in that light as fully as you can. All you need to do is imagine that you are a sponge and you can effortlessly absorb the life-giving light of the sun.

Now notice that a stream of light moves up from the very core of the earth itself and enters the bottoms of your feet. The light continues up into your spine, up your back and neck, and moves out through the top of your head, all the way up to the sun. Become aware of soaking up this earth energy, the other source of life, as if you were a sponge. Just let it happen, let it nourish every cell, every particle, every aspect of your being with life-giving earth energy.

Now imagine that you are a beautiful pearl threaded on these new streams of light. You are perfectly held, perfectly balanced, reaching to the sun and grounded within the very core of the earth itself. Take a few moments to be present with the energy of these two streams of light and notice your response to being held so profoundly within such life-giving energies.

Be sure to notice any mixed feelings you might have, simply notice how you feel.

Now take a moment to review your experience before coming back. Remind yourself that these streams of light and energy are available all the time, and that you can draw life-giving nourishment from them no matter where you are, no matter what you may be doing.

Allow yourself to wonder how your experience of these streams of light might affect the quality and tone of your daily activities, thoughts, feelings, and sensations.

When you feel ready, come all the way back to your environment and wiggle your fingers and toes to make sure you're really here, in this moment, in your body, ready to go on to whatever is next.

It's a Lifetime Relationship

Throughout all the stages of development, your experience of yourself as *bodymind* shapes who you are and how you live in the world, supporting—or undermining—your sense of self-esteem. To be grounded in a loving, grateful relationship with your own body, to be present in everyday experiences, provides a solid foundation of well-being with which to engage the world.

While you can't completely control what happens to you in your life, you can seek to be *present* in response to whatever experiences come your way. To disown your body is a recipe for disaster. It is impossible to be safe in a world where you are disconnected from your most immediate and profound source of knowing.

At this moment in the world's history, we have extended the mind-body split beyond our individual selves to encompass the globe: most of us are shockingly out of touch with our physical/ecological world, much to our collective peril. The work of creating and preserving physical health individually and globally requires an ongoing, conscious relationship with our bodies and our world: we must be willing to *be here*, in the present moment, aware of whatever may be happening, in order to be able to respond to whatever is needed. To say the least, this is much easier said than done. In the next chapter, we will explore *mindfulness*, a state of mind and being that helps us remain conscious of ourselves and the world around us . . . moment to moment.

Chapter 5

PRACTICING MINDFULNESS
Living Consciously

Each thought, each action in the sunlight of awareness, becomes sacred.
—Thich Nhat Hanh

Practicing mindfulness can truly transform the quality of daily living. Not only do we become more present to our ongoing experiences—more grounded in an awareness of our responses, choices, and actions—we also learn how to move through experiences more easily and "elegantly."

When I first learned about mindfulness, I was struck by how obvious and simple it seemed—but soon discovered how complex, challenging, and rewarding an undertaking it was to bring mindfulness into my daily life. The simplicity I first glimpsed is contained in its single-pointed purpose: to focus attention on the present moment, right here and right now. The complexity is that few of us are accustomed to being *all here* when we are here.

By definition, mindfulness is *awareness of awareness*. For example, as I write these words in a mindful state, I focus my awareness on being fully present to the task. I notice the sensations in my fingertips as they tap the keys on the computer keyboard. A twinge in my leg draws my attention to my body and how I am sitting in the chair. As I continue writing, my attention is drawn to the silence that surrounds me right now. It is early morning and the hum of the computer and clicking of the keys are my only companions in this moment. Even the birds are still, and the day's traffic noises haven't yet begun.

Throughout the few moments described above, I attended to the ever-shifting, ever-present array of sensations that constantly move through my experience—and everyone else's. It's like imagining that you are sitting on the bank of a stream, watching the water flow by even as you also notice what floats on its surface. Whether there are twigs, leaves, garbage, or other debris doesn't matter. Even if you would *prefer* only twigs and leaves—or nothing at all on the surface of the water—you continue to notice what *is*. In time, with practice, you would observe what is floating by without judgment.

It is the same with your ever-moving stream of consciousness. Mindfulness makes no demands about what *kinds* of thoughts, feelings, and sensations float through you awareness. Instead it asks you to notice *whatever* arises in your experience, to bring awareness to the moment that is occurring right now. Even when something dramatic or ugly appears, analogous to a large tree limb floating by on the stream, all you have to do is continue to notice what's moving along on the surface of the water. By staying on the bank of the stream and not jumping into the water—not getting swept away by your thoughts, feelings, sensations, or impulses—you avoid being carried away, swept outside the center of yourself.

As the image of sitting on the bank of the stream implies, an intrinsic characteristic of a mindful state is *non-at-*

tachment. For most of us, this is a new and challenging attitude to bring to our internal experience. As a general rule, we become quite caught up in, and concerned about, the drama of our lives. By practicing the Buddhist principle of non-attachment, we notice the never-ending, ever-changing flow of our thoughts, feelings, sensations, and impulses without clinging, grasping, holding onto, or fending off our experience. There is no struggle one way or the other. There is just awareness.

For example, as I continue to write, I notice that I'm starting to get restless. It's not time yet to stop writing, so I simply notice the sensations moving through me. There is no need to respond to these awarenesses. I simply notice them and go on writing. They will pass and something else will come up. There's no need to *do* anything but continue to write and be aware.

Another example of mindfulness in action happened to a friend who recently had the annoying experience of losing her luggage on an airplane flight to a distant city. She would have preferred not to have had this experience, but her skill at mindfulness allowed her to be present with what was happening without struggling against it. Initially she felt disbelief and a conviction that the experience was *not* happening to her. Once she recognized that she was struggling with a situation she couldn't change, she let go of her reaction and decided to focus mindfully on her experience. When she got irritated, for instance, she noted her response without either feeding it or pushing it away. It passed, only to be followed by a feeling of helplessness, which also came and went. Finally, she did what had to be done to have her bags delivered to her hotel when they arrived on another plane.

In addition to preventing her from being swept into a swirl of feelings and reactions, she also noticed how the practice of mindfulness fostered a sense of humor, an ability to laugh at the absurdity of the situation. Even as she moved through irritation, helplessness, and surrender, she found herself laughing at her inability to do anything about her lost clothing and toiletries…and, her luggage arrived at her hotel by midnight of the same day. Prior to learning mindfulness meditation, she would have engaged the experience with deadly seriousness, escalating her own upset, and losing the opportunity to play with the challenge of moving through the experience with awareness.

Awareness of Awareness

A basic premise of mindfulness practice is that the contents of consciousness—all the thoughts, sensations, feelings, fantasies, and anything else you can name—constantly change. When we begin to bring awareness to what is flowing through us, we discover that, moment to moment, nothing remains the same. In fact, over time it is possible to discover that just about the only time feelings, thoughts, or sensations persist—get stuck or blocked—is when we tighten around them, fight with them, or try to make them go away, rather than watch them arise and flow through awareness.

Bringing awareness to awareness also reveals the extent to which we spontaneously evaluate our thoughts, feelings, and impulses—how we judge them as good or bad. From a perspective of mindfulness, the very process of judging creates increased distress. Developing a capacity to notice judging as just one more awareness—no more meaningful or important than any other—fosters a shift. We naturally become less attached to evaluating the contents of consciousness and, instead, focus more on observing what comes and goes, even when what's coming and going happens to be a judgment of something as good or bad.

When you change your relationship to judging and lessen the need to categorize experience as good or bad, you engage a shift in response that is truly transformative. Take a moment to think about how pervasive the tendency is to evaluate nearly *everything* as valuable or worthless, better or worse, appealing or disgusting, happy or sad, supportive or hurtful. Recognize how deeply most of us *believe* that these judgments reflect an absolute truth.

For example, let's say I'm irritated with a cab driver for taking the slow route to my destination. If I am practicing awareness of awareness, I might simply notice my irritation, feel it, and let it move through me. It is what's happening at that moment; I can label it for what it is and let it go. If, on the other hand, I am caught up in judging, I might either get annoyed at myself for being irritated or escalate my annoyance at the driver for irritating me in the first place (as if the driver were the source of my irritation and not my own reactivity). Whichever road I take with my judgment, I'm going to have a rougher journey than I would have if I had been able to observe my feelings without becoming caught up in the judgments about them.

Becoming skilled at observing awareness of awareness brings practical and grounded benefits to daily life. How many of us spend much of our time carried along on the currents of fantasies—of mental dialogues with people, thoughts about what's coming up tomorrow or next week, ruminating over past mistakes, making lists of future projects we have to complete, thinking far into the future when, we hope, our dreams will have come true? Most of us spend a good deal of time caught up in our internal chatter and unfolding drama, not really aware of what's happening in this moment, right now. Mindfulness makes us conscious of where our awareness is focused and, in doing so, returns us to the present.

As a meditative practice, mindfulness teaches us how to know we've left this moment and gone off into our fantasy life—gotten caught up in some thought or feeling that takes us away from what's happening right now. Thich Nhat Hanh, a Vietnamese Buddhist monk, teaches mindfulness practices geared toward Western sensibilities. He has translated a meditative approach into a grounded and simple way of being in the world. What I like about his approach is its practicality and usefulness for bringing awareness of awareness into the regular activities of everyday life. For example, washing dishes is an activity many of us do at least once a day. When you wash dishes mindfully, what may have been a chore, drudgery, becomes an opportunity to experience yourself as alive and present. By focusing on the sensations in your hands as you feel the water, soap, and the surface of the dishes, you bring yourself fully into what you're doing. An immediate benefit of being mindful in this way is that it's hard to be bored when you're paying attention to your ongoing experience. The elements of the experience itself convey a sense of aliveness that isn't there when your mind is wandering and you wash the dishes automatically.

Imagine how the quality of your life would change if each moment were interesting and had your full attention — even those moments that were unhappy or uncomfortable. In the same way that awareness can shift physical pain, focusing on the moment-to-moment flow of the elements involved in any daily activity brings to life everything you do in a new way. That doesn't mean you suddenly feel *delighted* to clean the toilet, but cleaning the toilet does feel different when you use the task as an opportunity to practice mindfulness.

Adding Logs to the Fire

In recent years, I have added a metaphor to my work with clients around the issue of how they feed — or don't feed — their activation and upset. I invite clients to imagine that their response or reaction is like a bonfire and ask them to notice how they feed it, how they keep it alive. This is a useful exercise because, when allowed to, thoughts, feelings and physical sensations tend to arise, move through, and move on when given the space to do so. The problem comes when we begin to do one of the following:

- If we struggle with what's moving through us, asking it not to be there, we add energy to it in our attempts to push it away.

- If we have a preference for *not* feeling what we actually are feeling, we add energy because we are fighting what is present in our experience.

- If we begin an inner dialogue that says this shouldn't be happening to us, or it's not fair, we are also adding energy, which increases and prolongs our discomfort.

- If we tense up around an experience and allow that tension to mount without doing what we can to relax, we add fuel to the fire, as well.

- And, if we want something to continue that isn't able to continue, our desire also adds energy to whatever distress we may feel in the face of the inevitable movement of this moment into the next.

Mindful awareness offers us a way to notice what's moving through us without adding any energy to it. In this way, we may have moments of noticeable discomfort, but those moments may be much more short-lived than they would be if we added struggle to them. By noticing where we add logs to the bonfire, and pulling ourselves back from that stance, we support the natural tendency of flashes of activation to fade on their own.

A surprising experience for many people is to discover how much they *don't* want to let go of the thoughts, feelings, tension and other responses related to the upset. The habit of feeding our emotional experience is an old and well-established one for most of us. It's important to know that there are times we just don't want to let go of a reaction that tells us we've been treated unfairly, or when we don't feel able to release the tension we carry in our bodies around given upsets, insults, and other disturbing experiences. When that happens, the opportunity arises to get to know, even more intimately, how we add fuel to the fire of our activation.

MAKE IT REAL EXPERIMENT #1:
Rehearsing Being Present

This experiment invites you to take a few minutes to settle into a brief inner journey. Before you begin, bring to mind a task you usually experience as boring or annoying, one you generally want to avoid doing.

- As you imagine doing the task in the usual way, notice the thoughts, feelings and sensations that accompany your boredom or irritation. For example, you may notice the thought, *I don't want to do this!* Fine. Label it as a thought, let it go, and notice what comes next. You might experience tired muscles or chapped hands. Fine. Label the sensations, let them go, and notice what comes next.

- Now shift your attention and imagine it's the next time you have to do this same task, only *this* time you've chosen to use the experience as an opportunity to practice mindfulness.

- Begin by imagining that you gather together whatever you need for the task, paying special attention to how your body moves, the textures your hands encounter, whether or not you are breathing comfortably, as well as becoming aware of the quality of your thoughts and feelings. Are you focused on the task and sensations at hand, or is your mind wandering to the next obligation or recreation awaiting you?

- Envision yourself moving through the task, being present and mindful the whole time, and notice how the quality of your experience takes on a new tone as you stay with it mindfully. As they arise, pay attention to your thoughts, feelings, and sensations.

- Notice how boredom or annoyance become *awareness* when you stay present to your experience.

Empowering Choice

When you are present in each moment, a powerful element in developing self-esteem and well-being comes into the foreground. Suddenly, you have a *choice*, moment to moment, about how you want to move through the experiences of your day. While it's often not possible to control or change what's happening, or to make circumstances different from the way they are, you *do* have the power to choose how to engage what you encounter along the way.

There is never a moment when you are without the power to choose to be aware of your experience, unless you are rendered unconscious, or are simply overwhelmed by an experience that hijacks the observing part of your brain. As you practice mindfulness and discover that labeling moments as good or bad becomes increasingly meaningless, a delightful paradox emerges: when you are fully present to what is occurring, and do not struggle, resist, grasp, or cling, you pass through uncomfortable experiences more quickly and easily and savor good moments more fully. This is because engaging experiences mindfully creates all the internal room you need to allow your responses—your thoughts, feelings, sensations, and impulses—to move through you. Furthermore, the more you practice mindfulness, the more you recognize that experiences constantly shift and change, moments endlessly come and go. You know, without doubt, that distress won't last forever and that joy, too, will surely pass.

Living mindfully also gives you an opportunity to experience more fully, and assess the quality of, the internal and external life you live. You may feel that the stress in your life is completely beyond your control. Many of us feel this way. Practicing mindfulness can change your experience of the stress, even if the stress itself doesn't change. I remember an article in the *New York Times* about all the woes and horrors of having inconsiderate, noisy neighbors and the pitfalls of apartment living. One woman who was interviewed said that she felt she had kept her sanity in the face of particularly noisy neighbors through her practice of mindfulness. She allowed herself to be present with the noise and notice her responses to it. While she certainly would have preferred to change the situation and did everything within her power to do so, the only choice available to her—short of moving—was to engage the circumstance with her full awareness.

If you are someone caught up in a lifestyle in which you always have too much to do, and never seem to have enough time to sit in the stillness of your "quiet mind", you have before you an important choice: you can continue to move through your days reactively pulled this way and that by endless external demands, or you can get into the driver's seat of awareness. Were you to choose the latter option, practicing being present to your experience, moment to moment, you might discover that new awarenesses about your situation arise and new choices about how you want to live your life emerge. Or you might discover that you move through projects more quickly and effectively when your full attention is present, which then leaves you with some time to spend doing nothing at all.

If you are someone who tends to react strongly to interpersonal encounters or the inevitable hassles of everyday life, getting easily swept up in worries or feelings, learning to live more mindfully can give you an opportunity to observe these responses and then let them go. You may discover how much *less* stressed you feel when you have to go out in the world and interact with others, as you experience your transactions and exchanges with a new kind of ease you hadn't suspected was possible.

My psychotherapy clients and workshop participants have consistently reported how this kind of moment-to-moment awareness changes the quality of their daily experience. Where once they might have been swept away by a given situation, they now can bring awareness to it, which shifts the quality of the experience. They also report how different it is to discover that feelings really do keep moving and then fade when allowed to do so. Feelings that before seemed too uncomfortable to tolerate become one more thing moving through awareness

A woman with whom I had worked years ago called me recently to give me an update on events in her life. At one point, she told me how much her work with mindfulness had paid off, particularly during an especially challenging time in her life when she had had to deal with the hazards of office politics. She described a situation at work that had been going from bad to worse, with a colleague challenging her authority and position within the company. Because she was able to observe her reactions and feelings over the course of numerous meetings, phone calls, and memos, my former client stopped herself from overreacting and, eventually, prevailed. She felt certain that if she had gotten caught up in her defensive feelings, she wouldn't have been able to manage the politics involved in resolving the onslaught from her co-worker.

Another person, a colleague who occasionally meets me for mutual "mental health conversations," consistently reports how practicing mindfulness has helped him deal with the ups and downs of being in private practice. Instead of succumbing to the uncertainly of ever-changing clientele, he now observes his fears when they come up and then notices when fear is naturally replaced by some other feeling. Before developing a mindful perspective, he often felt overwhelmed and anxious. Now when these feelings arise, they aren't nearly as strong and they pass much more quickly than before.

Even when events are utterly out of your control, the choice of how you want to respond is still yours. Do you allow yourself to be swept away by whatever arises, or do you bring awareness alive to guide you, like the rudder on a sailboat, through your experience?

Mindfulness and Equanimity

A major benefit of becoming more mindful is the *equanimity* it promotes. The world is an easier place to be when we bring awareness rather than reactivity to our experiences. When caught in traffic or standing in a long line somewhere, bringing mindfulness to the experience can shift your state of mind and thereby alter how you experience the event.

A colleague of mine has noticed that her practice of mindfulness has elicited a new response from her when she finds herself stuck in any of the interminable and inevitable lines that form almost anywhere in New York City—in stores, at theaters, at the bank. When she finds herself unable to change the situation and she has to stay put until her business is complete, she hears herself saying, "Ah, well!" Just that – "Ah, well!" Sometimes she feels a chuckle ripple through her awareness, too. She's given up telling herself that the lines shouldn't exist or she shouldn't have to wait. Instead she either reads or simply notices what it feels like to wait. She reports that the time seems to move more quickly and she leaves the experience free of the wear and tear caused by the irritation and helplessness she used to feel.

A friend who is extremely busy, with many demands on him, uses a strategy based on mindfulness and self-hypnosis when he feels particularly overwhelmed by all he has to do in any given day. First, he notices the time pressure he feels when he looks at all the tasks waiting to be done. He allows himself to be present with the physical sensations of tension and discomfort. He notices his thoughts and feelings—how he tells himself he'll never get everything done and how worried he is about falling down on the job. Then he takes a breath, settles into a moment of quiet, and tells himself, *I have all the time I need in the time I have to do what needs to be done.* This is a powerful self-hypnotic suggestion that allows him to breathe more easily. Then he goes about his tasks mindfully, and when he finds himself feeling worried or pressured again, he simply notices his responses and lets them go, reminding himself that he has all the time he needs. Often he surprises himself by getting tasks done not only on time but sometimes with time to spare.

Of course, there are those occasions when there just *isn't* enough time and no amount of giving yourself suggestions to the contrary will make the slightest bit of difference. At those times, being aware of that fact allows you to bring mindfulness to your responses. The equanimity that comes with being present to the fact that you've tried but just can't meet your deadline can ease whatever distress you may feel. The tendency to overreact to time pressures lessens naturally and gradually, and often without your realizing that you have made such a significant shift in the quality of your internal life.

MAKE IT REAL
EXPERIMENT #2:
Bringing Mindfulness to Everyday Experience

Here is an experiment to enhance your awareness of *choice* and *equanimity*.

- The next time you find yourself in a situation that normally elicits a struggle, resistance, or overreaction, give yourself permission to notice and observe what's going on in you.

- If you have an urge to act, to *do* something, simply notice that, as well. Then, if you choose to act, do so consciously, with full awareness of your choice.

- Over time, notice what changes occur in your responses—if, perhaps, you are less reactive without making any special effort. You may notice that what used to be a source of stress or upset is now just one more aspect of the ever-changing experience moving into, and then out of, your awareness.

As with all the experiments in this book, it's helpful to remember to give yourself permission to be curious about what you will discover and how your discoveries will affect the quality of your daily life. In the recommended reading list at the end of the book, there are a number of books that deal with mindfulness practice. You might want to look at some of them to increase your understanding of the process and to find out what others have to say about how to bring the practice of mindfulness to daily living.

EXPERIMENT #3:
Slowing Down

One of the most powerful ways to encourage mindfulness in daily living is to *slow down*. Whenever you act more slowly, you offer yourself an opportunity to become more mindful.

- Choose an activity you do all the time, only now deliberately do it *slowly*. For example, if you walk to work, allow extra time and walk more slowly. Give yourself time to notice the feeling of your feet on the ground, the way your body moves as you lift one foot and put down the other. Then you might notice how your body balances itself as you move from foot to foot and the sensation of your arms swinging. Later, pay attention, as well, to what your mind, eyes, and ears do as you walk.

- If you choose a task of some kind, such as cleaning, typing, filing, reading, or doing housework, *slow down* and notice the many elements in your actions that usually are outside your awareness.

  Allow yourself to be creative and have fun with this experiment. It's an invitation to a state of awareness that is impossible to achieve when you rush or hurry through an activity. Most of all, give yourself permission to be surprised at how different these tasks and activities can be when you are fully present with what you are doing—how much more satisfied or centered you may feel as you move through your daily activities.

EXPERIMENT #4:
Making Room for Feelings to Flow Through You

The next time you find yourself caught up in feelings that threaten to overwhelm you, explore what happens if you use the following imagery process as part of becoming mindful of your experience.

- Begin by focusing on the physics principle that nothing is as solid as it seems. In unseen levels of reality, everything is comprised of molecules and particles that are in constant motion, and there is vast space between these molecules and particles.

- With this in mind, become aware of the fact that your body, too, comprises countless molecules and particles dancing in a pattern that gives your body its shape and form. Imagine the dance of motion and space within your body.

- Now imagine that you can spread out these molecules and particles even more and make extra room for your feelings to move through you. Just expand yourself so that there is nothing for the feelings to bump up against, no place for them to get stuck.

- Take a moment to notice your experience when you make enough room for feelings to move through you. Over time, you may find that whenever you overreact or feel overwhelmed, you can automatically shift your awareness, become "quantum" in your approach, and make more room for the feelings to move through you.

EXPERIMENT #5:
Dealing with Delays Mindfully

The next time you find yourself caught in traffic or having to wait in a long line when you're short of time, explore the following possibility:

- First, take a moment to be *fully* present, right where you are. Bring your awareness into your body and notice any tension that may be present.

- Next, notice your thoughts and feelings. Are you telling yourself that you shouldn't have to wait, that it's unacceptable to be stuck where you are, or that you are stupid for having gotten yourself into such a situation? Pay particular attention to what happens when you struggle against your current experience. There is nothing to do. Just be present with yourself. Observe and acknowledge *all* that you feel.

- Notice that becoming caught up in agitation doesn't solve anything anyway. It only creates more agitation. *Awareness*, on the other hand, naturally dissipates the feeling, and you may be surprised at the calm that follows in its wake.

- Experiment with what happens when you give yourself permission to use the time you spend waiting to deepen your awareness and your capacity to be fully *in* the present moment. When you do so, it doesn't matter what happens, or what you think or feel. *All* of it becomes yet one more reminder to be present to yourself and the fullness of your experience.

Mindfulness Meditation

The mindfulness practices we've explored derive from Buddhist approaches to meditation. Typically, these approaches involve a formal meditation practice, too. The key element in mindfulness meditation is the process of continually returning to your chosen focus for the amount of time you have committed to do so. For example, if you decide to center your awareness on the gap between one breath and the next, or on the flow of thought as it arises from one moment to the next, *this* is the focus to which you constantly return. Also, if you decide to sit for twenty minutes, part of the meditation itself is to stay with it for the full time. If you feel like finishing after fifteen minutes, then you may discover that the focus of meditation for the remaining five minutes is on the thoughts, feelings, and sensations that come up around having chosen to stay put. Sitting comfortably in a position that allows you to remain alert yet relaxed, you observe the natural, rhythmic inflow and outflow of the breath—if that is your chosen focus—as well as the ever-present stream of thoughts and ideas, or the various sensations and any feelings that may arise. Once you become aware of what is passing through your consciousness, you just let it keep going, as you return to your chosen focus.

If you become bored, notice the experience of boredom and continue to bring your attention to your chosen focus. If you get a cramp in your leg, notice the discomfort and observe how it develops or fades. If you find you must move, then do so with full awareness, noticing your decision to shift position, as well as all the sensations that arise when you do so, and then returning to your chosen focus. When you suddenly feel caught up in an obsessive thought, bring your awareness to that fact and continue to return to the breath each time you discover you have gone off, yet one more time, into the thought.

Current research demonstrates that it's the process of noticing you've left your focus and bringing yourself back to it that generates neurons in the brain. Mindfulness has been shown to enhance what we call the "executive function" of the brain, that part of our awareness that supports conscious choice.

This doesn't mean you won't find yourself caught up in thoughts, feelings, or sensations that strongly captivate your attention. For example, if you have recently lost a loved one, had a medical emergency, or discovered that a member of your family is struggling with an addiction, chances are that constantly going off into these concerns will be an inevitable part of your meditative experience. It is important to know that moving away from your focus is normal—inescapable, in fact.

I have a friend who constantly bemoans the fact that she feels she isn't doing her meditation "correctly". It turns out that, for her, *correctly* means achieving a clear, focused mind with no interruptions, no wandering into stray thoughts, feelings, or sensations. She doesn't yet understand that the practice *is* the process of discovering she has gone off into the contents of her consciousness and then returning to her chosen focus. I recall a meditation teacher saying that he had been practicing meditation for twenty-five years and wondered when he would get good at it!

The most important element here is that you not struggle with the fact that your mind *will* wander. I remember when my grandmother taught me meditation when I was young. She said at the time I would be lucky if I could stay focused for a few seconds at a time. I think she was being optimistic!

As you practice mindfulness, a healthy dose of compassion for what is called the *monkey mind*, as it scampers here, there, and everywhere, enhances the possibility that you will find the meditative process calming and stabilizing. Your mind will wander *constantly*. The goal is not to have perfect concentration or to focus your awareness "successfully" without interruption. Instead, it is to come back continually to the chosen focus of meditation whenever the mind wanders, to invite yourself back into an awareness of awareness. It is the continuing return to awareness that deepens your capacity to live mindfully.

Whatever kind of meditation practice you choose to follow at any given time, it is important not to expect every meditation to be a satisfying or pleasant experience. There will be times when you will be unexpectedly focused and move through your sitting or walking meditation with real satisfaction and ease. There will probably be more times when you discover that you just can't seem to sit still, or your mind wanders each time you take a step, or the time drags by unbearably slowly. It is important to know that difficult or unsatisfying meditations are normal and to be expected. They are all part of returning to awareness of *whatever* is happening, without demand, without expectation, without labeling the experience as good or bad.

Over time, your capacity to focus will improve, but that doesn't mean you won't still have meditations in which you can barely sit still, or be present to your walking, and you finish with a feeling of frustration or discomfort. It's helpful to remember that mindfulness practice isn't meant to make you feel good. *It is intended to teach you a state of mind that allows you to live in the world with greater ease, to suffer less, and to be more present in the life you are living.* And, as I mentioned above, with recent research we now know that mindfulness meditation changes your brain in ways that actually do increase a capacity for what is called "skillful living". The key is to know that the process of meditation itself may not always be a pleasure, but that the impact of the process on your brain creates a very positive outcome.

MAKE IT REAL
GUIDED MEDITATION #1:
Basic Mindfulness Meditation

Mindfulness meditation can be done sitting, lying down, or walking. I recommend a sitting meditation at first, because it is more likely that you will be both alert and relaxed at the same time in this position. For some people, walking or other forms of movement meditation are better suited to their natural style, so use this kind of approach if sitting doesn't work for you. If you have never meditated before, start with five minutes and see how that goes. Many people make it a habit eventually to sit for 20 minutes or so, at least once a day. I recommend beginning your day with meditation, because it will allow you to go out in the world with a more centered state of mind.

To begin, notice your breathing without attempting to control it in any way. Just become aware of its in-and-out rhythm. You might expand your awareness to focus on your nostrils and notice that the air on the inbreath may be cool and the outbreath somewhat warmer.

Now begin to notice any thoughts, feelings, and sensations that arise as you focus on your breath. There is nothing to do with these awarenesses. Just note them and return to your focus on your breath. Be sure to avoid any struggle with the process. Simply notice, without judgment, when your mind has wandered away from the breath and gotten caught up in some observation that is moving through your awareness.

Be aware that several seconds of uninterrupted focus on the breath is a real accomplishment. But the goal is not to see how long you can stay with the breath. Rather, the point is to be aware enough to call yourself back gently when you have wandered. Then simply notice where you've been as you return to your focus on your breathing.

The point of mindfulness meditation isn't to get anywhere or to accomplish anything more than being aware of awareness. What it offers is a means to strengthen your inner observer, the part of you that notices without becoming caught up in things. The more you have access to the *compassionate neutrality of simple awareness*, the more easily you can move through experiences without being swept away by them.

GUIDED MEDITATION #2:
Walking Meditation

Walking meditation can be done indoors or outdoors. When you're outside, you have an opportunity to connect with the earth in a nourishing way, but walking indoors also provides a more focused experience of being completely present to the movement of your body.

To begin, stand with your feet slightly apart and become aware of being fully present in your body, from the top of your head to the tips of your toes. Pay special attention to the bottoms of your feet, to their contact with the surface under you. Sway a bit, putting your weight on one leg and then the other. Do so gently, and as you do so, notice how it feels in your belly, in the area of your navel. You might discover that there is a natural feeling of balance that comes when you focus your attention in the area of your navel.

Now begin to take a step, and as you do so, be fully focused on the movement of your foot off the ground, the motion of your body as you step forward, and the contact of your foot as you complete the step. Also notice the other foot, how it slowly comes off the ground as it follows the motion of your step and then how it connects with the ground when the step is completed.

Spend ten or fifteen minutes walking mindfully. Take lots of time to move through each step, being fully present with your whole body and the surface underfoot as you move.

EXPERIMENT #6:
Practicing Non-Judgment

One of the automatic effects of becoming more mindful is a lessening impulse to judge and criticize. In this experiment, allow yourself to explore what it feels like, for a given period of time, to choose *not* to indulge in judgments about yourself or others.

- When you first do this experiment, choose an hour on one day during which you will stop any judging you may find yourself doing. If you find that an hour is too long, give yourself permission to begin the exercise with whatever amount of time you are capable of committing to do the experiment. Simply notice the judgments and then let them go, like leaves floating by on a stream. *Be sure not to judge yourself for judging.*

- When you feel you are ready, expand the experiment to include half a day of non-judgment. Over time, continue to increase your awareness of judging and criticizing—and letting go of those thoughts and reactions.

- Notice what fills your awareness when it isn't taken up with judging or criticizing.

As you work with this experiment, become aware of how the quality of your relationship with yourself, other people, and the world around you shifts as your tendency to judge lessens.

Spacious Awareness

I remember the first time I was on an airplane on a cloudy day. The plane took off in the midst of a gray dreariness. Within seconds, we broke through into a bright, sunny day, the sky a vivid expanse of bright blue. I recall my amazement at how I had forgotten that, during daylight, the sky is *always* blue and clear behind the clouds.

Many years later I learned that the image of a clear and cloudless sky is commonly used to describe the state of awareness that emerges from mindfulness practice. The more we return to the witnessing stance of simply observing, of bringing awareness to awareness, the more space we create in ourselves for allowing the contents of consciousness to move through us—as naturally as the clouds move across the sky.

A major characteristic of holding an expansive point of view is the pervasive awareness of the transitory nature of thoughts, feelings, sensations, and impulses. They are as constantly shifting as a sky during a storm. When the clouds finally clear, no matter how ferocious the storm, the blue sky remains—unchanged, ever-present.

When the mind is like a clear cloudless sky, there is nothing for thoughts, feelings, sensations, or impulses to bump into, push away, or grasp. There is just a spacious, open awareness that notices what's coming and what's going. There's also a quality of clarity and an expanded perspective that allows you to see the bigger picture, even as you focus on the details of life when they require your attention.

I often do hypnosis with people who are preparing for surgery, cancer treatment, and other medical procedures. Nearly always, I teach these clients about "sky awareness"—about accessing a spacious state of mind with which to engage treatment. One young man undergoing chemotherapy found this kind of spacious awareness particularly helpful when dealing with the inevitable needles and physical discomfort of the procedure. He allowed the pain to become clouds passing through his "sky awareness", which resulted in a more relaxed experience both emotionally and physically.

MAKE IT REAL
GUIDED MEDITATION #3:
Being the Sky

The following meditation offers you one more way to experience or imagine having a clear mind.

Begin by settling into a position that allows you to be comfortable and alert at the same time. Focus on your breath and travel with the next exhalation all the way down to the bottom, to the still point that exists there. Spend a few moments with your breath in this way, settling even further with each exhalation.

Now imagine a brilliant blue sky on a clear, sunny day. There may be some clouds in the sky, or perhaps there is an airplane, some birds, or gusts of wind blowing by.

Focus on whatever primary qualities of the sky you experience. You may notice that the sky is open and spacious, clear, has an all-encompassing quality, is ever-present and unchanging. What moves through the sky may change, but the blue expanse remains the same. For some people, the sky is a comforting presence, knowing that it encircles the entire planet with the atmosphere that makes life possible.

As you spend a few moments pondering the sky, be sure to allow any mixed feelings that may come into your awareness. If, for you, the sky seems too vast to represent a comforting presence, notice what happens as you imagine that you are the sky, that there is no separation between you and that vastness. As you imagine that you are the sky, allow your consciousness to become one with the sky as you explore the qualities of your vast blue space.

Notice how there is nowhere you can get stuck when you are the sky. There is nothing to cling to and there are no obstructions. Whatever moves through you comes and goes, and the sky remains what it is, what your mind is . . . clear, open space. Even air pollution disappears when the wind blows it away, revealing what has always been there . . . a beautiful, clear, blue sky.

Imagine, now, clouds moving by. They may be white, puffy clouds or dark, threatening ones.

Next, as the sky, imagine that great thunderheads form and powerful storms move through you. There may be thunder and lightning, gusty winds, rain, snow, or hail. Allow the storms to move on their appointed course as you notice their passing. Notice that they move through you, but they aren't you. They may bring noise and turmoil, which may disturb you, but they can't hurt you.

Eventually, storms always move on and leave you, the sky, clear once again, unchanged and ever-present. There is nowhere for anything to get stuck, nothing for anything to cling to. The sky and simple awareness . . . so much in common.

Next, be the sky filled with beautiful, white puffy clouds in all shapes and sizes. Perhaps one cloud looks like an animal, or an angel, or a butterfly. Maybe another cloud seems like a castle, cauliflower, or whipped cream. As you imagine the clouds moving and shifting, become aware of how beautiful experiences also keep moving and eventually fade, to be replaced by whatever comes next. As the sky, there is nothing to hold onto, not even the puffy, white clouds.

Spend a few moments simply experiencing clarity, spaciousness, and a larger perspective. Notice how it feels to remember that it doesn't matter what moves through you, the sky. Eventually everything blows by and the sky, your awareness, remains as it has always been — clear and open.

Notice the vast perspective you have as the sky. You have the capacity to look out over the landscape below and see the larger picture, the overview. Notice, also, that as the sky, you go all the way to the ground. Allow yourself to come down to the landscape now, and carry with you the clarity and spaciousness of the sky all the way down with you. Imagine yourself in a landscape that is comfortable to you. Notice the quality of your surroundings, paying attention to the colors, textures, and shapes that enter your awareness. As the sky, you can be as close to, or far away from, any detail in the landscape of your inner world. As the sky, you make the choice.

Now take some time to imagine what it would be like if you were to have the same perspective as the sky, the same clarity, the same awareness that no matter what moves through your experience, good or bad, it is temporary. Eventually, any awareness will give way to rediscovering an ever-present state of mind that simply notices whatever moves through it. Imagine what it would be like if you were to have greater access to that clarity and perspective, even in the midst of feelings, thoughts, or sensations that used to sweep you away.

When you feel ready, come back from the journey and bring with you whatever useful states of awareness you may have touched as the sky.

EXPERIMENT #7:
Practicing "Sky Awareness"

- Above and beyond accessing a state of mind that is useful and soothing in and of itself, the above meditation can be applied to any number of situations. All you have to do is choose a feeling or issue you want to understand from a larger perspective. Then become the sky and look down on it from that point of ever-present clarity. You may be surprised at what you discover.

- Another application: when you choose to explore an issue more deeply, bring the quality of sky consciousness all the way down to the ground with you and take a look at the situation up close. Remember that, in reality, the sky is everywhere, above and below. When you maintain the perspective of the sky, you can get as close in as you need to without becoming caught up in the momentary "clouds" or "storms" that may be passing through your thoughts or feelings.

EXPERIMENT #8:
Moving Through Irritation with "Sky Awareness"

Mindfulness practice can make difficult living situations easier to handle. As we've seen, because mindfulness brings awareness to *whatever* is happening, without a demand that the situation be other than the way it is, it is possible to move through annoying or distressing experiences with greater ease.

- As an experiment, the next time you find yourself confronted with an unexpected or irritating noise, notice what happens if you shift your focus and become the sky. Pay particular attention to the ways in which you can create enough space in yourself to allow the noise to move *through* your awareness without getting stuck anywhere. There is no need to push away the noise, no need to deny that it has impinged on you and perhaps distracted you. Just notice *all* your responses, even as you allow them—and the noise—to keep on moving through your awareness.

- Ask yourself what other situations might be helped by being in a mindful "sky awareness."

GUIDED MEDITATION #4:
"Sky-Writing"

In this meditation the metaphor of sky-writing offers yet another way of experiencing mindfulness and the passing nature of the contents of consciousness. Before you do the meditation, bring to mind a thought, feeling, urge, or impulse that has come up and is unresolved or still has the power to throw you off center.

Begin by settling in and focusing on the still point between one breath and the next. Bring to mind the thought, feeling, urge, or impulse you have chosen as the focus of the meditation.

Now imagine the sky on a brilliantly clear day—a sky that is vast, blue, and open—and notice that a small airplane begins to spell out your thought, feeling, urge, or impulse in clear, puffy white letters that appear across the sky. Allow the letters to be as big or bright as they need to be in order to convey the energy you have invested in this chosen focus.

Notice how the ever-present winds in the sky begin to dissipate the letters soon after the airplane has written them ... how quickly the letters at the beginning of the first word become blurred and increasingly difficult to read.

As you continue to observe, notice that by the time the plane has finished the whole job of sky-writing, all the letters—even the last ones written—are beginning to disappear. There is nothing at all you have to do. The wind currents naturally blow them away, just as the natural flow of awareness automatically dissipates the contents of your consciousness. Arising and then disappearing, all your thoughts, feelings, urges, and impulses are no more solid or permanent than the sky-writing that, even now, is only as substantial as a white film spread across the vast blue sky.

Now the sky contains only a trace of the thought, feeling, urge, or impulse, if there is any hint of it at all.

When you feel ready, come back to your surroundings by wiggling your fingers and toes.

Anytime you have troubling or repetitive thoughts, feelings, urges, or impulses, allow them to become sky-writing and then watch them fade. Do the process as often as you need to remind yourself that the contents of consciousness are no more lasting or solid than a puff of smoke.

And so . . .

Of all the concepts, techniques, and approaches offered in *Sacred Practices*, developing mindfulness in daily living is the most potentially life-changing. The presence of a mindful attitude alters virtually any experience. It is a doorway for bringing the sacred into everyday life. Mindfulness supports more conscious living by creating a reliable, compassionate witness that moves through events with equanimity, even as it promotes an ability to be present without becoming swept away by what moves into and through your life. Becoming more mindful offers you an opportunity to shift how you engage, interpret, and respond to life experiences in a fundamental way.

Imagine a world where most people live mindfully—where awareness of awareness is the norm and each person is fully conscious of his or her choices. The fact that mindfulness meditation and practices are becoming so popular in the West—that increasing numbers of people are becoming more conscious of their thoughts feelings, sensations, and impulses—speaks of a revolution in consciousness that has the potential to create a better world for all of us.

As their mindfulness practice deepens, many people notice that they spontaneously begin to experience increased gratitude and generosity. By being more present more of the time, you are able to notice the many small things that are going right: the fleeting moment of encountering a butterfly whose beauty takes your breath away; receiving an unexpected smile from a stranger; the bus driver who waits the extra minute to let you get on board, and on and on.

As we move through the next chapter, we will explore the many ways in which gratitude and generosity flow from mindfulness.

Chapter 6

GRATITUDE AND GENEROSITY
Engaging A Prosperous Life

…in our willingness to give that which we seek, we keep the abundance of the universe circulating in our lives.

—Deepak Chopra

It is useful to keep in mind that life is basically a messy business, that it's not at all neat and tidy. Everyday living is organic and unpredictable, no matter how much we may try to nail it down and get all our "ducks in a row". Within this ever-changing context of never knowing what will happen next, it is all too easy to get caught up in the hassles of daily life, to focus on the many things that *don't* go as expected, on moments that are difficult or irritating.

When you begin to live more mindfully, it becomes increasingly likely that you will notice how many things go *right* during any given day. These supportive, easy, or satisfying moments come in all shapes and sizes. On the simplest level, you might take the time to notice that you wanted cereal for breakfast and there was just enough milk left in the refrigerator to make that possible. Perhaps you needed to schedule a meeting with a hard-to-reach colleague and he happened to be in the office when you called. You may have locked yourself out of your house and the neighbor with whom you traded keys happened to be home.

On a more dramatic level, the accident you were certain was about to happen didn't; the illness you feared was serious turns out to be nothing more than a twenty-four-hour bug; the person you had dinner with last week seems to be interested in a deeper relationship—just when you'd given up thinking anyone new would come into your life.

Your awareness of gratitude might extend to include all the people involved in bringing food to your table or clothing to the store—all the workers in all the various phases of getting these essentials into your hands. You might begin to pay more attention to the service provided by store clerks, firefighters, teachers, and other people who serve the public. There is no end to the number of things that can go right in our lives.

Sometimes events for which we are most grateful aren't apparent until we have the benefit of hindsight and can see a larger, more complex picture. My favorite example of this kind of gratitude is a story told by Bob Mandel in his book *Wake Up to Wealth*. He tells how his wife, Mallie, who has a severe allergy to bees and wasps, was stung one day and went into anaphylactic shock. During her visit to the hospital's emergency room, her doctor insisted that she carry a syringe filled with adrenaline at all times, in case she were stung again. Sometime later, she and Bob were on a dinner cruise when a guest had a violent allergic reaction to shrimp. A doctor was on board, but the ship was in the middle of a river and he didn't have the needed medical supplies. Mallie came to the rescue with her ever-present syringe. When the woman thanked her, Mallie's reply was, "Don't thank me. Thank the wasp that stung me."

Gratitude and Generosity: Two Sides of One Coin

The more aware we are of things going right, and the more we make gratitude a part of our everyday experience, the more likely we are to express generosity as well. Generosity and gratitude dance together and support each other. The presence of both depends on an open, compassionate heart, a willingness to share life's bounty, and a basic belief in life's abundance. An abundant state of mind assumes we will have what we need, even when we haven't a clue from where it will come.

When our hearts are closed and we focus on life's problems, we are more likely to experience a world characterized by *scarcity*, in response to which we form a belief that we have to hold onto what little we have because there won't be any more. While scarcity can be a reality in nature and human affairs, when it becomes a chronic *state of mind*, we feel frightened that there won't be enough to go around even in times of plenty.

In many ways, abundance and scarcity represent states of mind even more than they reflect objective fact. Most of us know people who, with very little by way of material resources, are able to give more than others who seem to have more than enough of everything they need. I have a friend who is extremely generous. If I'm moved to give a dollar to someone, I notice that she has already given five. I am learning from her example to stretch beyond my usual caution, to expand my sense of abundance and generosity.

Even as I write this section, my mind says, *But there are people who have nothing, who are starving, living on the street, whose world is a stark reality of profound scarcity, and it's not about a state of mind—it's about social conditions, inequality, and the forces of a whole economy that overlook the needy.* One of my unresolved and powerful conflicts around money is what it feels like to have enough when I think of all the people who have so little. I don't have answers to the glaring economic inequalities that exist in the United States and around the world. As we continue our exploration here, I invite you to allow your own mixed feelings to emerge and, perhaps, become more clearly defined. I find myself wondering if it's possible *not* to have mixed feelings when there are so many people in need, while a relatively small number have so much.

One of the ways I deal with my conflict is through a fantasy I've carried in the back of my mind for many years. It's a dream, but I just can't make it go away. In it, I wonder what would happen if every person alive could be convinced of his or her right to abundance, to *expect* to have enough money, or whatever resources may be necessary, to meet basic needs and wants. I find myself wondering if the force of such a belief would somehow redistribute, in unexpected ways, all the money circulating in the global economy. So many of us have learned to believe that it is inevitable and reasonable to live in a world of *have's* and *have-nots*. If we were able to change this basic belief, might we find ourselves part of a slow, subtle revolution in which the power of a collective conviction—that *everyone should have enough of what he or she needs*—exerts its influence on our underlying collective relationship to the world's resources? If we also held the idea that this redistribution of wealth would consistently serve the greater good, who knows how the world might look in the future?

In response to this dream, I have come to feel that if each of us, as individuals, can develop a mind-set of abundance, truly believing that each and every person deserves to have enough, then we will play at least a small role in creating such a shift in human consciousness.

When we engage in acts of generosity, or when we allow ourselves to receive from others, it is highly likely that we will experience some mixed feelings. For this reason, one of the necessary elements in creating an abundance mind-set is a willingness to face and accept these feelings as they arise naturally around issues of giving and receiving. To some degree or another, most of us harbor feelings of jealousy, envy, greed, selfishness, arrogance, and other competitive or "grasping" feelings.

As we explore gratitude and generosity, we will look at some detailed examples of dealing with mixed feelings. For now, it is important to know that an experience of living consciously requires you to acknowledge and deal with all these feelings as part and parcel of your being. Having a mind-set of abundance supports your capacity to give and receive freely and easily. As you explore the material that follows, keep in mind that gratitude and generosity are interrelated and that one cannot be experienced or expressed fully without the other.

MAKE IT REAL EXPERIMENT #1: *Affirming a Generous Life*

- Use the following affirmation each day for a month and notice what, if any, changes you experience in your interactions with other people. Pay particular attention to those moments when you are spontaneously generous—when you surprise yourself with your willingness either to receive or give generously.

  I live in a world that is characterized by generosity and abundance, where there is always enough to go around. In my world, I give and receive openly and willingly.

- As with any affirmation, allow yourself to change the words in whatever way makes them most alive for you. The key to the affirmation is activating your willingness to experience the generosity of both giving and receiving in positive and constructive ways.

EXPERIMENT #2:
Giving Things Away

- Choose one day in which you will give things away. For example, give away some of your time to a friend who needs help with something, give money to homeless people on the street, give clothing to the needy, give someone a book you enjoyed, send someone a card or a note, remember to say thanks to people who help you.

- Be sure not to limit yourself to material things. The *generosity of spirit* you bring to your interactions with other people is tremendously powerful.

- To do this experiment fully, it is important to explore how you feel when you give willingly and generously, especially if you are surprised by a request that requires a generous response from you.

- Be sure to pay attention to any mixed feelings you may have as you allow yourself to give to others: any reactions of greed envy, selfishness, anger, or fear you may feel when someone needs something you have. Just notice whatever responses come to the surface of your awareness and remember to embrace whatever comes.

- Be sure to notice how centered you may feel when you willingly share with other people.

- After you have done the experiment, you might want to choose one day a month for the activity of giving things away, of sharing generously in a whole range of ways.

Gratitude in Daily Living

Paying attention to the small things that go right in your life changes the quality of daily living. Individual moments become more meaningful and valued for what they add to your experience when you allow yourself to be aware of the gifts they carry. When you live from a perspective of gratitude, even the bad moments offer surprisingly useful gifts.

Adversity is a powerful teacher, a taskmaster that forces us to stretch beyond our previous capacities. Think of a time when a crisis demanded that you experience what you may have felt to be an unfair burden. Then, as you moved through the experience, you found yourself coming out the other end stronger in some way. These kinds of situations happen all the time, and if we pay attention, we can use the experiences to enhance our learning even more.

I recall a friend who had a bout with cancer. During her illness, she found herself having to be more assertive than usual. By the time she had undergone all the procedures and was resuming her everyday life, she had developed a new capacity to ask for what she wanted. Would she rather not have had cancer in the first place? Definitely. Was she glad to be able to be more assertive? Absolutely.

Some people have a strong negative reaction to the suggestion that gratitude can become a transforming part of daily life. For them, being grateful means that all the bad things that have happened in their lives are overlooked, forgotten, or in some other way invalidated. When you read the words, *gratitude is a state of mind*, what is your response? Do you find yourself thinking that you don't have much to be grateful for—after all, look at all the people and events that have hurt you in the past not to mention all the things that seem not to be working out right now? If I were to ask you to list all the things that haven't gone the way you wanted them to go, but for which you are grateful, what would be your initial gut response? Would you think I wasn't making any sense? Would it make you angry to imagine being grateful in the face of distressing events?

Being grateful doesn't mean ignoring what is hurtful. When life isn't going well, the mind-set of gratitude doesn't require you to deny that things are not great. What it does do is provide an opportunity to recognize that life is a complex affair that is rarely totally positive *or* negative. Living from a mind-set of gratitude allows you to experience this complexity, to discover what *is* working for you, or what lessons *are* available, even when it seems circumstances couldn't get much worse. I always think of an example offered by nature, when a terrible forest fire promotes new growth of vegetation that wouldn't have been possible without the extreme heat and destruction of the fire.

One of my close friends has been out of work for an extended period of time. As a writer who previously had a thriving free-lance business, it was a blow to both her ego and self-confidence to suddenly be unable to generate work, even though her loss of clients was due to budget cuts in the corporations she served and not to the quality of her work. At first, she struggled to generate business in ways that were familiar and comfortable. Soon, though, it became apparent that this strategy wasn't working. Each month, it seemed things couldn't get worse, but they did, and she had to dig deeper inside herself to come up with new ways to market herself to potential clients.

Through a process of change that occurred during this time, my friend increasingly focused on what worked *for* her and she learned important lessons that reordered the priorities of her life. Where before she had been hard-driven, making little time for family and friends, she now values close ties with other people. She has learned to reach out and ask for help, and has had to stretch her creative potential to generate new ideas and products for her business.

She finds herself with new resources and attitudes that she describes as real and lasting gifts that have come from experiencing familiar doors close, as new ones are forced open.

This kind of experience demonstrates that even the worst situations can produce unexpected benefits for which we can be grateful. In natural disasters, when so much destruction and harm occur, there are always stories of people whose heroism and selflessness are an inspiration to others. Does this mean it was a good thing that the disasters happened? No, but it does suggest that even in the most terrible moments, something of value can be found.

Gratitude as a Gift to Yourself

Becoming more grateful isn't something we do only for others. It is a deeply personal shift in awareness that affects the quality of our moment-to-moment lives much more than it affects others who are the beneficiaries. Cultivating gratitude is like taking vitamins, exercising, or any other self-care activity. The only difference is that gratitude is a tonic for our state of mind, for our ongoing experience of the quality of our lives day to day. *It is nutritious psychological and spiritual food.*

This isn't to say that you should overlook bad circumstances that need to be changed. Saying that you can be grateful for using an experience that lets you deepen your understanding of yourself and others doesn't mean accepting situations that you *can* change or that need to be changed. *It means that finding what is useful in any given experience allows you to be even more aware of what is good for you and what isn't.*

I always pay close attention when I hear clients, workshop participants, friends, or colleagues mention how grateful they are for some difficulty that has come their way. I know they have developed a different relationship to adversity: it has become a teacher, and the lessons learned are gifts for which they are grateful. I also pay attention to stories like Mallie's where there is the hidden "blessing in disguise." When we recognize that stressful experiences may hold gifts, this expectation alone can ease the way and generate a more constructive, empowered state of mind with which to engage daily living.

The experience of gratitude is a deeply personal one. What seems a gift to one person may have absolutely no meaning to someone else. I'm often accused of making lemonade out of lemons, no matter *how* sour the experience. That's fine with me, because my personal preference is to engage what's working in life. What feels natural and real to you might be entirely different. It is important to give yourself permission to find your own style of living with gratitude. Even if no one else could possibly understand how you arrive at being grateful for a given experience, allow yourself to recognize the gifts that come even in adversity and discover what may be useful to you in ways you might not have recognized before you began to pay attention to gratitude.

Gratitude as a New Habit of Mind

Learning to focus on what's going right in your life often means creating a new mind-set or "habit of mind". Basically, you need to remind yourself to pay attention to those events, developments, and circumstances for which you can be grateful. Creating a new habit of mind is like creating new muscle. At first, it may seem to take a lot of effort to become aware of what's operating to support you. So many of us have a habit of focusing on difficulties and hassles that it can feel artificial at first to notice what's going right. That's a natural response; you need to keep practicing gratitude even when it feels like too much work or as though you are glossing over the "real picture."

What may surprise you is how your experience of gratitude will develop as you pay attention to it. It's like learning to find four-leaf clovers: once you develop the ability to identify them, they aren't so hard to find. It's as though a new perception clicks into place and more spontaneously orients your awareness to what's going right for you. Over time, you create a new habit of mind in which you automatically look for the support, potential learning, and gifts hidden in daily life experiences and events.

MAKE IT REAL
EXPERIMENT #3:
Looking For What's Going Right

- In this experiment, allow yourself to take one day a week to focus on noticing at least one element in that day that goes right for you. It can be as small as noticing that the traffic light turned green when you got to it, that you had enough water pressure in the shower or the water was hot enough, that the clothes you wanted to wear were clean and not wrinkled when you took them out of the closet before work, or something you usually take for granted—that you had enough to eat that day. You may notice surprises like messages or gifts from friends, or unexpected kindnesses from people you meet sometime in the course of the day. That's the totality of the experiment: *just notice at least one thing, one day a week, that works in your favor*, that offers you something lovely you didn't expect, that in some way nourishes and supports you.

- As soon as it feels comfortable, invite yourself to notice two events or circumstances that went right that day, and so on. Then, add a second day to the experiment. Over time, you will develop a new habit of mind in which you more automatically recognize an abundance of events and experiences for which to be grateful.

EXPERIMENT #4:
Expanding Your Awareness of Gratitude

In this experiment, take one of the events from Experiment #3 and explore it in more detail.

- Notice the complexity of elements that went into creating the experience for which you feel grateful. For example, when you go to the grocery store and buy some produce, or a product that is packaged and ready to go, acknowledge all the people who were involved in bringing that food to the grocery store: the field hand who picked the produce or the factory worker who prepared the food; the people at the processing plant where the food was readied for shipping; the truck drivers who brought the food through each phase of its journey, from its beginnings to the grocery store; the stock clerk who put the food on the shelf; the checkout cashier who was the last step in your purchase of the food, and so on.

The important focus in this experiment is recognizing how many outside forces come together to create the circumstances that make your life easier and for which you can be grateful. This awareness not only gives you an opportunity to feel grateful for all that goes into meeting your needs but also reinforces the fact that you are not alone. You are part of an amazingly complex whole that usually operates outside conscious awareness. That awareness, in itself, can be a powerful gift.

Nurturing a Generous Spirit

As I mentioned earlier, the practice of generosity is closely related to gratitude. Generosity is more than something you do—*it is a way of being that pervades both* doing *and* being. Generosity connects you with a sense of being part of a larger interactive context and constantly reinforces the fact that no one of us lives in this world alone. Generosity is a powerful way to honor the sacred in everyday life, a spiritual practice of profound proportions. It offers an opportunity to share ourselves with others to acknowledge how much the efforts of others constantly support our well-being, even when we are totally unaware of the contributions of people we've never met. To live generously draws on an awakened, alive sense of compassion and connection to others.

To be generous is to move beyond having fears of scarcity; it is even beyond connecting with other people with our hearts open. When we can give of ourselves or our resources with a spontaneous feeling of gratitude that we have enough to give, a circle is completed: *we are both givers and receivers.*

Take a moment to recall a time when you were generous with someone—whether you gave a gift, a smile, some needed support or reassurance—or a time when you felt moved to give something of yourself to another. Is it natural for you to be generous, or is it something you have to think about and consciously decide to do? Do you find that when someone asks you for something, or you feel moved to give to someone, that you have mixed feelings—that part of you feels comfortable with giving and another part wants to hold onto what is yours?

A number of years ago, when I started to explore generosity at a deeper level, I was in Central Park, in New York City, reading and taking notes when a young man came up to me and asked if he could borrow my pen. Reflexively, I said, "No." I immediately felt ashamed of myself, as I realized that I had plenty of other pens with me. The discovery that I felt threatened when he wanted something from me was a shock, since I thought of myself as a generous person. The experience revealed a quality in me that had been outside my awareness until that moment. In a very real sense, the young man was like the meditation teacher who taps the student with a stick, should the student begin to fall asleep during meditation. The young man's request, and my response, became a wake-up call.

As I explored this experience, I became aware of an underlying, previously unrecognized fear that other people would have things I didn't. Looking more deeply, I realized that my feelings were about the world of childhood, where I interacted with siblings and playmates. In my internal world of memory, I recalled experiences that had left me feeling there wouldn't be enough for me of whatever desired "goodies" were being passed around. This was a powerful moment and my disappointment in myself was softened by an excitement that this wake-up call offered an opportunity to heal a response that I hadn't realized held so much energy.

During a discussion on generosity in a workshop, a participant described how angry and indignant he became every time a person on the street asked him for money. As we explored his feelings he discovered that underneath his indignation was a pervasive fear of having no income himself. He had needed to believe that homeless people or panhandlers who were out of work were lazy and dishonest or drug addicts. Then he could blame them and reassure himself that *he* would never be in their situation.

I don't know if this man ever worked through his discovery to its final conclusion, but I can say that he, too, got a wake-up call during the workshop. If he used it to learn more about himself and deal with the underlying fears of his own neediness, my guess is that he may feel less anger toward others who are in need.

As you explore your own experiences with generosity, *it is essential that you be generous with yourself*. If you find you have mixed feelings about being generous—or even notice certain situations in which you are downright uncomfortable giving to others—allow your responses to guide you to a deeper understanding of yourself. Only with an open heart and a willingness to love yourself in spite of your shortcomings is it really safe to face these uncomfortable kinds of responses. When you can do so, the experience of psychological wholeness and ease of being increases.

Learning to Receive Generously

It is not just in giving that generosity offers useful lessons. It is equally important to be able to *receive* generously. For many people, learning to receive with ease and grace is a surprisingly challenging task. For example, how many times have you heard someone minimize a compliment by saying something like, "Oh, this old thing? I've had it for years."

I recall the many times I have heard about people who walk through a door to find themselves the "star" of a surprise party and who respond with anger and embarrassment. What is going on when we need to fend off being celebrated? If we take a moment to observe how children naturally respond when they receive attention, it seems in every respect a positive and pleasurable experience. I have heard stories of people who always insist on treating others to dinner, and who won't allow anyone to treat them. What is the reason for needing to be the only one who is allowed to give to others in this way? Then there are the stories of people who don't tell anyone it is their birthday, anniversary, or some other special occasion because they cannot bear to receive gifts. What creates the need to avoid receiving acknowledgment from others?

While the answers to these questions are complex and individual, we can imagine that the person on the receiving end of an interaction is in a more vulnerable position than is the person who does the giving. In many families, whoever has the capacity to acquire and give gifts is the person in power. In these families, gifts become tools of manipulation or authority rather than sources of real pleasure. In other families, gift giving becomes part of a dysfunctional pattern of interacting, leaving family members with deeply mixed feelings about both giving and receiving. Religious value and early training may also be elements in the discomfort of being on the receiving end of an interaction, as when a religion teaches that it is always better to give than to receive. What we may not have learned is how much pleasure it gives people when their gifts are *received generously*. To accept someone's gift with pleasure and thanks becomes, in itself, a gift in return.

Whatever your reasons, if you are uncomfortable when people want to give you support, gift, compliments, or help, ask yourself what you need to learn or resolve that will allow you to receive more generously. Ask yourself to recognize that when you don't allow people to give to you, you take away something from your relationships. In fact, relationships in which one person consistently does the giving are lopsided; there is a good chance that the recipients will be one-down or disempowered if they are consistently blocked from reciprocating. The process of give and take among equals is a gift to everyone involved and enhances the quality of interpersonal exchanges for all concerned.

MAKE IT REAL
GUIDED MEDITATION #1:
Interweaving Gratitude and Generosity

As with all the explorations in *Sacred Practices*, be gentle with yourself. Bringing love, compassion, and an open heart to your explorations of generosity and gratitude can make the experience one of discovery and deep satisfaction. This meditation invites you on a journey whereby you can weave gratitude and generosity into your daily life.

GRATITUDE AND GENEROSITY

Begin by finding a place where you can settle for a few moments without being disturbed. Focus on your breath, finding your way to the still point at the bottom of the breath, between the out-breath and the next in-breath. Spend a few moments settling into the still point, remembering to allow your whole being to be present: all your thoughts, feelings, and sensations.

Now focus your attention in the area of your heart and notice whether your chest is soft and open or tense and closed. Notice what happens when you invite yourself to open your heart.

Take a few moments to think about gratitude and generosity. Simply allow your mind to wonder about these concepts, becoming aware of your understanding of them, and how they play out in your current life. Pay particular attention to the qualities you associate with gratitude and generosity. Allow an awareness of these qualities to build slowly as you contemplate them.

Next, let a symbol, image, or color that represents the qualities of gratitude and generosity drop into your awareness. Allow whatever comes to arise spontaneously. Let yourself discover a symbolic representation of these qualities that fits for you.

If you find you feel blank, ask yourself, "If I could be aware of an image to represent the qualities of gratitude and generosity, what would come into my awareness?" Remember that a visual image is only one way of working with this kind of process. Your way may involve sensing, hearing, or tasting it instead.

Take a moment, now, to enter into the symbol, image, or color that has come to mind and allow yourself to explore what it's like to be the qualities inherent in the image or sensory experience. Engage this part of the meditation without preconceptions of what gratitude and generosity "should" look, feel, sound, or taste like. Allow yourself to be open to being surprised by what drops into your awareness.

Now shift your awareness into your body and notice the particular spot in your body where you feel the qualities of gratitude and generosity in the most alive way. Is it in your heart? Your solar plexus? Your head? Give yourself a few moments to absorb these qualities into yourself, giving yourself permission to discover how you can allow them to live in you even more powerfully than they do already.

Next, imagine yourself in the midst of your daily activities, perhaps in a situation where you express the qualities of gratitude and generosity spontaneously in a way that feels good to you. Take a few moments to "rehearse" how it would be for you to express these qualities.

When you feel ready, come back to the sill point at the bottom of the breath. Notice that you can bring the symbolic representation to mind any time you choose to, and in this way, you can reconnect with the qualities of gratitude and generosity as they live in you.

Finally, review your experience and come all the way back to a fully alert awareness of the present moment—fully alert and grounded in your body-mind being. Wiggle your fingers and toes to bring yourself all the way back.

Expressing Generosity and Gratitude to Ease Suffering

Since most of us interact with others in some way or another during the course of daily life, there usually are a number of opportunities to express generosity and gratitude in our interactions. Imagine the number of times in any given day when a smile from you could be the best thing that happens to someone you don't even know. Or, imagine how a small act of kindness, such as helping someone pick up something she dropped, could ease suffering and add to the other person's good feeling about the world; or how remembering to say "thank you" to someone who helps you can acknowledge the value of his assistance.

Take a moment to reflect on how often you unintentionally add to others' suffering by being inconsiderate or insensitive, by not paying attention during your interactions. Most of us assume that these actions—or lack of them—go unnoticed, but it may be that *not* stopping to help someone, *not* smiling when it would be as easy to smile as to frown, *not* saying hello to someone you know adds to the suffering of others, if only in a small way.

Think of the last time you were in a store, a restaurant, the bank, or some other place where someone helped you get what you needed. Did you remember to look the person in the eye and thank him or her? Did you pay attention to the fact that someone else's efforts helped you accomplish your goal? Did you acknowledge—if only to yourself—that without the assistance of the other person, you wouldn't have been able to get your needs met?

As you get into the habit of noticing the sources of the tremendous amount of help you receive each day—help you may have previously taken for granted—you may also discover that the habit of taking the time to say "thank you" develops right alongside. Even when it's not appropriate or possible to say "thank you" to the person directly, you can acknowledge it to yourself and send your appreciation as a thought in their direction. The very process of expressing gratitude on any level nourishes your capacity to notice the contributions of others.

Do you notice how the qualities of compassion, loving-kindness, mindfulness, and living with an open heart all weave together to create a continuous way of being in the world? Generosity and gratitude are the natural offspring of these states of being and are powerful sacred practices in their own right.

MAKE IT REAL
EXPERIMENT #5:
Easing Suffering Through Generosity and Gratitude

This experiment is another one in which you are invited to change a habit of mind and explore how your generosity and gratitude, or lack of them, ease or cause suffering in others.

- Choose a given day of the week and make a decision to monitor your level of irritation, frustration, distraction, tension, or any other "negative" response that might ordinarily spill over into your interactions with others. If you find that contemplating an entire day of this experiment seems too daunting, feel free to pare it down to whatever amount of time you can manage. Then, as you work with the experiment, you can add more time as you go along.

- Make a decision, on that day, not to express your negative responses in your interactions with others. You can choose to tell people you're in a bad mood and thereby "own" your response instead of externalizing it, but you can also decide not to act on your feelings by refraining from expressing them in any form.

- Instead, *decide to be kind no matter how irritated, frustrated, depressed, or put out you may feel.*

- Then, notice the difference in how interactions unfold throughout the day and in the responses you receive from others.

    Generosity and gratitude tend to be contagious, but in case you run into someone whose bad mood spills out onto you, choose to notice it and experiment with what happens when you maintain your decision to be kind. Keep in mind that *kindness is a powerful form of interpersonal generosity*. If you find yourself slipping into responding with irritation or acting in ways that add to the suffering of others, explore whether it's possible for you to stop midway. Be sure to bring kindness to yourself, as well. If you find that you cannot shift your attitude, you have yet another opportunity to practice being generous with yourself as you explore what got triggered in you and how you came to respond as you did.

Gratitude, Generosity, and Money

We have been exploring gratitude and generosity as qualities that can permeate interactions in everyday life. Here we'll explore the relationship between gratitude, generosity, and money. Take just a moment, at this point, to notice your responses to the subject of money. As I mentioned earlier, most of us learned how to relate to money in our families, communities, and religious institutions, and our relationship with it is influenced by powerful beliefs and conflicts. In many families, money is a source of power struggles, a means of reward and punishment, a way to show love, and a variety of other complex and emotionally charged interpersonal dynamics. Either not having enough money *or* having a great deal of it can create powerfully mixed feelings. For these reasons, few of us are neutral about the subject of money. Because money has such an emotional charge for so many people, let's take a moment to do a quick survey here. Ask yourself the following questions and notice what responses come spontaneously into your awareness.

- If you imagine that money is energy in the form of matter, and that this energy constantly circulates—changing form but never ceasing to exist—what is the quality of circulation of money in your life?

- What is your primary attitude toward money and how it circulates in your life? Are you anxious about it? Do you take it for granted? Does it frighten you to spend it, or do you feel powerful when you buy something?

- Does money come to you easily and then flow unobstructed into the places you intend it to go? Or does it elude you, not quite coming to you in sufficient quantities to allow you to feel secure or bountiful?

- Does money flow to you and then disappear because you don't pay attention to where it goes?

- Are you grateful when you have enough money to meet your needs, and does generosity in the form of sharing your money enter into your relationships with others?

- Are you *mindfully aware* of the flow of money into and out of your life?

    As you cultivate generosity and gratitude as more active elements in your life, you will find that your relationship with money automatically becomes something with which you must come to terms. By necessity, as you increase your capacity to be more generous in any way, you are also likely to discover whether your beliefs about money and other resources are based on assumptions of scarcity or abundance. Some of us, for example, are so intent on giving money away to others that, ironically, we create scarcity in an otherwise abundant life, putting ourselves at risk. This kind of relationship to money and generosity sometimes reflects a discomfort with having it, or a childhood family rule that said it's bad. Putting ourselves at risk is as problematic as living within the confines of a scarcity consciousness in which we're afraid to let go of any money.

It is important to remember that money is concretized energy. In and of itself, the energy of money is neutral. *It is what we do with that energy that makes money a problem — or not.* Money is no different from anything else in our lives for which we are responsible, such as what we do with our bodies, how we use words, how we express our sexuality, what we eat, how we work, even what we do during our recreational time. If generosity and gratitude permeate our lives, they also touch our relationship with, and use of, money.

MAKE IT REAL
Experiment #6:

This experiment invites you to explore an abundance mind-set—creating an assumption, held at deep levels of your being, that there is enough to go around, that you will have what you need when you need it. Allow yourself to get in touch with whatever reservations or mixed feelings you may have about living with an abundance mind-set. There is no "right answer"—there are only the responses that arise in you and your willingness to allow your responses to guide you to an ever-increasing openness to an abundant life. You may not always get what you want exactly when and how you want it, but that doesn't mean you can't *expect* your needs to be met.

- To begin this experiment, allow yourself a few minutes of uninterrupted time to be especially aware of the responses you have to the following statements. Be sure to invite and allow mixed feelings.

- Repeat the following statements to yourself, either mentally or out loud, and notice the immediate thoughts, feelings, and physical sensations that arise in response:

  - *I am learning that I can have enough of whatever I need or want.*

  - *I always have enough resources to take care of all my needs.*

- *I live in a world where I always have enough money to meet my own needs and wants, and to share generously with others.*

- Notice what happens over time as you allow yourself to consider the above statements. Shifting into an abundance mind-set, away from one that assumes scarcity, allows you to engage generosity and gratitude even more powerfully. Notice how this engagement emerges in your life as you work with this experiment.

EXPERIMENT #7:
Practicing Generosity and Gratitude with Money

In this experiment you have an opportunity to acknowledge and express gratitude for the money that flows through your life. As you become more grateful for this money, you can also remember to share your good fortune with others.

- Choose a particular day on which to focus your awareness on the money that circulates through your life. As before, if an entire day feels like too much to tackle at the beginning, give yourself an amount of time that seems manageable. Then, gradually, keep adding time until you do spend an entire day with this experiment.

- Whenever you handle money, be it paper or coins, take a moment to acknowledge how grateful you are to have it in your life. In whatever ways you use it, allow yourself to be grateful that you have the money you need for the exchange at hand.

- When you get paid for your work, be aware of the reciprocity that goes on when you receive money for your services: you give of yourself and you receive money in return. What attitude do you bring to the reciprocal relationship between what you offer and the money you receive?

- If you are someone who receives money for other reasons, such as inheritance or support from sources other than work, do you experience gratitude when the money flows into your life?

- Once you've explored how you acknowledge money or take it for granted, notice what it feels like when you give money away, whether you give it to homeless people, to charities, to family members, or to friends. Simply become aware of the feelings that move through you when you share money with others. Do you feel grateful to be able to share? Do you feel a sense of having less? There is no right answer here. Just become more aware of how you feel as money flows into and out of your life.

GUIDED MEDITATION #2:
Fostering a Dynamic Relationship Between Money, Generosity, and Gratitude

In this meditation, you have an opportunity to deepen your understanding of money as a concrete form of energy that you can access in positive and constructive ways, and to enhance your comfort with sharing your resources responsibly with others.

Begin by settling down in a place where you will be undisturbed for a little while. Allow yourself to focus on the still point between the out-breath and the next in-breath. Remember that this is "home base," a place from which to begin any deepening experience.

Imagine now that it is sometime in the future—perhaps several months or years from now—when you have learned to ex-

press gratitude and generosity with money in your everyday life. Be sure to allow yourself to notice how you have learned both to give and receive money comfortably and naturally, and how you allow money to circulate through your life in ways that are both responsible and satisfying. Recall that even when you save money, it circulates as the savings institutions use it to fund economic activities of many kinds.

Pay particular attention to the ease with which you share your resources with others because you live with an abundance mindset: you assume there will be enough to go around. If you have trouble imagining yourself with this attitude toward money, think of people you admire for the way they use their money. Recall the qualities about them that, to you, represent their generosity with themselves and others.

Next, imagine that you are back in your present life and it's the next time you are presented with an opportunity to share money with someone. You might use the example of a homeless person who asks for some money. In your imagination, explore how fortunate you are in having enough to be able to share a quarter, a dollar, or whatever. Be especially aware that it is the presence of an abundance mind-set that allows you to give and receive so freely.

Bring your meditation to a close by imagining that it is some time after you have shared money freely and the main quality you notice is that you still have enough to meet your needs. There is always enough to go around.

And so . . .

The most powerful point to remember is that experiencing gratitude and generosity—as a state of mind and as a way of being in the world—creates even *more* gratitude and generosity. The more openly you can give and receive generously, the more you will notice how much you receive in any given day. As you deepen your relationship with gratitude and generosity, allow yourself to be curious as to how you will notice their increasing presence in all aspects of your experience. Whenever any one of us expresses or experiences gratitude and generosity, everyone around us is automatically affected. In the next chapter, we will explore how the context of *collective consciousness* offers a constant opportunity to contribute to, and draw upon, the combined wisdom of our species.

Chapter 7

ONENESS AND INTERCONNECTION
The Interplay of Collective Consciousness

> *We drop like pebbles of each other's souls, and the*
> *orbit of our ripples continues to expand, intersecting*
> *with countless others.*
>
> —*Joan Borysenko*

As we begin our exploration of the realm of collective consciousness, we shift our focus from individual attitudes and behaviors to the impact of these factors on the greater context of collective consciousness, which is shared by us all.

Modern physics suggests a number of tantalizing possibilities about the nature of the universe. Among them is the intriguing idea that reality may be more accurately characterized in terms of *information* than energy, although both are very much involved. In this premise, information is the foundation of the universe and energy is one of its manifestations. If this is true, then it is also possible that all the knowledge of all time, from all forms of life, surrounds us in the same way the air we breathe is all around us. We feel the negative consequences of breathing polluted air or the uplifting sense of well-being when the air we breathe is fresh and clean. In this chapter, we will explore the potentials and implications of how our collective psyche may affect our sense of well-being, even as our individual experience adds its measure to that collective.

As we delve into the themes of collective consciousness and oneness, we will also need to explore more deeply the characteristics and implications of quantum realities, those dimensions in which the parameters of time, space, and location are irrelevant—actually, nonexistent. From a quantum perspective, reality operates quite differently from how we perceive it. In other words, what we think is real isn't actually as real as it seems. For example, objects that we experience as solid, including ourselves, are actually made of constantly moving molecules with lots of space between them. When we enter quantum realities, we are confronted with a need to revise and expand our most basic assumptions about how our world operates.

Most of us were taught to think about the physical world as energy existing in different forms: solid, liquid, gaseous, visible and invisible light, and sound waves. When we shift to the idea of an *information* universe, the underlying foundation of reality shifts. This perspective describes the implications of the continuous presence of information—unbounded by time or space—that allows possibilities that go far beyond the familiar transformation of energy from one state to another, as when water turns to ice, and vice versa. One perspective doesn't invalidate the other; each describes different dimensions of reality, two distinct attributes of the whole.

In an information-based universe, none of us ever takes the journey into wholeness alone. We all are part of the enfolding collective consciousness of humanity that consists of the combined awareness, experience, and wisdom of every human being who ever lived, including both positive and negative elements of human consciousness. As a therapist who works with individuals in search of healing answers, I find deep hope and optimism in the dynamic possibilities available in an information universe—even as I find reason to be concerned. Within such a context, each of us has access to our shared wisdom, shared pain, shared *everything* as we seek to develop beyond our familiar achievements and ways of being. We also contribute, automatically and inescapably, to the sum total of our collective experience and consciousness—good and bad.

Morphic Fields and Morphic Resonance

There appears to be emerging support for the idea of collective consciousness from studies done by scientists whose work relies on the assumptions that underlie quantum physics. For example, Rupert Sheldrake, a biologist from Great Britain, has studied the transmission of information among geographically separated members of certain species of animals. In his controversial theory, *morphic fields* represent the reservoir of information that is available to all of us all the time. His experiments suggest that members of a given species may have ready access to the learning and experience of the information generated by all members of their own kind.

In one experiment, for example, the experience of laboratory mice trained to run especially difficult mazes seemed to "help" other mice of the same species—but at a different location from those who were trained—learn how to run the same kind of maze more quickly. On a more mundane and fun note, but perhaps equally significant, Sheldrake describes an experiment where people were asked to work a popular Sunday crossword puzzle on either Sunday morning, Sunday evening, or Monday. As it turned out, people who worked the puzzle on Monday consistently found it easier to solve. Sheldrake's hypothesis is that the solution may be easier to reach by Monday because the answers from those who solved the puzzle on Sunday then exist in a human morphic field of information, which can be accessed by the Monday puzzle solvers.

Does this experimental outcome, and others like it, prove that we humans participate in a collective information field? No, but it does suggest that we each have a tangible, measurable effect on one another every time we have a new learning experience. According to Sheldrake, without conscious intent we tap into a collective field of information through an automatic and unconscious process he calls *morphic resonance*. This resonance occurs when members of the same species are in tune with the accomplishments, behaviors, and information held by any other members of the species.

When I first read about this concept, an example immediately sprang to mind. I had recalled that, many years ago, I watched a young man break a record on the high jump. The television commentator had said that the young man was going to try a height that was impossible to attain, which is what sparked my interest in the first place. Not only did the athlete break the record but, soon after, others routinely matched his achievement and went on to break new records. The first young man's accomplishment seemed to open up the possibility for everyone else—as though his achievement literally stretched our collective capacity in some way.

A popular example of morphic resonance is the hundredth money phenomenon. The story goes that a female monkey named Imo, who lived on an island with her troop, took a yam to the ocean one day and washed it before eating. Soon her offspring were also washing their yams, as well. Within a brief period of time, all the members of her troop were doing the same.

It's not so difficult to imagine that these monkeys learned from watching Imo's behavior. What *is* hard to explain is how monkeys of the same species but living on islands separated by vast distances soon began to exhibit the same yam-washing behavior that had first been observed with Imo. Could it be that as more members of Imo's troop learned how to wash their yams, they created a critical mass in the morphic field of their species, thereby making this new learning more available to monkeys that were geographically separated from the troop? Though it is impossible to know what actually happened, it is tempting to apply this example to the idea of collective consciousness.

There are countless examples of all manner of achievement becoming commonplace once a person has shown the rest of us what's possible. On a less obvious level, we can wonder what the implications of morphic resonance are in relation to emotional and intellectual processes as well. Could it be that whenever someone stretches our understanding, as Copernicus did when he claimed that the earth revolved around the sun, the rest of us unconsciously stretch to include this idea as well?

Joanna Macy, a professor of philosophy and religion as well as a workshop leader on peace and environmental issues, sums up the theme we've been exploring when she says, "…every act we make, every word we speak, every thought we think is not only affected by the other elements in the vast web of being in which all things take part, but also has results so far-reaching that we cannot see or imagine them."

The "Raincloud of Knowable Things"

When I was young, my grandmother taught me about morphic fields, only she referred to them as the "raincloud of knowable things". Her spiritual beliefs and experiences of altered states of consciousness convinced her that all of us participate in a consciousness that touches everyone all the time. "At certain points," she explained, "ideas whose time has come emerge in a *raincloud of knowable things* and shower down on everyone all at once. During these times, certain people from a variety of backgrounds and interests seem to be especially receptive to the ideas." Describing morphic resonance, but calling it intuition, she talked about how these people seem to soak up the new awareness and then articulate it, generally receiving skepticism, or worse, in response. After a time, however, the ideas begin to emerge even more widely in numerous fields—science, art, education, business, spiritual practice, and other areas of human endeavor, as more and more people experience a resonance with the once unfamiliar notions.

Perhaps the most familiar example of the simultaneous emergence of an idea or movement is Einstein's theory of relativity. At the time, Einstein wasn't the only scientist to discover relativity, but he is the one history remembers. The theory was "in the air" and was registered by at least one other scientist, in a different part of the world, at approximately the same time. The annals of science contain many similar examples of concurrent discoveries in widely separated parts of the world.

The explosion of inner-child work is another example of the *raincloud* in operation. Although the method of identifying specific parts of the self and interacting with them had been integral to at least two schools of psychotherapy—Gestalt and Psychosynthesis—for many years, the concept of accessing and reparenting *child* parts didn't become widely popular until the early 1980's. It was as if many therapists had been working with the concept independently, most not realizing that others were doing the same. It was only as books began to appear and the public's response mushroomed that I became aware of how effectively the *raincloud* had done its job of showering our collective consciousness with this concept.

The Compelling Nature of Morphic Fields

An important quality of morphic fields is the notion that the greater the number of people who think or act in a certain way, the more available that way of thinking or behaving becomes to the rest of us. This has both positive and negative implications. For example, if increasing numbers of people were to express generosity in their lives, the urge and capacity to be generous might be strengthened in all of us. On the other hand, if more and more of us disregard the needs of others—from playing radios and television sets at deafening volume with no regard for neighbors to the random violence of rape, robbery, and other aggressive behaviors—we might find it easier, at unconscious levels, to act insensitively or violently toward others.

We need to become aware of the quality of the "psychic air" in which we live as a species. Do we function collectively in an overall state of consciousness that supports healthy thinking, feeling, and acting, or do we live in a toxic psychic environment that affects us in ways we don't realize? If the expression of mindfulness, compassion, and lovingkindness by increasing numbers of people would make it easier for others to tap into these ways of being, the same would be true in the opposite direction: more and more people immersing themselves in television shows, movies, books, music, and ideologies that espouse violence would increase violent responses species-wide.

Years ago, my concerns about the quality of our collective consciousness led me to develop a concept I called *psychoecology*. The basic premise of my thinking then was that our internal ecology of consciousness is every bit as important as the ecology of our physical world, and I still believe this is true. The problem is, I'm not sure what to *do* about it, except to help one person at a time improve the quality of his or her inner life. My hope is that if enough individuals change, their efforts will contribute to a developing critical mass of people who experience a greater sense of psychological wholeness. It has been my experience that people who feel more whole, more self-accepting, are less likely to hurt others. Through their willingness to resolve issues that would otherwise cause them to act out their internal distress and conflict in the world, people who are psychologically whole and living consciously become a source of healthy psychic nourishment for the rest of us.

For these reasons, it is essential to become aware of the quality and tone of your habitual ways of thinking and feeling. The internal states you slip into automatically attune you to particular aspects of our morphic field that resonate with those ways of being in the world. Feed yourself a constant diet of cruel or fear-laden images and your unconscious orients itself to these elements of collective emotion and behavior. Nourish yourself with images of kindness, open-heartedness, and delight and you direct your awareness toward quite a different way of feeling and being.

How can we protect ourselves from the toxic aspects of collective consciousness? Are there ways we can "inoculate" ourselves against the epidemic of violence and intolerance that is erupting all around us? Perhaps the most immediate step is to fill your awareness with constructive kinds of information and experience so that you support the spontaneous tendency to resonate with a sense of well-being, connection, and wholeness rather than what is toxic. To do this requires a certain degree of willpower, given that the media and popular sources of entertainment, such as movies, books, music, and video games, often depict negative images of abuse and worse.

Our *actions* also align us with either toxic or beneficent elements of collective consciousness. For example, when we are aggressive and move through the day pushing people around, literally or figuratively, we resonate more with aggressive aspects of the human morphic field. If we act in ways that show disrespect for ourselves or others—behaving destructively, selfishly, or in unkind ways—the tendency is reinforced by its morphic resonance with collective destructiveness, selfishness, or unkindness. If, on the other hand, our behavior manifests acts of generosity and other constructive qualities, that capacity is further enhanced by the resonance we experience with these collective ways of behaving.

For example, I recall a middle-aged woman who spent all her free time reading romance novels. When she eventually married, she was happy enough, but experienced an underlying tug of disappointment. When I asked her about this nagging feeling, she said that her husband would never measure up to the passionate men depicted in the books she read. The stories were harmless enough, but they unconsciously aligned her with a collective fantasy about love.

At the other end of the spectrum is a colleague who became so preoccupied with reading books on the long-term effects of child abuse that he began to experience secondary post-traumatic stress symptoms. He dreamed about abuse and seemed unable to carry on a conversation without focusing on the subject. His friends and colleagues began to avoid him, as he became increasingly immersed in images and stories of abuse. Eventually he had to reenter therapy and refocus his interests on less devastating elements of human experience.

Another person had a passion for helping others. She volunteered at a soup kitchen and gave time, money, and energy to social causes. What she discovered was that so many opportunities for service presented themselves that she had to learn to say "no". She was so attuned to collective need that it literally filled her awareness.

Yet another individual devoured biographical books and films. He naturally gravitated to life stories of people he admired and described himself as constantly uplifted, intrigued, and renewed by their lives. He avoided biographies of people whose lives were characterized by cruelty or violence. As he described it, he sensed that to read about these qualities as lived by real people would be toxic for him. His imagination was vivid and he preferred to feed it with collective experiences that nurtured a sense of honor.

Since it is impossible to be outside the reach of collective consciousness, we are faced with a constant opportunity to make a difference by cleaning up our small contribution to the human morphic field. No one else can do this for us; each of us must choose the quality of thought, feeling, and being we want to bring into our individual lives and, thereby, into the reach of everyone else.

MAKE IT REAL EXPERIMENT #1:
Choosing Your Resonances in Our Morphic Field

In this experiment, let yourself become aware of the general quality of your thinking and feeling. Are you someone who looks at the world primarily with an optimistic point of view, or do you tend to worry about what could go wrong?

- Review the quality and tone of your habitual ways of thinking and feeling, the internal states you slip into automatically. These attitudes and responses attune you to particular aspects of our morphic field that resonate with those ways of being in the world. For example, if it is your habit of mind to worry, notice what happens if you become more mindful of slipping into worrying. Notice the behavior and when you can, let it go and focus your attention on a situation or circumstance that is working right in your life.

- It may be that you are someone who feels angry or irritated a lot. Notice what happens if you deliberately attune yourself to aspects of our morphic field that support qualities such as calm and ease. You might focus on someone—a spiritual figure or a person you admire—and allow yourself to experience the world as you imagine that person would.

- Tune into the most constructive states of mind in collective consciousness in the same way you might choose to live in the least polluted area possible. This doesn't mean you need to deny, push away, or minimize those aspects of your life that aren't going well. It suggests, though, that after acknowledging a particular problem, it may be useful to focus on what is going well or what would be most helpful or in some other way to emphasize that your "glass" is half full rather than half empty.

After doing this experiment for a while, notice if there is any spontaneous shift in the quality of your mental and emotional life. Also note whether events in your life seem to run more smoothly in some recognizable way, or whether you are aware of any other details you might attribute to attuning yourself to a positive and constructive field of information. Most importantly, engage this experiment with compassion for yourself. Habits of mind take a long time to create and originate in powerful and compelling learning experiences we had when we were growing up. It takes time to shift from habitual ways of experiencing and interpreting the world. It might help to enter into this experiment with the thought that you can reach for a *small* change in thinking. Just as any journey is made up of all the steps along the way, changes in how you think and feel come about in small increments, as well.

EXPERIMENT #2:
Morphic Resonance and How You Spend Your Time

In this experiment, take a serious look at how you spend your time, realizing that the kinds of activities you engage in immerse you in particular aspects and qualities of collective consciousness.

- What kinds of movies do you see? What kinds of television shows do you watch? What types of books do you read? What is your favorite kind of recreation?

- Ask yourself if your activities are uplifting. Do they add to your basic sense of well-being—or not?

- What is the quality of collective consciousness that you imagine you participate in when you spend time with your usual and favorite activities?

The purpose of this experiment is to become increasingly aware of the morphic resonances you encourage through the focus of your attention and energy. Remember that each of us is immersed in an ocean of collective consciousness and parts of that ocean are more positive and healthy than others.

EXPERIMENT #3:
Your Contributions to the Morphic Field

In this experiment, take some time to decide what you would like to contribute to our collective morphic field. Then, once a week, take some time to sit quietly and generate the feeling, quality of being, or state of mind that you want to enhance for everyone.

For example, you might do a meditation on compassion, in which you offer your experience, thoughts, and feelings to the human morphic field. Or you might focus on your sense of humor, adding your capacity for laughter and delight to collective consciousness. Your awareness and the qualities you express go into the morphic field anyway, but this experiment allows you to *choose* to add your positive states of being to collective consciousness, which automatically increases—and intensifies the impact of—the information we all share.

GUIDED MEDITATION #1:
Attuning to the "Raincloud of Knowable Things"

Before you begin this meditation, choose a subject, issue, problem, or creative urge on which you wish to focus your attention. It can be anything, large or small. During the meditation, you will attune to the *raincloud of knowable things*, the morphic field of that which you wish to explore more deeply. In a very real sense, you will open yourself to inspiration from a larger, collective reservoir of wisdom.

Begin by finding a place to sit undisturbed for a while. Have paper and pen with you, or a tape recorder, so that you can make note of anything that comes to mind as you meditate.

Take a few minutes to settle into the bottom of the breath. Allow yourself to notice your breathing and follow your exhalations all the way down to the bottom of the breath. Allow the still point between this breath and the next to enter your awareness. There is no need to struggle. Just become aware of the still point whenever it comes to mind. Notice what it's like to allow the stillness to touch you in some way that feels good to you.

Now bring to mind the issue you've chosen as the focus for your journey. Simply recall it, think about it, ponder what you wish to know, experience, or realize about it. Take a minute or so just to be with the issue, keeping it in mind, mulling it over, looking at it from different angles.

Realize that you are building an information field of your own that begins to resonate with the larger collective information field. As your focus deepens, you become increasingly attuned to the larger morphic field, the raincloud that contains the information you seek, even when you have no idea what that information is.

Next, imagine a beautiful cloud of some color or texture that represents the larger information field from which you seek inspiration—the raincloud of knowable things. Remember that you don't need to have a visual image ... just let an impression drop into your mind that represents the cloud for you in some way that feels right.

Imagine that your thoughts become lighter than air and begin to rise up into the raincloud. You can envision your thoughts as all the words you are thinking, or as wisps of color or texture. Allow whatever image or impression that surfaces in your awareness to represent all the thoughts you are sending up into the raincloud.

It is as though you were "seeding" the cloud so that it will rain on you. In this case, you seed it with your questions, ponderings, and/or requests so that it will rain inspiration. It is best to have no preconceptions or expectations. Simply hold an attitude of open curiosity and notice what comes into your awareness.

You may find that nothing comes at first. You may discover, in fact, that it is only over time, long after your actual meditation, that you begin to receive the wisdom of the raincloud, the collective morphic field, in response to the issue you explored in the meditation.

When you feel your focus begin to wind down, or you have reached the end of the time you have allotted for the experience, take a few moments to record some notes, if you haven't already, even if you think you have nothing to write or say. You may find that a new awareness enters your dreams or appears during odd moments of inspiration during the day.

When you feel ready, wiggle your fingers and toes and come all the way back to an alert state of consciousness, aware of your surroundings and ready to go on with your next activity.

EXPERIMENT #4:
Continuing to Attune as You Sleep

To your meditative focus, add a request that you will continue to tap into the morphic field, or *raincloud*, during the nighttime. Ask yourself to focus on the issue as you sleep, to receive inspiration and new information during this time, and perhaps to have a dream about it. Then, when you awaken, take a few moments to record whatever comes to mind.

Be sure to keep a pen and paper near your bed—or a recording device of some kind—so that you can note whatever emerges, without having to disturb yourself too much, especially if you want to go back to sleep after you've recorded your experience.

Individual and Collective Empowerment

What would it mean to you if you truly believed that you were never alone in life? Can you imagine that no matter what challenges you have faced, suffering endured, delights encountered, or accomplishments achieved, you never move through them alone? All the varieties of human experience that enter your life are shared by every other person at the level of collective consciousness—and the experiences of everyone else are shared by you at a deep level of awareness.

If it unnerves you to imagine that you are aware, at some level, of the experiences of every other person, you are not alone! The comfort offered by the concept of collective consciousness often is offset by the potentially overwhelming idea that no one of us ever suffers alone either. When I first began to explore collective consciousness, I was both excited and daunted by the all-encompassing quality of the concept. My excitement grew from the idea that the accomplishment of any individual becomes a potential resource to everyone else. But I was also initially appalled by the thought that I am affected by the state of mind and emotions of every other person in the world. It is one thing to imagine that my own personal triumphs and healing can contribute to the journey others are taking into psychological wholeness and more conscious living. It is another thing entirely to imagine that the hatred, envy, greed, anger, and suffering of others inevitably affect my own deep consciousness.

As I have lived with this idea, I have realized that it need not be as overwhelming as it initially seemed. It helped me to remember that, just as our physical bodies distinguish us from the rest of the material world, our individual psyches differentiate us from one another at the level of collective consciousness. I found that if I could keep in mind that we have some measure of control over the kinds of collective awareness and qualities to which we expose ourselves, it became tolerable to acknowledge that we are all in this together. With the realization that we are inevitably connected through our human morphic field, I become increasingly committed to doing whatever I could to contribute constructively to collective consciousness.

Also, as an added comment here, as I mentioned in the new Introduction, these days I am more aware of the function of "frequencies" and that our focus of attention is like tuning into a particular radio station. We can choose the frequencies with which we seek to resonate, thereby lessening somewhat the impact of collective negativity on our individual consciousness.

It's important to know that being committed to contributing something positive to collective consciousness isn't just about being a "good" person. Instead it is about being *ecologically responsible*, except in this case we're dealing with the *psychoecology* I described earlier. Just as we have learned to pay attention to our physical resources by recycling them, we also have to pay greater attention to what we do with our psychological resources—our thoughts and feelings. For example, when you have the courage to look yourself in the eye, acknowledge your shortcomings, and dare to love yourself anyway . . . when you express compassion and lovingkindness to a stranger or someone you don't particularly like . . . when you spend quiet moments in stillness settled into your body—you are contributing, immediately and inescapably, to the possibility that others will be able to do the same.

This doesn't mean that your "bad days" are irreparably harmful. Getting angry, depressed, agitated, or anxious is bound to happen—lots! It took many years and many of us to pollute our major cities, so it helps to remember that your personal bad days don't have the power to devastate the emotional lives of others. It does mean, though, that your suffering isn't yours alone. It becomes part of our collective morphic field, available to those who resonate with it. In the same way, when you resonate with suffering, you tap into this collective experience, as well, offering your support to others.

While there may be great physical distance between you and someone you hear about in the news who experiences a great achievement, heroic moment, disaster, starvation, oppression, or some other event, there is really no such thing as distance. As I described earlier, it all becomes part of the human morphic field. And yet, while we are all subliminally affected by our collective morphic field whether we choose to be or not, we also are free to access these experiences consciously—as when we meditate on outstanding human accomplishments or extra-ordinarily feats, or focus on the least honorable or desirable of human qualities as portrayed in movies and books.

In the following guided meditation, you will have an opportunity to practice tapping into the collective *support* that is available for you as you seek to live more consciously, to achieve a greater sense of psychological wholeness, or to generally feel a greater sense of connection to what is constantly available in the human morphic field. Fortunately, there are always those who are ahead of us along the way, even as there are always those who have yet to arrive at the place we stand today, so inspiration is always available.

MAKE IT REAL
GUIDED MEDITATION #2:
The Path of Individual and Collective Empowerment

Begin by finding a place where you can sit for a while without being disturbed. Take a few moments to settle yourself, to travel to the bottom of the breath, noticing the stillness that exists between the out-breath and the next in-breath.

Now give yourself an opportunity to review your journey into greater self-expression, wholeness, conscious living, or some other development you've undertaken. Recall when you began the journey, how long you've been at it consciously, and where you have succeeded in meeting your goals in ways that feel good to you.

Also review those areas you know still need deepening, expanding, or nourishing or the aspects of yourself you need to embrace more fully.

Now imagine that you are on a very special path. It is the path of individual and collective empowerment, representing not only your own journey but that of every other person all over the world as well. You may notice just a portion of the path that relates to where you are at this time, or you may get a sense of the entire journey into a greater experience of wholeness that we are taking as a species.

Just let whatever impressions arise be there now. As always, there is no right answer. There is only your awareness, at this point in time, of whatever impressions hold meaning for you. Re-

member, you don't have to see any visual imagery for this to be a powerful experience. Allow yourself to sense whatever impressions are available to you as you do the meditation.

Now become aware of the surface of the path on which you travel. Notice the quality of that surface. Notice, also, whatever, sounds, smells, colors, or other qualities come into your awareness as you focus on this path.

Next, become aware of those who travel ahead of you, who are further along in accomplishing what you seek to achieve. What is your initial response to this awareness? Be sure to allow any mixed feelings that may arise.

What would it be like for you if someone up ahead were to reach back and offer you a hand? Could you accept the help? What would it be like to take that hand and let the person offer assistance? Just be present with whatever you experience as you allow the help that is available to be there for you.

Next, turn around and notice all the people who haven't reached the place in their journey that you have in yours. What is it like for you to realize that you have come further than some other people? Is it all right for you to be where you are and for them to be where they are? What mixed feelings, if any, arise as you look back?

If it feels right to you, allow yourself to reach back now and offer a hand to someone who is behind you. This may be someone you know, or it may be a stranger. It doesn't matter which. The important thing is to allow yourself to reach out and offer help, consciously and willingly.

Pay attention to your responses as well as to the responses of the person who takes your hand. Again, there is no right way to do this. Simply allow yourself to be aware. Remind yourself that, whether or not you are comfortable reaching out to those who travel along the path behind you, every step you take offers them support anyway.

Turn and face forward again now, paying attention to the people who travel at the same pace and in the same place as you.

Realize that you never travel alone, no matter how you may feel. There are so many others taking the journey with you.

For now, notice what happens when you give yourself permission to continue your journey and to accept and give help without even having to realize consciously that you do so. Within a context of collective consciousness, receiving and giving go on all the time naturally and automatically, without effort, without struggle.

When you feel ready, take a few moments to review your journey. Recognize that you can return to an awareness of the path whenever you wish. You may want to remind yourself that you never travel alone.

As you come all the way back to your surroundings, wiggle your fingers and toes. You may want to write down some notes or just sit with the quality of your experience, as you would the lingering tone of a bell just rung.

This guided meditation is one I have used in workshops for years. Often people report feeling a deep sense of connection with those whom they sense travel the same path with them in the morphic field, even as they recognize they will never meet most of those people in person.

As you do this meditation, be sure to allow yourself to have mixed feelings. You may feel inadequate when you imagine that there are people far ahead of where you are now, who have achieved goals some part of you may believe you will never reach. You may also feel deep gratitude that these people have gone ahead and, with their efforts, cleared the way, that their contributions to our morphic field will make it easier for you to achieve what you seek. You may discover feelings of sorrow or guilt because of people who are so far behind where you are today or who may never reach their most deeply desired goals. Whatever feelings you may have, remember that each and every step you take into living more consciously, into a greater sense of psychological wholeness and well-being, supports all who journey on the same path of self-discovery.

Also, if you discover that you have a feeling that you "should" feel more empowered in your life than you do, meet this feeling with compassion and lovingkindness. There is no need to be anywhere but here and now. In fact, it's not possible to be anywhere but here and now. There's no rush. The way ahead is clear and you have the support of all who have gone ahead of you.

Oneness

As we deepen our journey into living more consciously within a context of psychological wholeness, we open ourselves to the experience of being part of a larger "something" without which we could not exist. Experiencing *oneness* can be both profoundly comforting and terrifying, because there is a fundamental paradox we confront as soon as we approach it: even though our senses, thoughts, and feelings tell us we are all separate, they are also the gateway to experiencing oneness, which shows us that we are inextricably part of a much more complex, interrelated context of being.

In Buddhism there is a concept called *co-dependent origination*, which means that everything that exists is dependent on the concurrent existence of everything else. According to this idea, which is similar to an ecological perspective, each of us is an essential part of a dynamic whole. If any one part were removed, everything would change, just like the kaleidoscope. We exist in a web of interrelatedness, within which each of us is dependent on a diverse array of other parts that make life and survival possible.

Think about this idea at a very basic level. Whenever you sit in a chair, for example, you can ponder how, in order for the chair to exist, a long, long list of things had to happen. Initially, there had to be sunlight, dirt, the seed of a tree, insects, microbes, water, and many other elements that contributed to the tree's development. Then there had to be people and machines to make lumber from the tree, someone else to design the chair, and yet other people to actually make it. Next came the trucks that carried the chair from its origins to the place where you acquired it. Then there were all the people involved in the marketing of it, and any other elements involved in the journey the chair took from seed to completion. If any of these elements had been missing, the chair wouldn't exist.

What is true for the chair is true for *everything*: remove any one of the complex array of elements in the material creation of anything, and it no longer exists. Just as the chair can't become a chair without all the other participants along the way, you can't be you without an amazing, complex interconnection with all the contributors that make your life possible.

A metaphor for oneness is the hologram. What is particularly intriguing about a hologram, which is created by laser light and a special photographic process, is that every portion of the photographic plate, if broken into pieces, contains the whole picture. Drawing on this unique property as a possible representation of how an information universe might work, is it also possible that each of us, as individuals, contains the "whole picture" within ourselves, even though it is outside conscious awareness?

The metaphor of a hologram invites us to consider, once again, that we cannot *not* be part of a larger context of wholeness. Oneness is the foundation from which we emerge; separateness exists only as an illusion supported by the unique form we each take as human beings in physical bodies.

Another achievement that has become both a metaphor and a manifestation of oneness is the Internet. Through a global network of computers, we have created a continuous opportunity to experience oneness via the virtual community that is emerging within the worldwide web. In cyberspace, there is instantaneous communication among people in widely dispersed geographical locations and time zones around the planet. Time and space are no longer barriers to communication and, along with increased accessibility, comes a deepening sense of interconnection.

Within a context of oneness and co-dependent origination, each one of us is supported within the web of interconnection that contains us as surely as the oceans contain the drops of water that create them. In the exercises that follow, you will have an opportunity to explore metaphors for oneness, as well as the paradox of our co-existing states of individuality *and* oneness. As you work with the exercises, remember that tapping into a sense of oneness needn't negate your individual self. Instead, your sense of self can expand to include an awareness of your place within a larger context. As physicist David Bohm described, we are all like patterns on a continuous carpet: each a separate shape, texture and color, yet finding our place and meaning only within the larger pattern.

MAKE IT REAL
GUIDED MEDITATION #3:
On Being a Wave

This meditation and the next invite you to explore metaphors for oneness. As you do them, allow yourself to be aware of any mixed feelings you may have. At times, oneness may be an appealing, even comforting idea. At other times, it can threaten to annihilate your sense of self and may trigger fear or anger instead of greater ease. Simply be aware of the responses you have and notice whether they change from time to time.

To begin, allow yourself to settle in comfortably and focus your attention on the still point at the bottom of the breath.

Bring to mind a vast ocean. It may be one you feel particularly connected to already, or it may be one that comes to mind from your inner world of imagining. Become especially aware of the texture of the surface of the water and the movement under the surface. Recall that deep within the oceans are currents that rarely move up to the surface of the water. They flow in the depths, unseen.

Pay particular attention now to the surface of the water. Is the surface still or are there places where the water ripples? What color is it?

Now notice that a breeze begins to blow, creating small wavelets that appear, momentarily, on the surface. Remember that it's not necessary to see images. Just allow impressions to come. What is most important is that you sense the quality, the essence, of the experience.

For a moment, allow yourself to imagine that you are one of those small wavelets, that you move with the wave as it rises and falls, rhythmically following the currents of the ocean. Pay special attention to how you stay connected with the larger surface from which you emerge, or how quickly you return to it if you leap higher than the water's surface for a moment or two. When you experience yourself as the wavelet on the surface of the ocean, you are part of the water and yet are able to momentarily express yourself as separate from it.

Now notice that there are other waves that rise from the surface of the water. Some may seem to dance together; others jump off in improbable directions. Whatever each wave's unique direction and shape, all emerge from, are defined by, and return to the all-embracing water.

Take a moment now to imagine that your sense of a separate self is like the wave—rising up and dancing along the surface of the water yet always connected to the vast ocean from which you come. Pay particular attention to the feeling you have when you are a wave. How do you experience that sense of individuality, that freedom to express yourself?

Now notice what you experience as you settle back into, and blend with, the larger body of water. Play with the paradox of being both an individual wavelet and also part of the larger body of water from which the wavelet emerges. Notice that you cannot not be both: you are part of the ocean itself and the individual wave that dances along the surface of the water, even as it is never truly or permanently separate from the larger body of water which is its source.

How might this imagining affect your everyday life? What if you were to recall, during the day, that you are both separate from—and part of—every other living thing? What behaviors might you change? What beliefs or feelings might you experience differently?

Take a few moments now to be present with the sense of being a wavelet at the same time that you are also the ocean. Take whatever time you need to incorporate into your experience the sense of oneness and separateness, the inescapable relationship between the two. Notice, especially, how it feels in your body to experience this kind of unity in diversity, this oneness and separateness at the same time.

When you feel ready, review your experience and come back to your surroundings by wiggling your fingers and toes, bringing yourself into a fully alert state of mind.

GUIDED MEDITATION #4:
On Breathing

Begin this meditation simply by settling into your breathing. Notice the natural in-and-out rhythm of air as it enters and leaves your lungs. Become aware of the temperature of the air as it enters and leaves your nostrils. Do you notice how it feels warmer on the outbreath than it does on the in-breath?

Reflect on how your body expresses immense wisdom in its relationship to the air around you. It knows how to take it in, extract the oxygen that is needed to nourish your cells, and then release to the environment the carbon dioxide that is a waste product of your body.

Now recognize that all green growing things contribute oxygen to the air you breathe. In return, in a reciprocal relationship of support, your exhalations provide the world's vegetation with the carbon dioxide needed for its nourishment.

Imagine now that the air you breathe at this moment has traveled all around the globe to arrive at your nostrils right now. Ask yourself how many other beings have breathed this air also, and how many will breathe it in the next moment, once you exhale?

Notice how it feels to recognize that we share the air we breathe; it is one air. The air connects us in ways that are immediate and ever-present. Even as you breathe, you participate in an inescapable whole; you both draw from, and contribute to, the well-being of all the life around you.

Take a few moments to be present with your breath. You might wish to express gratitude that nature, in its wisdom, created the mutually beneficial relationship that exists between animals, insects, other life forms and the earth's vegetation. Without each other, none can survive.

Imagine for a moment the great currents that constantly move air around the planet. A dynamic dance goes on all around you in every moment of every day, even though you may live your life totally unaware of the profound interplay in nature that includes you.

Be sure to allow any mixed feelings that may accompany this exploration. Remember that part of wholeness is to invite every response to move into conscious awareness and simply be there.

When you feel ready, wiggle your fingers and toes and come all the way back from your journey.

EXPERIMENT #5:
Generating Metaphors for Oneness

In this experiment you have an opportunity to create your own metaphors for oneness. Pay attention to those that have special power or meaning for you. Once you have identified more metaphors for oneness, bring them into your meditations. Over time, notice how they affect the quality of your daily experience.

For example, in my office I have photographs of the earth taken from space. I look at these photographs many times a day, and they remind me that I cannot separate myself from the planet—that I am but one cell in an extraordinary collective.

Psychological Wholeness and Oneness

When exploring the experience of oneness, fears of engulfment and annihilation are as basic as fears of abandonment. These fears deserve—as well as demand—attention when they arise. They are primal responses—sometimes unavoidable and usually compelling in their initial conviction that we are about to be erased from the face of the earth!

Someone once said that you have to *become* a self before you can *transcend* the self. In terms of our exploration into psychological wholeness, I might say that you have to experience your individuality before you can comfortably enter oneness. While a deepening sense of well-being and comfort naturally emerges from an experience of unitive consciousness, you also need to have a solid enough sense of your individual self to be able to tolerate fears of engulfment or annihilation that may initially accompany it. Without a solid sense of self, you may feel that the initial merger into oneness represents a surrender of the individuality and autonomy that are so much part of Western cultural identity.

If you find that you are uncomfortable exploring unitive consciousness, pay attention to your response even as you recognize that it is the very presence of your individual self that allows you to register this discomfort. Your awareness itself is evidence of the fact that there is no actual loss of self when you enter an experience of oneness. Rather, *there is an expansion of how you define the boundaries and extent of who you are.* Remember that a sense of psychological wholeness brings with it a willingness to acknowledge *whatever* mixed feelings may arise. The important point to keep in mind is that there is no need to act on these feelings. Instead, their presence offers yet another opportunity for you to become self-aware, to be mindful of what is moving through you in the present moment.

I recall the first time I entered the experience of being both a wave and the ocean itself. Initially I had a flash of fear, a feeling that I would cease to exist. Being the ocean led to an awareness of how I couldn't exist apart from the oneness from which my individual self emerged. Shifting to an experience of myself as the wave brought its own kind of fear. I recognized the transitory, fleeting nature of my individual self. Interwoven with the experience, however, was an enveloping sense of well-being and rightness about it all, even as my self-protective impulses struggled to cope with the awareness of the eventual loss of self as the wave slipped back into the ocean.

The rightness of the experience emerged with my awareness of the context within which my being was held as securely as the ocean holds the wave. That the wave experience brought me face to face with my own mortality became an acceptable aspect of experiencing oneness. In fact, an awareness of inevitable mortality actually makes daily life sweeter. You recognize more immediately that each moment is a precious gift, arising with no guarantee of what will come next. We tend to live more fully when we willingly acknowledge that we won't be here forever.

To develop the capacity to move between an awareness of your individual self and that of oneness expands your experience of psychological wholeness. No longer limited to thinking of yourself as stopping at the boundary of your skin, the sense of who you are extends into the world around you. Rather than being annihilated or engulfed by something that is *not* you, now you are everywhere, in everything, even as you also continue to be your familiar, individual self. In addition, experiencing yourself as part of a larger context can serve to remind you that it *matters* that you are here. As part of a collective ecology of being, *you make a contribution that no one else can*, simply by being in the world and expressing your unique, *individual* self.

In the next chapter, we will continue to explore the relationship of the individual to the collective as we return to the realm of quantum physics. Within a context of shifting probabilities, synchronicities, and individual choice we can engage a dynamic view of reality that enhances our capacity to contribute to the collective, our experience of an ever-deepening sense of psychological wholeness, and our capacity to live more consciously.

Chapter 8

CREATING POSSIBILITY

The Dance of Intention and Synchronicity

> *What if you slept, and what if in your sleep you dreamed, and what if in your dream you went to heaven and there plucked a strange and beautiful flower, and what if when you awoke you had the flower in your hand? And, what then?*
> —*Samuel Taylor Coleridge*

Miracles are events that reflect a natural order that occurs outside the usual dimensions of physical reality. Spontaneous recovery from disease after a healer has done her work—something that occurs in many cultures—cannot be explained in everyday medical terms. Perhaps the healing represents a transfer of new information to the body-mind of the person who is ill, or maybe the healer transmits energy that the patient's body uses to heal itself, or there may be some other dynamic taking place that we don't even know how to imagine. Mental telepathy—in which information is shared instantaneously, nonverbally, and irrespective of distance—appears as another kind of miraculous event if viewed only within a three-dimensional framework of a reality bound by space and time. Yet people all over the world and across the centuries have reported accounts of telepathic experiences.

In this chapter we will explore the realm of the miraculous from the perspective of quantum physics and what it implies about the nature of reality. Our exploration will include the possibility that the information we carry in the form of thoughts and feelings may actually affect physical reality in some way.

To continue building bridges between our usual understanding of how reality appears to operate in our everyday world and the new perspectives suggested by the principles that govern quantum realities, you will need a healthy dose of curiosity. In addition, you need to be willing to suspend disbelief temporarily as you stretch the boundaries of what is possible beyond the confines of familiar notions about reality.

There is a story told about when the Spaniards first laid anchor in Patagonia, at the southernmost tip of South America. They went ashore in small boats, leaving their galleons anchored at the entrance to the natural harbor. Apparently, the native people of the region only became aware of the new arrivals when the Spaniards' small boats came into view. As the story goes, the Patagonians had never seen watercraft larger than their own small boats and therefore hadn't noticed the galleons—literally didn't see them on the horizon—until the large ships were pointed out to them by their visitors. Once the possibility of such large ships entered their worldview, the Patagonians were able to perceive the galleons.

Many of us are like the Patagonians when we are first exposed to quantum realities. Encountering possibilities we may never have imagined, we may not be able to perceive their presence until we've learned more. And, as with the

Patagonians, just because we are not able to recognize some of the new possibilities available to us in nonmaterial dimensions of reality doesn't mean they don't exist.

"Nonlocal" Reality

Most of us in Western culture grow up learning to experience the world in linear terms. Time proceeds from past to present to future. A journey moves along from a point of origin to arrival at a destination. Causes result in effects. Newtonian physics demonstrates how every action has a reaction, every cause an effect. In a world characterized by cause and effect, events unfold in a progressive fashion with a rational, observable, and predictable relationship between the source of action and its eventual outcome.

When we shift into a more multidimensional perspective—a point of view more akin to what quantum research begins to reveal and suggest—these kinds of cause-and-effect relationships don't hold up in the same way. In fact, some of the experiments done in quantum physics are truly mind-boggling in their demonstration of the limitations of what we all take for granted every day.

One of my favorite experiments was conducted by physicist John Stewart Bell. He wanted to explore what would happen to two sub-atomic particles that interacted with one another and then were separated. He demonstrated that once the particles had made contact—had interacted in some way—from then on, *a change in one of the particles immediately created the same change in the other, even when they were separated by vast distances.*

These results, now known as Bell's Theorem, provide powerful evidence for some kind of oneness or shared information field that exists between seemingly separate entities. It may be that we humans, as individuals, are connected by these same kinds of *nonlocal* realities. The fact that change in any one of us may affect all the people with whom we've ever interacted excites me a lot. It suggests that we have the means for creating change in ways that transcend the confines of cause-and-effect relationships—that the state of the world may *not* be dependent on what takes place in time and space but rather on whatever new possibilities we generate collectively in the nonlocal realms of shared information and instantaneous change.

Making Lemonade from Lemons

If we truly do affect one another in the mind-boggling, nonlocal ways suggested by Bell's Theorem, what happens to *free will, responsibility* and *personal integrity*? We will explore these concepts in more detail in a little while. For now, I'd like to suggest that *how we engage and interpret our experiences reflects the kinds of collective information with which we choose to resonate.* Recent research shows that an optimistic outlook leads to greater physical and psychological health. As we explored in the last chapter, it may also orient us to emphasize certain aspects of collective consciousness instead of others. For this reason, I tend to frame events and circumstances in a positive light whenever possible.

It is true that I make lemonade from the lemons life tosses my way whenever I can. I also honor and stay present with the shadowy side of life. It doesn't have to be one way or the other. Allowing mixed feelings, even as we look for the opportunities offered in events, provides a field of learning that is rich with possibility. Since we endow experience with some kind of meaning in unique and individual ways every moment, and since meaning gives a sense of purpose to our lives, it seems to me that we might as well frame our experiences in a way that most enhances our life's journey. To find life constantly sour and distasteful creates a context of meaning that can lead to discouragement and despair.

The worst of times and the best of times both offer choices. Within a context of psychological wholeness, nothing is ever wasted, even the most terrible moment. It, too, can be an invitation to increase the possibilities of how we move through life experiences. To create meaning that allows us to move through experiences with greater equanimity and mindfulness is a mighty gift we have the power to offer ourselves.

For all these reasons, as we continue our exploration of multidimensional realms—including concepts of *probabilities, observer effect, alternate realities,* and *the fluid nature of change*—I will emphasize the optimistic possibilities inherent in a quantum perspective. If my approach creates mixed feelings in you, be sure to allow those responses to help you clarify your personal worldview and how it shapes your expectations about, and interpretations of, life's events.

Probabilities and Shifting Circumstances

Most of us have been taught to understand life as a progression of linear events moving through time. We experience ourselves as young, middle-aged, elderly, and we learn that our material world operates from a foundation of cause and effect. All these assumptions get turned upside-down once we enter the quantum world. For me, one of the most exciting aspects of reality suggested by quantum research is the existence of *probabilities*, which means that we no longer can predict, with any certainty, the outcome of an event or action: we don't know what is going to happen until we actually observe an event unfolding.

This view of reality emerged in early quantum experiments with electrons. In these studies researchers discovered that an electron can appear either as a particle or a wave depending on the perspective of the observer. When scientists focus on marking the location of an electron as a particle, its wave aspect collapses. When the wave aspect is measured, the electron no longer appears as a particle, even though each electron has both wave and particle elements inherent in it. What researchers discovered was that the observer introduces an additional element into the behavior of electrons. According to some scientists, the wave-particle phenomenon suggests that there is an observer effect that literally plays a role in shaping reality. Based on these findings, we can imagine that while reality seems to contain many possibilities, this research suggests that the possibility we observe and expect is what becomes actual.

The observer effect is revolutionary in its implications. If the very act of observing or expecting a possible outcome somehow plays a role in actually creating it, what does this suggest about how change occurs? It suggests to me that, in a world peopled by humans who have the capacity to observe and be *aware* of our observations—a world characterized by probabilities rather than fixed outcomes—life's possibilities become much more open and fluid. Instead of being inevitable and locked in, our options are like paints on an artist's palette: we can choose which paint to put on a canvass, actively participating in determining what colors and shapes go where.

As a therapist working with people who seek to change and enrich their lives or cope with illness or trauma, I find the concept of a fluid reality comprised of ever-changing probabilities to be both useful and deeply meaningful. If we are, in a sense, like artists, then we aren't nearly as constrained by existing patterns as we think. The dynamic interplay of probabilities becomes the palette of colors from which we can choose to create the quality of life we want to have. The question is, *which* colors serve to paint the most positive and constructive life for you? Which colors create optimal opportunities for your self-expression and sense of wholeness? How do you know how to choose or engage a given probability to achieve what you seek?

The Dynamic Power of Choice

If the observer effect operates at the level of subatomic particles, who is to say it doesn't also play a part in the dynamics of other nonlocal aspects of reality, such as morphic fields? It may be that, within both collective and individual consciousness, there are infinite probable events and outcomes existing as potentiality every moment, all the time.

Because I believe in the very real possibility that this is true, I place a lot of emphasis on *choice*—on being mindful of the choices I make during the course of everyday life. Because our choices orient us to certain outcomes and engage us in particular activities, they help to create the quality and tone of our lives. Each and every moment, we face choices about where we will focus our attention, what actions we will take, how we will conduct ourselves. Even decisions *not* to do something represent choices that will have an impact on our quality of life. The choices we make affect the probabilities that become the reality we live moment to moment, and on a larger scale, the quality of our contribution to collective consciousness.

Yet, much of the time, many of us may feel caught up in circumstances beyond our control, over which we believe we have no real choice. In the larger sense this perspective holds a truth, as none of us can separate ourselves from the collective environment that constantly enfolds us. In fact, imagining that we are the sole creator of our experience would place us outside the context of collective consciousness, which is not possible. What happens in the world at large affects each of us individually. We can't escape that fact. We *can* do something, however, about how we experience and respond to the circumstances of our lives. What stands out as foreground and background isn't fixed or preordained. It is *here* that our choices make a difference.

Let's look at a specific example. Assume you are caught in a traffic jam and you have an important appointment you probably will miss because of the delay. Since you can't change your car into a helicopter, the one choice you have left is *how you choose to respond to your experience*. At the moment, there is an array of probable feelings you might have: anger, helplessness, panic, apathy, or any number of responses that will directly affect the kind of experience you have. When you choose to use the situation to increase your capacity to be present *mindfully*, you tap into a probability that includes *learning* instead of just being distressed. With this choice, you may still miss your meeting and have to deal with the consequences, but you will also have created a constructive experience for yourself.

Suppose you have a project that needs to get done, but you procrastinate and fail to complete it on time. Are you aware that you have played a major role in creating the situation you now experience? Or do you find yourself wrestling with feelings about how this proves life is too hard or you're no good? All along the way, you have made choices that have helped create the situation you now experience. When you first accepted or were assigned the project, there were a number of probable responses you could have had, each with a slightly different outcome. The probability in which you participated wasn't the only possibility—but it was the one *you* chose. Of course, there may be times when a project doesn't get completed on time because of what other people do. Here again, you have an opportunity to engage your participation as part of a collective in a mindful way, creating learning instead of stress. *When you can't control the larger situation, at least you can be in charge of your responses to it.* You can access a probability that serves you in the best way possible, given the circumstances.

Shifting into New Probabilities and Alternate Realities

Although I have no way to "prove" this point, I'm going out on a limb now to explore a dynamic I'm convinced occurs: the ability to shift from one probability to another and thereby enter what could be called an *alternate*, co-existing reality—literally changing the direction of our lives in the same way a subatomic particle moves into one or another probability as a result of the observer effect.

The idea of shifting probabilities became real for me when I moved from the West Coast to the East in 1981. I was aware of the fact that choices I had made prior to the move had set in motion a series of events that hadn't seemed possible before that time—that my very choices created, in turn, new experiences I had not previously believed possible. It's hard to describe, but I had a sense of knowing—without knowing *how* I knew—that something fundamental had shifted, that I had moved from one probability to another and entered a new, alternate reality.

This was more than suddenly discovering new opportunities. Instead, I was on a whole new course and could feel it. That doesn't mean I became an entirely reworked, unrecognizable person. Rather, it was as though my internal kaleidoscope shifted and aspects of myself became organized in new ways, emphasizing undeveloped talents and perspectives while shifting other, more familiar, activities and tendencies into the background.

Along with the natural changes in daily routine you might expect with a major move, I also experienced shifts in the quality of relationships that I chose, the tone of my everyday experience, and the focus of my work with people. Daily life took on a more meditative quality and intuition became a much more active and practical element in my moment-to-moment awareness and activities. Along the way, I discovered Ericksonian hypnosis and took an intensive training program over the course of a year that greatly enhanced my work as a therapist. My spiritual practice deepened as well, and began to influence my work even more than it had before my move East. While these changes may not have been so apparent to others as they were to me, I was astonished by how transforming they were and, in the years since, the shifts made at the time have continued to deepen and expand.

The main quality that identifies a probability shift in your life, as I discovered in my own experience, is that it "clicks into place". Suddenly, you enter what can only be described as an alternate reality that may appear the same as the prior one—the surface elements of how you look and sound remain the same—but actually you are a different person, expressing new qualities, seeking new opportunities and options. A friend of mine talks about an infinite number of probabilities or alternate realities existing, literally, side by side and undetected by most of us. As she describes it, "Walking down the street, you probably assume the person next to you shares the same reality, but that's not the case. You share the same parameters of time and space, but within the unbounded realm of your interior worlds, very different and unique probabilities are unfolding."

When you first engage a new probability, you may have only a vague awareness that a shift has occurred—or you may experience an immediate and strong conviction that things have changed. You may not be able to explain it—you just *know* that things are different. Doors open to you that, before, you wouldn't have noticed. Your perspective on yourself and the world changes and you find yourself gravitating toward new kinds of friends and activities. Creative talents that were dormant suddenly awaken and demand attention.

Over the years, my conviction that it is possible to shift into a different probability has grown stronger, and I've heard stories from other people who've had similar experiences. One of my friends decided to close down a successful business that offered career-counseling services. She had been an educator but wanted to turn to some kind of alternative healing work. At first, she felt only a vague pull in a new direction. In response, she began to take vacation trips to healing spas and centers. During one trip, she felt something click into place—a shift in probabilities, as she described it later. From that point, as she looks back on it now, she can track how events began to fall into place, relatively quickly and easily, to allow her to reorganize her life. She relocated to the Southwest, trained to be a massage therapist, and is now happy in a new career.

When we shift into a new probability, the relative ease with which elements that support this change fall into place doesn't mean there aren't significant challenges as well. Change is stressful, even when it's positive and constructive. Shifting probabilities bring their own measure of mixed feelings. Often, in order to create what is new, we must break free of what is old and outgrown. I've often said at workshops that if I had had any idea of the amount of change and challenge that would enter my life when I shifted probabilities, I'm not sure I would have leaped into the experience as readily!

Just as the moment-to-moment choices we make orient us to particular morphic fields, they also orient us to engage certain probabilities over others, even though we may be completely unaware of the emerging orientation when it initially begins. Perhaps our choices have an observer effect: they affect the focus of our attention in the same way observers of subatomic particles affect the outcome of the particles' actions. For this reason, it is important to be aware of the quality of your choices—those that are significant as well as those that may seem of no real importance.

Together with *intention*, a subject we will explore in some depth in the next section, choice is the single most powerful and active element in engaging life in a dynamic, co-creative way. Sometimes, for example, making the choice to take a class may prove to be just the catalyst you needed to open yourself to a whole new probability shift. I recall a colleague who decided to take an acting class because she wanted to explore the possibility of joining her community theater. She soon discovered that the challenge of exposing her emotions in front of other members of the class required her to choose repeatedly to be more open and take risks. These choices created a fundamental shift in her way of being and came together to create what she felt was an opening into a new probability. Soon, other opportunities presented themselves and she consistently chose to enter them with a willingness to stretch herself beyond the previous confines of her self-expression.

This sounds like a familiar description of the kinds of changes brought about by therapy and any number of other approaches that focus on self-realization and self-development, doesn't it? I think it is exactly that—and that many of the truly transformative changes we achieve when we choose to explore our inner life come about because of probability shifts. Can I demonstrate this? Not at all. Does this way of explaining things increase my willingness to take risks, add to my enthusiasm in helping people to change, and fuel my creativity? Absolutely. Perhaps it will do the same for you as you keep in mind that the very existence of the possibility of probability shifts means that none of us ever needs to feel stuck, locked into a life we find unsatisfying, or settle for being less than what we have the capacity and desire to be.

As you work with the exercises and meditations in this chapter, give yourself permission to wonder about how you limit your sense of what is possible if you believe change can come only one step at a time, over a long period. Notice what you feel when you consider that the choices you make today may be the keys to opening the door to new, more constructive and satisfying alternate realities.

MAKE IT REAL
EXPERIMENT #1:
Reviewing Your Choices

Do this exercise at the end of the day, before you go to bed. Be sure to come to it with open curiosity, and make an agreement with yourself that you'll put aside any criticism or self-blame you may feel as you do the exercise. Remember that the quality of your moment-to-moment choices orients you to probabilities within which your choices can play themselves out even more effectively. Your goal here is to increase your awareness of habitual ways of choosing how you move through daily life.

- Take some time to review your day, from the very beginning right up to the present moment, focusing your attention on the choices you made throughout it. At first, you may find that it's difficult to recognize where you made choices, because old habits of thinking allow you to attribute the day's experiences and outcomes to external circumstances that had nothing to do with you. For example, as you began the day, did you have something to eat? What attitude or mood did you bring to the experience of feeding yourself? Were you mindful or distracted? Were you grateful for the food or did your attention focus on the many tasks awaiting you? As you ask yourself questions like these, keep in mind that how you engage these moments represents small but meaningful choices that set the tone for the day and orient you to a reality that reflects and strengthens that tone.

- Sit quietly and pay attention to the choice points that come easily to mind. Note them and allow yourself to acknowledge the relationship between those choices and the quality and outcome of your experience. What you are asking yourself to make more conscious is how your moment-to-moment choices affected the *quality* of your experience, regardless of what actually happened. You are not responsible for all the circumstances of your life, for there are experiences in which you are but one participant in a complex dance.

- Ask yourself how an experience might have affected you differently had your choices been different from what they were. For example, if you got annoyed at the man who sells newspapers because he was caught up in a conversation with someone and didn't notice you right away, what quality did that irritation bring into the rest of your day? How might the next few hours have been different for you had you chosen another way to respond to the newspaper vendor?

- Also pay attention to larger decisions. For example, did someone offer you an opportunity today or ask for a favor? How did you respond and what did your choice bring to the overall quality of your day—or to how you feel about yourself right now?

Once you have finished your review, which need not take more than ten or fifteen minutes, put it aside and let it go. The point of the review is not to ruminate or worry about what you did or did not choose. Its purpose is solely to increase your awareness of the choices you will make tomorrow—to help you recognize moments of choice *as they happen*.

EXPERIMENT #2:
Making Choices More Consciously

- In this experiment, choose one day a week when you will be especially aware of your choices, from the beginning of your day all the way through until you go to bed. If it helps, use a small notebook to jot down your choices as you become aware of them. For example: "honked horn at car in traffic"; "thanked bank clerk"; "snapped at assistant for his error", and so on.

- Then, at the end of the day, review how the choices you made affected your inner state as well as the specific outcomes of your experiences and interactions. For example: "driver shouted at me and I felt angry and threatened"; "bank clerk's face lit up and I got a warm feeling inside"; "assistant was offended and I was tense the rest of the day."

The Power of Living Intentionally

When you get up to begin the day, do you take a few minutes to decide how you want to engage whatever awaits you and whatever you choose to accomplish? In general, do you have an underlying sense of who you want to be in the world, of the qualities you seek to express?

The process of deciding *consciously* who and how we want to be and what we seek to accomplish depends on our becoming aware of the *basic intentions* we hold about ourselves and our lives. *Intention gives shape and texture to our choices*. It is a blueprint that allows us to take responsibility for our choices and action, and it reminds us—within the larger context of our lives—that we have a contribution to make as individuals.

Living intentionally is intimately related to living mindfully, for it requires that we take the time to be aware of our choices and consider our goals. Any activity undertaken with intention becomes more focused and creative. When intention guides both the conscious and unconscious aspects of our lives, we can move through experiences like a boat with a sturdy rudder rather than succumbing passively to whatever waves and currents life may bring our way.

The intentions you create can be simple—a decision, perhaps, to exercise today—or they can be complex—an acknowledgment that you have a purpose in life and a commitment to do all you can to express it fully in the world. Intentions can be long-term or related to a brief period of time. The power behind creating intentions, whatever their subject, is the activity of focusing our conscious and unconscious resources for achieving the outcomes we seek.

At the beginning of workshops, I often ask participants to create an intention for being there. I suggest that they begin the intention by acknowledging their choice to be present and then express what they each hope to achieve. I explain that meeting specific personal or professional goals they may have is less important than having the opportunity to co-create the workshop experience—to take personal responsibility for participating. In fact, the process of creating an intention and recalling it from time to time is, in itself, one of the central learnings of the day: if participants can remind themselves that they are in a particular context because they have *chosen* to be there, their participation is likely to have a more empowered quality than if they feel they are there due to outside pressures, requirements, or demands.

An intention held over time has the potential to create a positive self-fulfilling prophecy. It acts like a self-hypnotic suggestion, which supports our deepest urges and potential to follow through on the quality and tone of the intention. Making the commitment to be conscientious about the intentions you create is equally important. It is not enough just to say that you're going to accomplish this goal or act that way and then not give it another thought. Being mindful of your intention gives you the further opportunity—or challenge—to honor your commitment to yourself. A surprising benefit of following through with your intentions is the boost to self-esteem that comes when you act in line with your conscious choices.

Living with intention doesn't mean setting up endless resolutions that you then feel compelled to keep. There is a difference between creating an intention and burdening yourself with one more *should*. An intention is a heartfelt choice, a decision based on a willingness to do or be something that feels right. You follow through as best you can, and when you don't, you can use that as an opportunity to learn more about yourself.

Because living intentionally is a creative process, intentions may shift over time. It's important to remain open to the possibility that you may outgrow an intention or need to modify it. Perhaps you have learned something that has expanded your understanding and added new elements to the outcomes you seek. When this happens, you can choose to release an old intention and create a new one or allow an existing intention to evolve to include previously unrecognized possibilities.

I recall a friend who created a general intention to express his full self as much as possible each day. For him, this meant meeting whatever risks and responsibilities his job required, as well as being available to his family and friends. Over time, and in ways he hadn't expected, my friend's love of art developed and he surprised himself by developing a blossoming talent. His experience of expressing himself fully had gone beyond what he initially thought possible when he created his intention, especially when he took the risk to allow his artwork to be shown in a local gallery. As a result, even though the actual words of his intention remained the same—*Each day, it is my intention to express as much of my full self as possible*—his understanding of the meaning behind it expanded.

When you create an intention, there is no need to anticipate how you will accomplish it, nor do you need to feel that you have to control the outcome in order to fulfill the intention. What it does mean is that you need to honor your choices by consciously creating intentions about how you want to be in the world and then do your best to follow through on the commitments you have made.

Take some time to see whether you think you really can give your whole self to what you have chosen to create as an intention. Be honest with yourself. It is better in the long run to create a less demanding intention than to set yourself up for failure. Remember that every journey is made up of a succession of small steps. For example, if you want to create more free time in a busy schedule, begin by adding fifteen minutes or a half-hour to your day by getting up earlier. Then, over time, you can continue to expand your recreation time until you have fulfilled your intention to have *enough free time to nourish yourself in satisfying and healthy ways.*

Another example: before going to an important meeting, you might find it useful to create an intention about how you would like to engage the experience and what you would like to take away with you when it is complete. Your intention for the meeting could encompass absolutely anything that is meaningful for you. It may be that you want to participate more actively. If so, your intention might be something like this: *It is my intention to speak clearly and dynamically. I will make eye contact with the people present. Most importantly, it is my intention to allow the process to be a useful learning experience.* Creating an intention ahead of time can help focus and center you. It also provides an opportunity to convey a request to your deeper, unconscious wisdom to mobilize your resources in the direction of your intention.

When you create an intention that is more general and far-reaching—such as, *It is my intention to invite novelty and discovery into my life*—there is little you can do consciously to fulfill it. It is possible, however, to remind yourself, often, of what you intend. Then, life's synchronicities—a subject we'll explore in the next section—can bring you and the focus of your intention together in spontaneous and unexpected ways.

As you ponder the kinds of intentions you want to create, keep in mind that those that are most alive and powerful spring from a *heartfelt* sense of what you seek. When you repeat the intention out loud, notice your response. Is there a feeling of rightness to it? Or, does it bring mixed feelings? If your intention is right for you, you will feel moved in some way, because a right intention will automatically orient your thoughts, feelings, and actions toward achieving what you seek. If you find you have mixed feelings, explore what it is about the intention that doesn't quite fit what is right for you at this particular time. You may have reached too far, exceeding your current level of comfort or sense of possibility. Revise the intention until you can say it with that feeling of rightness.

Once you have created an intention and said it out loud to yourself—or to others, if it is part of a group intention—allow it to settle inside you. Depending on what works best for you review it once a day, once a week, once a month, or only occasionally, to make sure it still "fits" you. Creating an intention is like planting a seed. You water and feed it whenever you review it in a heartfelt way, whenever you reawaken your internal sense of connection with the choices it contains. Then you can allow it to develop in its own way and seek new seeds to add to your garden.

MAKE IT REAL
EXPERIMENT #3:
Beginning Your Day with Intention

Work with this experiment each day for a week. It will help you remember that you make choices all the time *and* that you can create intentions about the choices you want to make on an ongoing basis.

- When you first awaken, notice your state of mind and the quality of your expectations. Do you look forward to the day, or is your first thought one of dread and anxiety in anticipation of a day filled with hassles and difficulties?

- Next, before you get up, take a few moments to ask yourself, *What is my intention for today?* You might want to experiment with what happens if you begin the day with an intention to notice and receive consciously the good things that happen—perhaps you will encounter some kind of gift you hadn't expected, or an event or experience that adds to your sense of well-being, or a learning experience that gives you a feeling of being supported.

Whatever intention you choose, keep in mind that it has the power to orient your perception to whatever may be the focus of your intention and thereby become a positive self-fulfilling prophecy.

EXPERIMENT #4:
Beginning Small

This experiment offers an opportunity to work with *chunking down* your intentions—creating intentions that encompass the smallest steps possible on the way to achieving the outcomes you seek. It is important to know that in regard to intentions, bigger isn't necessarily better.

- To begin, bring to mind something you want to change in your life. For example, maybe you would like to spend more time engaged in creative pursuits; or perhaps you would like to get a project done that, till now, has felt too big to tackle.

- Write down your intention. Now identify the *smallest possible aspect* of the outcome you've chosen. Let's say your initial intention is to clean out your home office. Your chunked-down intention might look something like this:

    It is my intention to put away or throw away five pieces of paper this week.

    You might think this is a bit mundane or silly as an intention. If you do, remember that living mindfully means being conscious of our choices and actions in *every moment*. Even the smallest moments matter, and creating intentions around these small moments can increase your capacity to be more mindfully aware.

- Read your intention to yourself. Notice how it feels inside you—in your body, in your mind, in your feelings.

- Now read the intention aloud. Anytime you feel even a twinge of discomfort, think about what you may need to change about the wording of the intention. Keep revising it until you feel comfortable with, and empowered by, the way it sounds to you.

- When you have accomplished what you set out to do, allow yourself to create an intention that covers the next smallest step. Notice how you feel about yourself each time you successfully follow through on your intention.

- Also notice how you can turn a failure to follow through into a learning experience simply by being aware of the choices you made that led you to putting aside your intention and how you felt in response.

EXPERIMENT #5:
Creating More General Intentions

This experiment deals with broader intentions that address general quality-of-life issues—big changes you want to make that have to come from the inside out, or developments you would like to see unfold in the future. These intentions can become meditations in themselves—positive affirmations that "work on you" deep inside and create constructive self-fulfilling prophecies. Recalling them from time to time reinforces their power to help you develop new attitudes, new behaviors, new ways of experiencing yourself and your world. Here are some examples:

- *Each day, I will pay attention to, and be grateful for, the good things I used to take for granted.*

- *It is my intention to shift from reactions of fear to a deepening trust and faith in myself and my world.*

Even as I write these examples, I am reminded of the deeply personal nature of intentions. There is no way I can give you examples that will contain the power and commitment you will need to feel if an intention is to express something that is true for *you*. For this reason, I encourage you to take these intentions as starting points only and develop them to fit your personal needs.

- Once you have created your intention, say it aloud to yourself. As in the last experiment, give yourself permission to work with the intention until you really *experience* a willingness to commit to its fulfillment. As a final part of the experiment, give yourself a few moments to feel open to, and curious about, how your intention may affect you immediately and over time.

EXPERIMENT #6:
Nourishing the Sacred

In this experiment, create an intention that nourishes the sacred in your life in some way. You might focus on a particular state of mind:

- *Increasingly, I take time to recall that I am one with all things.*

- *It is my intention to acknowledge the sacred spark in myself and in everyone I meet.*

Or you might choose to focus on your actions:

- *I choose to be mindfully aware of my daily actions and make even the most mundane activity a meditation, a celebration of the sacred.*

- *It is my intention to create enough time in each day to meditate or in some way, to spend time in stillness and contemplation.*

Or you might want to strengthen the expression of the sacred in your everyday activities:

- *Each day, it is my intention to become increasingly aware of opportunities to be generous in my interactions with others.*

- *It is my desire, each and every moment, to ease suffering wherever possible.*

Whatever intentions you create, it is important to experience them as energized, alive and able to move you. Notice when you become aware of having fulfilled an intention. If it is an ongoing commitment, simply reinforce it once in a while, even as you create new intentions over time.

Intention and Synchronicity

Intentions become magnets, drawing to themselves experiences and opportunities that further their actualization. Included in this dynamic are so-called coincidences—chance meetings or conversations, for example—that seem to appear with increasing frequency and in some way support your intentions. Sometimes these coincidences are subtle and barely noticeable. At other times, they may be so vivid and unmistakable that you can't possibly miss them. The way in which creating intentions seems to activate coincidences points to an important element in the dynamic relationship between our choices and the lives we live. That element is known as *synchronicity*, which is defined as *meaningful coincidence*.

Synchronicity is a familiar dynamic in everyone's life, even if the word itself is not. While no one really understands *how* synchronicity works, *that it does exist without question*. It is as ever-present as the air we breathe—and often as invisible, until we stop to pay attention to it. In fact, the more we pay attention, the more likely we are to notice synchronicity occurring. Once you focus on it, the presence of synchronicity may seem to increase in surprising ways. Does it really increase, or have you just begun to notice how often meaningful coincidences bring you together in time and space with your desired outcomes?

What distinguishes moments of synchronistic occurrences from mere coincidences is the meaningful nature of them. They are more than "running into someone". If the meeting means something to you—as when you need to ask a friend a question and there she is, unexpectedly standing in front of you—then synchronicity is at work.

In some way we don't yet understand, synchronicity emerges from our collective context to create moments of unmistakable meaning. I recall a story I heard about a young couple who had just married. They had met "by chance" in a coffee shop, having been seated next to one another by the hostess. Two other "chance meetings" took place in a gym and on the bus. From the moment of their first meeting, the man had a strong sense that he had to get to know this woman. By the third time they bumped into each other, he could no longer contain his urge to ask for her telephone number. They couldn't begin to explain how these coincidences had happened, but they became aware of "something" bringing them together in a meaningful way.

The complexity involved in synchronistic events can be truly stunning to watch. There was a time when one of my relatives needed to find an apartment in a large West Coast city. A complicated series of events ensued, including an injury that kept this relative laid up for six weeks. When she was again able to look for a place to live, one of her first phone calls brought her into contact with a young woman who told her about an apartment complex where residents shared meals and social activities. As it turned out, there was one apartment available—the first in many months—and, after moving in, no further vacancies appeared for nearly a year. She had slipped into the building during a brief window of opportunity, made available to her by a number of meaningful "coincidences."

Learning some of the ways in which nonlocal aspects of reality interact with everyday life—and synchronicity certainly is one of these—can have practical benefits. All that's required is to be willing to suspend disbelief and participate in dynamics that make no rational sense. If you are willing to let go of linear thinking, some intriguing results are possible.

For example, I have a friend I seem to run into whenever she needs to see me. It can be anytime of the day, when I'm walking any number of places in my neighborhood. Each time I come upon her, I experience a moment of surprise and then she tells me she's wanted to talk to me. Does she *cause* me to come to her, or does her intention to connect with me set up some pattern of synchronicities that brings our paths together?

Another friend has developed an intriguing relationship with the fluidity of time and space that she calls on when she has to use the New York City subway system. Whenever she is particularly rushed, she creates the intention that she will arrive at her appointed destination on time. In her mind, she "tells the train" when she needs to arrive and then lets go and allows synchronicity to take over. Usually no matter how crowded the train or how last minute her timetable, she arrives on schedule.

For many people, my friend's intention and the train schedule that happens to coincide are totally unrelated and represent simple good luck. That in fact, may be true. Or it may be that something is going on at nonlocal levels of reality that bring together my friend's need and the train in a meaningful way. I'm not saying her intention to be on time *causes* the train to come. Remember that nonlocal events are governed by *probabilities*, not by cause and effect. My best guess—and that's all it can be—is that reality is much more fluid and pliant than we realize, and that we enter a different realm, governed by different possibilities and rules, when we engage aspects of reality unconstrained by time and space considerations.

Recently I danced with synchronicity without realizing it ahead of time, and without creating any kind of intention at a conscious level. One Saturday I discovered that I had to get an important paper in the mail right away, but first it had to be signed by a bank officer. At the time, my regular bank didn't have Saturday hours, so I went to one that does. Unfortunately, no one was there who was authorized to sign. I resigned myself to running the errand the following week, well past the date when I needed to get the paper in the mail. On my way home, I passed my bank branch and happened to notice that it was open for a special children's day. I went inside and a bank officer signed my paper in five minutes. An important element in achieving my goal was that I paid attention to the synchronicity in the unexpected fact that the bank was open. Instead of walking by, assuming no one would help me because it wasn't officially open, I went inside, responding to the opportunity.

Inviting Synchronicity into Your Life

Part of engaging synchronicity more actively is learning to develop the habit of responding to opportunities and unexpected "invitations" when they arise as I did with the bank. The more we respond to synchronistic events, the more they appear in our lives. For example, pay attention the next time you decide to call someone, only to find that he calls you at that exact moment. Or notice how you have what seems to be a casual conversation with someone, and you later discover you've heard a piece of information that proves to be important. Seemingly negative events also can represent meaningful coincidences, as happened when my relative hurt herself and couldn't look for an apartment right away. The meaning she took from the experience was that her apartment wasn't ready yet and she needed to be delayed in her search until the time was right.

Often you will need the benefit of hindsight before you can discover that a coincidence was meaningful. Also realize that what may appear meaningful to you may not make the least bit of sense to anyone else. That's fine. Trust your own responses and just keep noticing synchronicity as it dances through your life. Your awareness is like an invitation to elicit more meaningful coincidences which, in turn, support the choices and intentions you create.

When you give yourself permission to experiment with nonlocal reality by inviting synchronicity more actively into your life, you may be surprised to discover how natural it is to draw on it. You may come to expect the support of meaningful coincidence in getting you where you want to go in life. In the exercises that follow, allow yourself to have some fun and discover the delight inherent in stretching the possibilities of what you can achieve.

MAKE IT REAL
EXPERIMENT #7:
Creating a Synchronicity Log

In this experiment, notice the synchronicities that occur in your everyday life and then record them in a log or journal. In doing the experiment, pay attention to the smallest moments of surprise or "ah-ha"—as well as the unmistakable miracles or events that transform your life in unexpectedly helpful or meaningful ways. Make sure you also notice how, at times, you are in what seems to be the wrong place at the wrong time in ways that may be upsetting but still personally meaningful. You're looking for synchronicities of *any* kind.

- Once a day, take a few minutes to write down any meaningful coincidences that have occurred. They may be positive or negative events or interactions that initially seemed random, or they may make immediate sense as being related to you in some meaningful way. Your goal here is to develop a habit of noticing synchronicities as they emerge.

- There may be times you want to determine how you may have caused—or could have prevented—a particular coincidence. That's a natural response. For this experiment, though, understanding the cause is less important than discovering the meaning a coincidence may have for you. Be sure to remember that there will be coincidences that seem to have no meaning to you. That's fine, as well.

- Over time, be sure to keep a record of how synchronicities coincide with intentions you have created, and notice how meaningful coincidences emerge consistently to support the fulfillment of the goals you seek to achieve.

EXPERIMENT #8:
Synchronicity, Intention, and Affirmation

In this experiment, create intentions about synchronicity that can become affirmations you say each day. Below are samples. Yours might be quite different. Remember to create intentions that are alive and heartfelt for *you*. The idea is to let the unique meaning of the affirmation's underlying intention bring more supportive, constructive synchronicities into your life.

- *I actively invite synchronicity into my life to support my deepest intentions in positive and constructive ways.*

- *In my world, synchronicity operates freely to support and nourish my experience of well-being and the unfolding of my heart's deepest desire.*

- *In every way, synchronicity supports the fulfillment of my deepest life purpose and enhances the quality of my daily life.*

GUIDED MEDITATION #1:
Enhancing Your Relationship with Intention and Synchronicity

To begin, sit in a quiet spot, the place where you usually meditate or spend the most time creating intentions, or anywhere else that you feel comfortable and focused. Settle in and allow yourself to find whatever position allows you to be physically at ease and mentally alert. Take a few moments to settle in at the bottom of the breath, connecting with "home base" as your beginning point.

Imagine that you are entering a sanctuary of some kind. It may be a temple or some other kind of building in which you sense you have entered sacred space. Become aware of your willingness to be in this sacred space. It is a space characterized by conscious intentionality.

Using the metaphor of the artist, discover an empty canvas and a full palette of colors—or a box of colored pencils, tubes of paint, pastels, whatever form the colors take in your imagination. You have every shade and hue available that you could possibly want or need to create an imaginary work of art that represents an intention you want to bring into your life. This is a magic canvas. It exists in a world characterized by synchronicity. Whenever you create an intention here, synchronicity is automatically activated to interact with and support what you intend.

Before you begin to imagine creating your intention as a work of art, take a few minutes to meditate on the potential impact that living intentionally might have on the quality of your daily life. For these moments, contemplate or ponder the implications of living your everyday life from a foundation of conscious choice.

For example, if you were to begin each day with an intention to learn as much as the day offered to teach you, how might this affect your state of mind and interpretation of your experiences? This is a form of "reflective" meditation that allows you to develop a deepening understanding of your relationship with intention.

Now, bring to mind an intention you would like to create or an existing one you would like to empower. If the "energy," "character," or "quality" of your intention were represented on the canvas as a landscape, a picture of something, a geometric design, streaks or swirls of color, or any other graphic form, what would it look like? If you are not a visual person, imagine what you would create if you could see the canvas. Allow your work of art to be as simple or complex, as complete or vague as naturally emerges in your imagination. The goal isn't to create a beautiful imaginary picture; rather it is to allow a symbolic representation of your intention to appear spontaneously on the canvas.

To invite synchronicity more dynamically into your life, do the following: create a thought or a prayer that conveys something like: I am willing and eager to notice meaningful coincidences in my life and to have synchronicity help me achieve the outcome of my intention.

Then, release the thought into the surrounding space, as you might a helium-filled balloon. As the prayer travels in nonlocal dimensions, it activates a response from synchronicity in whatever mysterious ways such interconnections happen.

Spend a few moments holding an expectation that synchronicity will help you achieve the outcome conceived in your intention.

When you feel ready, let your awareness return to the sacred space. Become aware again of the canvas. At any time you can alter the work of art you have created in any way that feels right for you.

Recall the intention that has been the focus of this meditation. Review it and pay attention to any responses, mixed feelings, or bodily sensations you experience. Remind yourself that the intention represents a conscious choice you have made to participate actively in creating the quality of your experience in your daily life.

Now come all the way back, wiggling your fingers and toes to bring yourself into a fully alert state of mind.

Group and Collective Intention

There is a powerful "side effect" of learning to engage the dance of intention and synchronicity in everyday life. As we allow ourselves to focus on the mystery of meaningful coincidence and the choices we make on a moment-to-moment basis, we have an opportunity to reinforce our awareness that we are part of an unimaginably complex collective consciousness—a whole, within which we find our ground of being.

A paradox emerges when we become aware of the immense complexity within which synchronistic events emerge to give personal meaning to unexpected developments and experiences. On the one hand, our personal intentions activate nonlocal possibilities which, in turn, attract meaningful coincidences to support our goals. On the other hand, as parts of a much greater whole, there probably are collective intentions creating events over which we have little or no control.

Even so, the amount of individual freedom we *do* have to choose who and how we want to be in the world warrants our best efforts to create intentions that support the most positive and constructive probabilities available to us. One of the ways in which I have worked personally for many years to translate my willingness to take the next step in my journey toward wholeness and conscious living has been through accessing my optimal future self. In the following chapter, we will explore how to tap into the realm of future possibilities to create an intention that your life will follow the most positive pathways available to you.

Chapter 9

OPENING TO YOUR OPTIMAL FUTURE

Saying "Yes" to All You Can Be

> ...when... consciousness operates at the level of
> information picture not only is it no longer bound
> by the confines of space or distance, but it is also no
> longer restricted by the one-way flow of time... the
> human biological organism possesses the ability to
> leap into the future, to actually tap into information
> about future events and process that information in
> the present.
>
> —Michael Talbot

When we engage the dance of probabilities, choice, and synchronicity, we also tap into the dynamic realm of *possible futures*. Just as the fluid quality of nonlocal aspects of reality allow life to unfold within a context of shifting probabilities, the existence of possible futures allows us to tap into new states of being in nonlinear ways. Because tapping into the future self is about *experiencing* a different possibility, much of this chapter is devoted to experiments and guided meditations. Through a direct taste, as it were, of new states by being, thinking, and feeling, we can move beyond old habits and familiar responses more quickly.

In exploring the realm of the future self, we will encounter concepts and possibilities that don't make sense when looked at within the framework of three-dimensional reality. We need to focus our "quantum eyes" to peer into the timeless reality in which the future is able to touch the present. Along the way, we will consider ideas that can't be explained fully. I offer them as suggestions of what may be possible, as we learn more about how to tap into quantum realities.

Since 1982, much of my personal growth process has centered on accessing, and then becoming, my *optimal future self*. In this manner, I have incorporated changes that probably would have taken much longer to consolidate otherwise.

The *optimal future self* is one way to talk about a deep inner wisdom we each carry inside. This wisdom knows more than we do, within our conscious levels of being, about what's possible for us to achieve. When thought of in terms of a *future self*, these possibilities become more tangible and more easily grasped. For example, several years ago a *future self* emerged in one of my meditations. This *future self* had absolute confidence that problems could be solved, messes cleaned up, and life's challenges met with greater ease than I had ever imagined. I was able to experience how my body would feel when I truly understood that things eventually work out. This was a new learning for me, and I welcomed it. What I didn't realize was how synchronicity was going to bring me face to face with an abundance of problems and challenges so that I could learn how to move through them more easily, to bring into my everyday experience what my *future self* knew already.

This example points to an important point: *if you don't*

want to change, don't do future self work. If you do want to change, be willing to be challenged, to let go of outworn but familiar ways of being, and most of all, be prepared to feel a lot better about yourself in the long run. In some way I can't explain, accessing the *optimal future self* activates our inner wisdom and elicits a response. It is a way of saying *yes* to our most positive possibilities, something we'll explore in more depth later.

There are a number of ways you can think about your *optimal future self*. You can visualize it as an internal blueprint, an inherent potential that exists within you—within all of us—from the very beginning, just as a blossoming flower exists as potential within the seed. You can think about the *optimal future self* as a positive self-fulfilling prophecy, a constructive self-hypnotic suggestion. Or you can conceive of the future self as a representation of a source of deep inner wisdom that guides you in powerful ways.

As we begin our journey into the future I want to point out an important distinction to keep in mind. *Having the intention to open yourself to your deepest potential is different from wishing you could be more than you are today.* As we saw in the last chapter, *intention* is an active willingness to engage in creating change and arriving at desired goals. In contrast, *wishing* usually implies that we are yearning for outcomes we actually doubt we can achieve. For this reason, it is important that you connect with your *optimal future self* with the clear intention of opening yourself to actualizing your fundamental talents and capacities—to be open to whatever aspects of yourself are ready to blossom at this time.

Accessing the Information Universe for a Better Future

Using the construct of your *optimal future self*, you can create a means by which to access information contained in the human morphic field. Whatever you seek to develop, change, or bring into your life, chances are that some other person—somewhere, sometime—has achieved what you seek. Through the *future self*, you have a means of accessing and translating this information, of making it available and personally meaningful to your present-day awareness.

I often ask workshop participants to get a glimpse of how they will feel and think when they have achieved an outcome they seek. What happens consistently is that most people become aware of something they haven't experienced before. It's as though their intention to access a new awareness becomes an antenna that attracts what they seek directly from the morphic field, where they draw the experience from collective consciousness. Within the guise of the *optimal future self*, the experience is then shaped to meet each person's individual style and unique way of being.

The *future self* can also give you new information about how you live in your body. Remember, you are a bodymind, and your physical experience has a lot to do with your sense of psychological well-being. Through your future self, you have access to more empowered, more centered body states. I have worked with large numbers of people—clients and workshop participants—who have experienced greater comfort, ease, and self-confidence by tapping into the body of their *future self*. Once their bodies have a chance to "try on" new states, it is as though something awakens within them and becomes their own.

For one woman, the experience of her *optimal future self* was a true revelation. She was excitable—people and situations quickly stressed her and she had difficulty calming herself. When she experienced her *future self* from the inside and accessed a calmer body state, she had an opportunity to get a flavor of what it was like to be less agitated. In fact, she described her internal experience as "quieter, more still". Once she touched the experience directly, she knew what it felt like to be less easily agitated. She also sensed that her *future self* interpreted events in a different way—a style in which her inner dialogue eased, rather than escalated, her anxieties.

Accessing the *future self* is like entering a timeless library where you can discover outcomes, possibilities, and ways of thinking, feeling, and acting that are an inherent part of your potential—that increase your sense of psychological wholeness—of which you were previously unaware. Sometimes the new information emerges into everyday life slowly, over time. Months or years may pass as you naturally grow into what you have glimpsed. At other times, you just "get it" and adopt new states of mind and being instantaneously. Then it is a matter of practicing the new resources you now have available.

I recall a time I was on my way to my office and I was worrying about a delivery I expected that day. It was snowing and I became increasingly convinced the delivery wouldn't happen. As I obsessed, a thought drifted into my mind: *I wonder how my future self would handle this moment, right here, right now?* Immediately, I felt a shift occur in my thinking as I accessed a calm, unconcerned state of mind. It came over me in one moment as my internal dialogue shifted to one focused on reassuring myself that the delivery would be made eventually—if not today—and, in the meantime, it wasn't nearly as big a problem as I created in my own mind. My body state shifted, too, into a surprisingly calm and centered quality. I went on to my office the delivery arrived as scheduled, and I suffered much less wear and tear than usual. Since that morning—and it has been maybe years since then—the way of thinking I accessed has become a reliable presence in times of stress.

There is no "right way" to access information from the *future self*. Each of us will do so in our own way. The important thing to know is that the *future self* offers an impacting means of obtaining new information—possibilities we haven't yet activated on a conscious level—that supports who and how we want to be in this world.

Connecting with the Optimal Future Self

Certain characteristics show up repeatedly in people's reports of their journeys into the *future self* and appear to accompany the experience of accessing the *optimal future self*. The most important is that the *future self* takes whatever symbolic form most strongly communicates its qualities. For example, while most *future selves* are symbolized in human form, that's not always the case. Some appear as animals, some are balls or patterns of light; some are cross-gendered or younger than the present-day self; and some take no form at all. When a *future self* does not take a symbolic form and instead is *sensed*, it is as though a telepathic communication occurs. There is a feeling of knowing, an intuitive awareness, that conveys the qualities, thoughts, and feelings of the *future self* to the present-day self.

As is true with any inner symbolic work, it is important to accept your first impressions, even when they may seem off base to your rational mind. Remember that accessing your *future self* is about tapping into awareness and developments you haven't yet achieved. For this reason, it's not unusual to be surprised by the image or quality that comes to mind.

I remember a workshop participant who had a *future self* who was a horse. The image troubled him and yet, when I asked how it had felt to *be* the horse, he reported that it was wonderful. The horse conveyed a physical exuberance, a sense of power to go where it wanted to go. Once he was able to talk through the experience, he realized that the horse had a great deal to offer. Over time, the image may have shifted to a human representation, but in that moment the horse carried the most alive way of representing his potential in his conscious awareness.

For another person, the *optimal future self* was symbolized by a white light that didn't have any specific form. Her first response to this image was one of fear that she was going to die. But as we talked about it, she realized that the quality conveyed by the light was one of vibrant aliveness, an energizing feeling she experienced throughout her body when she *became* her *future self* and experienced her from the inside. The more time she spent allowing herself to explore how the light translated into her everyday awareness, the more comfortable she became with it.

These examples point to a second essential characteristic of the *optimal future self*. Until you have become this new part of yourself—given yourself a chance to enter the image and experience from the inside, in your body and psyche—you won't have a complete sense of what your deeper wisdom is revealing to you. It is important to have an opportunity to think with the mind of the *future self*, see with the eyes of the *future self*, feel with the emotions and responses of the *future self*, and experience the body of the *future self*. Once you have moved through these states of awareness, you will have a sense of what your *optimal future self* has to offer or teach you.

I recall another workshop participant who was quite put off by the way his *future self* looked. He described an old man dressed in tattered clothes. When I asked him what the *future self* felt like from the inside, he said, "Oh, he's completely comfortable with himself, totally unselfconscious." When I asked about the underlying intention this participant had created for his journey, he said it had been to resolve his constant worry about what people think of him. As we talked, he realized that the message wasn't that he would grow old and sloppy but that he could become comfortable with himself no matter how he looked.

The man's experience underscores the fact that when working with the *optimal future self*, its *form* is usually less important than its *essence*, its qualities. Even when an image appears whose form is important in and of itself, it is the underlying experience of how it is to *be* the *future self* that carries the greatest impact for change in the present. For example, a client reported that her future self had a completely different hairstyle that caught her attention because it was so unlike her usual look. The new hairstyle turned out to be an important symbol for the change that was to come, as this woman moved into a greater sense of psychological wholeness. Even though she did eventually change her hair in the way reflected by her *future self*, the more significant issue was the shift that took place in her way of being in the world: the new hairstyle represented a greater dynamism and level of activity.

One other common experience comes to mind. Often in workshops some participants draw a blank during the *future self* exercise. I've learned to trust that usually it is just a matter of time until a conscious awareness of the *future self* emerges. For example, a participant at one workshop let me know that she'd come the year before and hadn't gotten any impression of her future self at that time. Then, six months later—in the midst of a crisis—her future self unexpectedly appeared in her imagination and had been available to her ever since. She was as impressed as I that her deeper wisdom *had* used the workshop experience successfully, even though she had received no evidence of it at the time.

Optimal future selves may represent *any* span of time. In my own experience, some are years ahead of where I am now; others have been only weeks or months ahead of me and I "became them" easily and without much struggle. For example, I recall an early *future self* who appeared to me with a change in hair color. This *future self* had blond hair at a time when mine was still dark brown. Again, the hair was suggestive of the fact that *change* was available through accessing the *future self*. The essence of that change was her complete confidence when speaking in public. Over time, as years passed and I began to highlight my hair to cover the gray, I recognized the presence of this *future self* in me as I became increasingly at home in front of audiences. It took about five years from my first impression of this *optimal future self* until I actually had become her.

One of the "quickie" *future selves* appeared as a very large earth-mother type with a halo of long, black, curly hair. She was dressed in a long full skirt and blouse and her essence expressed a mature and grounded femininity. She was the color of a well-polished violin and I sensed a depth to her comfort with her earthy "woman-self" that was new to me. Within several months of connecting with her, I felt the effects of her influence as I experienced my own maturing "woman self." The experience has continued to evolve ever since.

The paradox I experienced in connecting with my various *optimal future selves* is similar to what others who have done this work also report: even though they exist as someone I haven't yet become, their power to create change in the present moment is immediate and tangible. Accessing their perspective—their way of thinking and feeling about a situation, their deepened sense of equanimity, or any of the other qualities I have found in these wiser, more mature parts of myself—has changed the quality of my daily life in profound ways. Through these experiences, my sense of time has shifted and I sense past, present, and future as part of the *now* through which my whole self expresses and lives.

Why Emphasize an "Optimal" Future Self?

Consistent with the idea that reality is made up of a constantly available array of probabilities, one of the assumptions in working with the *future self* is that *there are as many possible future selves as there are probable realities existing in the universe.* Research demonstrates that most of us have a variety of possible selves we project into the future as fantasies of what might become of us. Some of these fantasies are negative—as when we fear we may become homeless—and some are positive—as when we experience ourselves attaining hoped-for outcomes.

For this reason, when you create intentions to connect with a *future self*, it is important to keep in mind that you want to access positive, constructive, *optimal* outcomes and states of being. If you find yourself connecting with a *future self* that is in any way abusive, shaming, critical, or otherwise represents a shadow or negative aspect of yourself, stop the exercise and let go of the image. Usually a negative *future self* emerges because there is some issue that needs to be resolved and is getting in the way. If this happens, let go of the *future self* exercise and go back and take the quality of the negative *future self* into your shadow work. You are likely to discover that, after you have explored the issue that emerged, subsequent *future self* journeys will move along in positive directions.

Also, one of the concepts derived from quantum physics that attracts me most is that time becomes much more fluid and creative when we move outside—or beyond—the constraints of three-dimensional reality. Research into quantum realities has helped me to more deeply sense the flexible nature of time.

Accessing your *optimal future self* allows you to play with time—to move it around, transcend it, focus it in the past, present, or future—and to stretch your sense of the possibilities inherent in moving out of the time-bound physical world.

There are quantum experiments, some noted in Michael Talbott's books, that suggest that the future affects the present. What this suggests to me is that it may be that a response or way of being that already exists in the future may be able to reach into the present and affect what's possible here and now. For me, *the memories of the future self become the inspirations, hunches, and leaps of insight in the present moment.*

I find this idea tremendously appealing, and encourage the people I work with to actively ask the future to offer solutions to problems they seek to resolve in the present. The metaphor of an *optimal future self* provides a grounded and immediate way in which to translate what the future may have to offer.

The bottom line is that you want to invite *the very best you can be* at this point in time. What is best for you may be represented by a seemingly small step or by a change that feels revolutionary to you. Big or small, remember to emphasize that the steps you take into the future will enhance your sense of psychological wholeness and well-being, your capacity to live more consciously. Know that an indication of a negative *future self* is a call to do additional shadow work, not a prediction of a negative future.

As you focus on optimal outcomes, remember that it often takes time to notice the changes your *future self* is actualizing. A man I worked with used his *optimal future self* to access and then practice mindfulness. He was having trouble learning to let his thoughts, feelings and impulses move through his awareness without acting on them—or reacting to them. By connecting with his *future self*, he tapped into a different way of perceiving moment-to-moment hassles. He discovered that his *future self* didn't take problems or irritating circumstances so personally. His *future self* had learned that there were some things he just couldn't control and that breathing through them was much more comfortable than falling into old patterns of anger and agitation. For many months, this previously impulsive, irritable man practiced connecting with his *future self's* more mindful attitude and slowly learned how to achieve it himself.

Hindsight offers a perspective that allows you to notice how change has made its way into everyday life. Sometimes the shifts are so natural and gradual that you don't realize you've come as far as you have. I have an exercise where I ask people to find themselves on the path of their current *optimal future self* and to look back at how far they have come since first connecting with this part of themselves. Many people are quite surprised by the distance they have covered. I recall a woman who came to a workshop a year and a half or so after her first *future self* experience. Initially her *future self* appeared in a different locale from where she was living at the time and seemed to be engaged in a deeply satisfying line of work, the nature of which was unclear. A little more than a year later she had moved to a different city and her professional life had taken an unexpected turn. Instead of being a nurse in a hospital setting as she had been for years, she now spent her time making home visits. The absence of the kind of hospital job she had wanted became a doorway into what she now considers to be a much more meaningful use of her skills. As she described it, the transition happened so naturally, with each step emerging almost without planning, that she hadn't really registered the magnitude of change until she was actually settled in her new residence and working at her new job.

Keep in mind that you have an opportunity to access a *succession* of *optimal future selves*. As changes find their way into the time and space of your everyday life, you will become your *optimal future self* in the same, natural way that tomorrow becomes today and today becomes yesterday. As you notice that you have achieved your goals, remember to orient yourself toward your next *optimal future self*, who represents the next steps you are ready to take.

There are times when an *auxiliary future self* may appear that represents a quality or way of thinking that you are picking up "along the way." At these times, you may discover you have more than one *future self* in your awareness. *Auxiliary future selves* often appear on side paths or in some other way that lets you know they are but one aspect of your *optimal future self*. A friend of mine had an *auxilia-*

ry future self appear in the form of a flamenco dancer. The energy and quality carried by this *future self* were just what my friend needed at that particular time and for a very particular and circumscribed reason: she had a role to play in a community theater production and feared she wouldn't be able to access the flair she needed in order to be convincing. Accessing this *future self* and spending time with her each day for several weeks allowed my friend to internalize the flamboyant qualities carried by this previously untapped part of her.

If it seems odd to think about having more than one *future self* at a time, keep in mind that your present-day self has many parts, or ways of being, that also co-exist. As you access the best you can be, you want to give yourself permission to encompass *all* the parts of you that are available to change. Let your need be the guide. When you feel lacking or not up to a task, ask your *optimal future self* to reveal the quality that carries what you want to develop or express.

MAKE IT REAL
GUIDED MEDITATION #1:
Reaching Out to Your Optimal Future Self

This is a simple meditation, designed to orient you to your *optimal future self*. As you do the meditation, be sure to allow yourself to accept whatever comes.

Begin by settling in and focusing your attention in the still point between breaths. Spend a few moments connecting with the stillness.

Focus on your feeling of willingness to connect with your optimal future self, with the part of you that represents a wiser, more evolved you. Now imagine that your future self walks up to you and stands in front of you. Become aware of your first im-

pressions, of the qualities conveyed by your future self. Remember to allow whatever springs to mind. Avoid any impulses you may have to change to an image you like better.

Be sure to allow any mixed feelings that arise. Bring your whole self on the journey.

Take a moment now to become your optimal future self—to experience this part of you from the inside. Notice your thoughts, feelings, perceptions, and body sensations. Pay particular attention to how the characteristics of the future self may differ from how you, as your present-day self, experience the world.

Imagine how these changes or differences might affect your life in positive ways, how you might handle things more constructively or creatively with the added wisdom and ways of being of your optimal future self.

When you feel ready shift back into your present-day self, while the optimal future self continues to stand in front of you. Be sure to hold in your awareness the qualities the future self has conveyed to you. Even now, you are learning at deeply unconscious levels, to be the future self.

Come back to your surroundings and wiggle your fingers and toes. Jot down a description of your optimal future self and the qualities and essence she or he conveyed to you.

Alternate Selves

A colleague asked a question at a conference where I presented a talk on the *future self*. She wondered why I didn't call this construct an *alternate* self. Immediately, I realized the benefit of her idea: an *alternate self* is nonlinear in nature, "right here and now" but in another dimension, a present-day source of untapped potential. Rather than being defined in terms of a temporal progression as a *future self*, an *optimal alternate self* conveys a wiser possible self that *co-exists* within a parallel universe. For this reason, tapping into an alternate self is more like taking a step sideways than it is going forward.

For example, if you wanted to access your capacity to speak in public more comfortably, you might imagine that an *optimal alternate self*—who already enjoys public speaking—could step into your awareness from an alternate reality. Then, by accessing the experience of that *alternate self*—his or her body state, ways of thinking and feeling about public speaking—you would begin to create changes in yourself at both conscious and unconscious levels. Over time, the changes you sampled would emerge into your everyday experience.

All of the characteristics of the *optimal future self* also apply to *optimal alternate selves*. The process and dynamics are the same. The only difference is that you have a choice about which construct feels most alive to you at any given time.

Saying "Yes" to Your Optimal Future Self

Underlying all my work with the optimal future self is an assumption that shapes much of what I do: *life needs us to be all that we have the capacity to be in order for it to express itself fully through us.* By creating an intention to say *yes* to the potential within us, we send a message to our inner wisdom that conveys a willingness to stretch, change, and move beyond present limitations. Once we willingly *choose* to take whatever steps will allow us to express more of our potential, synchronicity and our own inherent talents and uniqueness then come together in a dynamic, if mysterious, interplay.

One way of empowering your choice to expand or enhance your unique self-expression is to say *yes* to your optimal future self. When you do so, you activate a response that awakens aspects of yourself that were previously dormant. The *yes* becomes a wake-up call that stirs latent aspects of ourselves—talents, interests, personality traits, and more.

I recall a young woman who came to see me specifically to work with her *optimal future self*. She felt stuck in her job and wanted to return to school to prepare for another profession. During her first journey to meet her *future self*, she experienced this part as filled with enthusiasm and self-confidence. While this young woman wasn't sure whether her *future self* was in school or working somewhere else, what she *did* know was how empowering and satisfying the *body state* of her *future self* felt to her. When I suggested that she say *yes* to the intention of becoming her *future self*—and thereby express her heartfelt willingness to be guided by her own deep wisdom and the workings of synchronicity to create this outcome—she reported a powerful experience. As she said *yes* to herself, she felt a kind of "thrill" run through her body, just like an electric current. Then she felt her heart open "as if it were a flower." It was as though she could literally feel herself blossoming.

As we talked about the experience later, she still felt the thrill of saying *yes* and was confident she had shifted something inside herself. I suggested she take a few minutes each day to reconnect with her *future self* and repeat her *yes* many times.

For one workshop participant, saying *yes* to his *optimal future self* brought some mixed feelings and deepened his understanding of an unresolved conflict he had brought to the exercise. A long-term and very close friendship was ending, creating a great deal of pain for all concerned. Even as he knew that the changes in the friendship were irreversible and the result of the natural growing apart that sometimes happens to even the closest of friends, he had difficulty finding a comfortable way of accepting the change. His *future self* offered a new way of experiencing the loss of such a close friendship, so he eagerly said *yes* to this new part of himself. As he did this, though, he also heard a quiet but insistent *no*. Paying attention to his mixed feelings, he looked more closely at the *no* and discovered that there was a step he had to take between where he was in the present moment and the resolution offered by his *future self*. He needed to grieve the loss first, and that was what he had been struggling to avoid. Until he dealt with his disappointment and feelings of loss, he wouldn't be able to fully embrace the comfort offered by his *future self*.

This man's experience points to an important element in saying *yes* to your own deepest potential: you also need to be able to say *no*. To overlook mixed feelings wastes time: while part of you says *yes*, another part holds back and prevents you from bringing into your everyday life the full measure of what it is you seek to achieve. Living consciously requires bringing along your full self. To do so demands that you listen to your response of *no* and explore the underlying reasons for your resistance to a particular change. As in the example above, often a response of *no* serves to bring to light a situation or issue that needs to be understood or resolved before your response of *yes* can be wholehearted.

Ultimately, the changes that occur as you become your *optimal future self* will emerge in the specific ways, and at a pace, perfectly suited to what is possible for you. The entire process is guided by your own deep wisdom, so that even when you feel stretched or challenged beyond your usual level of comfort, know that you wouldn't ask yourself to become more than what you have the capacity to be.

MAKE IT REAL
EXPERIMENT #1:
Getting to Know "Yes" and "No"

Sit in a quiet place where you can do this experiment for a few minutes, just to notice your automatic responses to the words *yes* and *no*.

- Once you are settled, begin repeating the word *yes* to yourself mentally. There is no need to attach anything to the *yes*. Just say it to yourself over and over, and notice whatever you experience in your mind, body, and feelings.

- Next, clear your mind for a moment allowing the *yes* response to fade. Then begin to say *no* over and over, mentally repeating it to yourself and noticing whatever responses arise.

- Now return to the *yes* response and repeat it to yourself for a little while. Notice any difference in your thoughts, feelings, and body sensations when you repeat *yes* and when you repeat *no*.

Sometimes it is essential to say *no* and sometimes *yes* means you have caved in to something that isn't right for you. For the purposes of saying *yes* to your own deepest potential, though, notice the following: saying *yes* to yourself tends to create a sense of opening, possibility, curiosity, and well-being. Repeating *no* tends to create a sense of constriction, of closing in on yourself, or shutting off the feeling of possibility, of being open to the supportive surprises life has in store for you.

EXPERIMENT #2:
Practicing Saying Yes

This experiment asks you to take an hour one day a week and use the word *yes* as a kind of mantra. For example, you might begin by using it during the first hour of your day, starting by saying *yes* to the day as soon as you awaken. There is no need to think deeply about anything. Just begin the day by saying *yes* to it and to yourself. Then, for the next hour, say *yes* to yourself. After that, let it go and simply notice whether you experience the day differently from others.

GUIDED MEDITATION #2:
Saying *Yes* to Your *Future Self*

Before you begin the meditation, choose an issue that involves healing, change, development, or some other outcome you seek at this time or in the near or far future. There is no limit to what you can choose as your focus. The important point is that you concentrate on an outcome you really want to achieve, something to which you can give your heartfelt willingness.

Take a few moments to settle in at the bottom of your breath without seeking to control it in any way. Just be aware of the still point between breaths. It's always there to receive you when you turn your attention to it.

Bring to mind the issue you want to explore on this journey and find yourself on a path that represents the process involved in achieving what you seek. Recall that your inner landscape is infinitely vast and varied and that your deeper wisdom can choose any place you need to be for this journey. Also remember that there is no need to have a specific image. It's fine to have a felt-sense, an impression, of where you are and the qualities you discover there.

Especially notice how it feels to move along the path deliberately, willingly. You are taking steps toward a desired outcome and offering your entire self to that purpose.

As you walk along the path, begin to say "yes" to yourself. Keeping the outcome in mind, allow the "yes" to resonate through your entire bodymind, becoming a source of nourishment that supports your capacity to achieve what you seek.

Up ahead, notice that your optimal future self approaches. As before, there is no need to see this part of yourself. It's enough to have an awareness of the essence of your future self, a felt-sense of this wiser part. This is the part of you that has already achieved what you now seek. Become aware of the most powerful qualities of this part of yourself. What is your response to this part?

Take a few moments now to become your optimal future self, to blend with this part of you. Experience yourself as if you were this part, thinking with the mind of the future self, having the feelings of the future self, and sensing the body of the future self. Pay particular attention to any differences you notice between the bodymind of your future self and that of your present-day self.

When you become aware of the differences that feel positive and good to you, allow yourself to say "yes" to them with your whole being. Notice how it feels when you open your heart and say "yes" from the deepest parts of your self. Sometimes the "yes" resonates as a ringing bell resonates—through you all at once, from deep inside to the surface of your being.

If you feel comfortable saying "yes" to developing these new qualities in your present-day self, give yourself permission to say it mentally a few times, paying particular attention to the feeling you get when you experience your willingness to accept the outcome you seek.

Take a few moments to feel the power of saying "yes" to your optimal future self. Remember that, as you continue to be one with this wiser part of yourself, your bodymind is learning to be this new way. It is as if you were a sponge soaking up all the new learning, the new ways of perceiving, feeling, and responding that come with achieving the outcome you seek.

Now allow yourself to be outside your future self again, focused within your preset-day self. Notice how your experience as the future self continues to resonate and reverberate within your present-day bodymind being. Say "yes" to the learning that continues to fill you even now. Then say "yes" to saying "yes".

Next take a few moments to review your experience. Notice that your future self continues to be present as a source of support and guidance. All you need to do is say "yes" to what your future self has to offer.

When you feel ready, come back to your surroundings, bringing with you a continuing sense of what it feels like to say "yes" to your deepest potential to achieve what you seek. Wiggle your fingers and toes to bring yourself all the way back. Continue to feel the "yes" reverberating throughout your being as you return.

You might want to write down some notes after your experience, to process cognitively the shifts you felt when you became your *optimal future self*. Taking notes gives you an opportunity to review details of your experience later, whenever you want to remind yourself of what emerged. It is also helpful to take a few minutes each day to recall the achievement you seek, to say *yes* to it and to the help and guidance available from your *optimal future self*.

Getting Unstuck and Choosing Your Optimal Future

If just saying *yes* were all it took to achieve our goals, most of us would have no problem expressing ourselves more fully in the world. The truth is, however, change usually brings its own version of discomfort or fear—fear of the unknown, the unfamiliar, the as-yet-to-be-discovered. It's natural to have mixed feelings about change, even when we are certain it will lead to constructive, satisfying outcomes, for the change may also require us to challenge old habits, beliefs, and rules.

For example, some families are bound together by very clear-cut notions of how one ought to live, down to which professions or trades the young adults should enter. If you come from such a family, as an adult you may find that the work you were encouraged to do doesn't really fit who you are. As you come to the realization that you want to move in a new direction, you also realize that to go forward will mean you have to turn your back, in a sense, on the values of your family, or your religious and cultural tradition, or the ways of being of the people in your chosen community. Sometimes it feels as though you will have to leave behind people you care about as you move toward your chosen goals.

At a workshop, a man told a story of his inner journey through the priesthood and how he eventually realized that it wasn't the right place for him. He had felt at home in his vocation until he reached the age of thirty-five, when something new began to stir in him. He found he was no longer satisfied with the restrictions of the priesthood, and after a period of agonizing self-searching, he left it eventually married, and became a school counselor. In doing so, he challenged his fears of losing his family, his religion, and the friends who had supported him while he was a priest. As he reflected on his experience, he was particularly grateful that he had followed his heart rather than his fears of rejection.

Fears of possible rejection, failure, or humiliation when we put ourselves "out there" can create in some of us an inability to move forward in our journey into wholeness. If you feel stuck, consider whether you learned from people close to you that it is risky to express yourself in certain ways. For example, I recall a friend whose immigrant parents felt profoundly self-conscious in their new country. They always told their children to be cooperative and quiet—to "get along". At one point in his career as a middle-level manager in a corporate setting, my friend decided to act on his love of writing and complete a novel he'd been working on for years. He became frustrated at his seeming inability to finish it for reasons he couldn't understand. The main character in the story was an angry young man who had lots to say about life in general and especially about subtle forms of discrimination. Eventually, my friend realized that the novel represented being noisy and contentious in a way that would have frightened and upset his parents.

It is not unusual for a sense of loyalty to become a basis for being unable to move forward into change. As I have worked with people over the years, I have found that when a process of moving forward comes to a halt, usually there is a belief, feeling, or fear that involves someone else. It doesn't seem to matter whether the belief, feeling, or fear is true. What counts is how much we *believe* we are doing something wrong if we express talents, skills, or expressions of empowerment that were not encouraged or celebrated when we were young. Whatever the reasons, whenever we want to move forward and can't, it's useful to explore whether some childhood learning or belief—or a need to stay connected or loyal to someone—is at the root of the problem.

In the guided meditation that follows, you have an opportunity to discover what is behind your own stuck feeling, if you have one, that keeps you from taking the next step into greater self-expression. You have a chance to say *yes* to change—to make the decision to go ahead anyway.

As with all inner journeys, bring your *whole* self along, mixed feelings and all. Your discomfort or stuck feelings can accompany you alongside the part within that is eager to move on, to accomplish all that you seek to achieve.

MAKE IT REAL
GUIDED MEDITATION #3:
The Fork in the Road

To prepare for this meditation journey, choose an issue about which you feel stuck, or some other development or goal you want to achieve but haven't been able to accomplish. This meditation has several important steps. I encourage you to take the whole journey in one sitting, so you may want to set aside at least twenty minutes to complete the entire meditation.

To begin, find a place where you can sit comfortably without being disturbed. As you settle, take a few moments to focus your attention on your breathing, moving to the bottom of the breath with each exhalation.

There, at the bottom of the breath, take some time to linger in the still point that emerges naturally between one breath and the next.

Bring to mind the issue you want to focus on in this journey. Simply recall it and allow yourself to be in touch with how it feels to be stuck, frightened, resistant, confused, or some other feeling that contributes to keeping you from achieving what you seek.

Now imagine a very special path somewhere in your inner landscape. This path represents the journey to resolve the impasse, to move beyond where you are presently stopped. Remember, it's enough to sense the landscape and the path. There is no need to struggle to have a clear image.

Allow yourself to sense what it would be like if you could become aware of your feet on this path, of the surrounding landscape, of the smells, colors, and textures there. Take a few moments to develop a sense of being on the path, and be sure to allow yourself to have whatever impressions come, be they vague or vivid, depending on what emerges naturally, without effort.

As you begin to walk along the path, notice that you take each step with the intention of resolving your current dilemma. Pay particular attention to the way it feels to place your feet on the path and to keep moving forward simply because you have chosen to do so.

Now imagine that you come to a point where there is a fork in the path. One path goes off to the left and the other goes off to the right. Come to a stop at this point and notice that this place represents your dilemma, the place where you are stuck right now.

Here, at the fork in the road, one path represents your optimal path and the other represents the elements that hold you back. That which holds you back may be someone you care about, an outgrown sense of loyalty, or some other pull on you that keeps you from going forward.

First, explore the path that holds you back. It is important to know that this path is not yours to walk. *It belongs to someone else, whomever she or he may be. It represents someone else's values, intentions, and choices.*

Though this path isn't yours to walk, it is important to know about it, to explore it. Notice, for example, the colors, shapes, textures and general quality of the environment through which this path travels. Be aware of the qualities of the path itself, whether it is straight or meandering, whether it is smooth or rough. Give yourself permission to be aware of any impressions you have that convey to you something about the qualities of the path that is not yours to follow.

Next, notice if the person to whom this path belongs is there with you now. What are your responses when you first recognize the true owner of this path? Be sure to allow mixed feelings and whatever reactions spontaneously arise. You need to know whose path this is and why you find yourself stuck here.

If you choose to be loyal to this person or situation, the best you can do is simply stay put and be there. Since you can't move forward on this path—since it is not your path—there is nowhere for you to go.

As you ponder your stuck position, what happens if you realize that the only thing you would need to leave behind, if you were to walk your own path, is your **belief** *that it's not okay to do so?*

Become aware of any feeling or thought you have that conveys a sense of "waking up"—a dawning realization that you've been caught in an old way of seeing the world and that it's all right for you to move on now.

When you have finished exploring the path that is not yours to take, turn your attention to the path that is rightfully your own. What are your first responses to it? What feelings do you have as you consider the path that awaits you?

Recognizing fully that once you begin to walk on your own path, you will have to leave behind the person or situation belonging to the other path, what happens as you step onto the path that is yours to walk? What responses arise?

As you walk along the path that represents your becoming more fully the person you have the capacity to be, how do you feel?

At some point, take a moment to look back at the fork in the road and notice what it feels like to have moved beyond the place where you were stuck. Allow yourself to realize that you can visit the person or situation related to the other path whenever you choose. The main point is that you don't have to stay in that old place anymore. You have the freedom to come and go now.

Turning your attention back to your own journey, notice that there is a line of light coming toward you from up ahead on your path. The line of light emerges from the heart of your optimal future self and reaches out, gently, to your heart. Allow the line of light to connect inside your heart and notice how you feel about that. This is a lifeline from your future self, a line of communication. Be sure to allow mixed feelings as you explore what it's like to let the line of light connect with you.

Next, notice that your future self approaches from up ahead on the path. There is no need to have an image of your future self; simply allow impressions to come to mind. Be sure to allow these impressions to drop into your mind without consciously thinking about them.

As this wiser part of you approaches, sense what kind of person this is. Be sure to allow mixed feelings as you pay particular attention to the differences between your future self and who you are today.

If it's okay with you, take a moment to step inside your optimal future self and blend with, become, this wiser, more mature part of yourself. Again, allow impressions to emerge without attempting to create them with your conscious mind. Just let them drop into your awareness.

What is it like for you to see through the eyes of your future self, hear with his or her ears, think with the mind of your future self, live in the body of your future self? Take a few moments to allow your mind, feelings, body—your whole being—to learn how to be that wiser you. There is nothing to do here except soak up the essence of the future self as if you were a sponge.

Next, ask your future self to show you what it is like to have fully resolved the issue that you brought on this journey. For ex-

ample, let your future self look back across time to show you how you finally moved on from the fork in the road, how you made the choices necessary to achieve your goals. You may or may not have any conscious awareness of what your future self shows you. That's fine. Just let yourself be open and willing to be guided and inspired by your deeper wisdom.

Now move outside your future self and make the choice, if it's okay to do so, to continue to walk forward with your future self as your guide. Take a few more steps and notice how it feels to continue to choose to resolve the issue about which you used to feel stuck.

To end your journey, take a few moments to review what you have experienced. Go back to the fork in the road and notice how it feels to be there now. Then go back to your own path and notice how that feels.

Give yourself time to get used to moving forward on your own path. Allow mixed feelings to resolve themselves naturally, over time.

Now, wiggle your fingers and toes to make sure you're all the way back and take some notes from your experience. Recall that you can take one of these journeys anytime you want to move toward expressing more of the talent that is inherently yours.

And, Speaking of Next Steps . . .

The *optimal future self* isn't our only source of guidance and inspiration on the journey into wholeness. In the next chapter, we will explore the realm of affirmation, prayer, and spiritual guidance. While these subjects used to be regarded as "out there", a source of ridicule and disbelief, research is beginning to catch up to what mystics around the world have known across the ages: activities such as prayer can and *do* have an effect on the material world. Once again, we'll travel into non-local aspects of reality and the information universe and discover even more ways to support our journeys into more conscious living.

Chapter 10

INTUITION AND WELL-BEING

Affirmation, Prayer, Guides, and Other Nonlocal Phenomena

There are two ways to live your life. One is as though nothing is a miracle. The other is as though everything is a miracle.

—*Albert Einstein*

One of the richest and continuing sources of inspiration in my life has been my relationship with intuition. When I was a young child, my grandmother taught me about ways of knowing the world that were considered by many people to be strange or downright foolish. I can still hear my grandmother's voice warning me not to share the taboo subjects so freely discussed in my home. Thankfully, in today's more tolerant and adventurous atmosphere, the subject of intuition is finding a more open reception. I think even my grandmother would feel more comfortable talking about her multidimensional, nonlocal experiences in the current climate.

The techniques and ideas that follow not only offer a means to enhance your experience of being part of a larger whole but also provide *practical* ways of tapping into a dynamic, grounded relationship with unseen worlds. Free of the limitations of time and space, new realms of awareness and experience open up that offer unanticipated opportunities to explore expanded aspects of ourselves and our world. Whatever your spiritual or religious beliefs, or lack of them, I encourage you to engage this part of the journey with an open mind and heart—and with an extra dose of curiosity.

Going "Out There" While Staying Grounded Right Here

It is important to take this kind of journey as our most grounded, practical selves. Sometimes we are tempted to use alternate dimensions of reality and spiritual practices as doorways to escape into a world of fantasy or "magical thinking". When this happens, we allow ourselves to sidestep everyday problems—intentionally or inadvertently—by focusing on "internal communications" or a "higher calling". Unfortunately, all we have found is a convenient place in which to hide from the problems and challenges of everyday life.

I encourage you to bring along a dose of constructive doubt, even as you give yourself permission to experiment with alternate ways of knowing the world. Doubt can be a healthy companion along the way, as it is one of the means by which you can measure the value of your excursions into nonlocal ways of knowing the world. If you haven't developed your intuitive skills already, in time you will discover a certain sense of *rightness* that accompanies accurate awareness.

Another important companion along the way is a willingness to be wrong—to find out how it feels when you're off track. No one can know this for you, so your doubt and sense of rightness are indispensible tools along the way. As with all things nonlocal, look for what is meaningful to you and ignore the rest until it proves useful—or not.

It helps to keep in mind that the states of consciousness and possibilities that exist in alternate dimensions are perfectly reasonable within the rules that govern nonlocal reality. You can't assess telepathic phenomena, for example, in the same way you would assess a physical event, such as who caused a traffic accident—the *how* and *why* of the accident. With a telepathic communication, you probably can't describe the how or why. Instead, you're limited to *what* happened and *when*.

The phenomena we will explore in this chapter represent valuable and dynamic sources of inspiration, information, and well-being when their applications are practical and grounded. In traditions around the world and throughout history, nonlocal ways of being and knowing have been used as sources of wisdom, healing, information, and guidance. Shamanic traditions, cultures where ancestors or nature spirits guide the hunt and harvest, dependence on nontraditional healers of many kinds, meditative approaches that create changes in everyday life—all represent activities that have a solid and practical place in nonlocal reality. What is important to understand is the difference between (1) what we can expect in a reality governed by the physical laws with which we are familiar, and (2) what is natural in a realm that is free of the constraints operating in the world of our five senses.

Intuition and Nonlocal Phenomena

And so, when we enter the realm of nonlocal reality, the rules change. No longer do we deal with information that emerges one word or idea at a time. Suddenly we step into an arena where ideas, thoughts, feelings, and sensations are known instantaneously, as if the information were taken in all in one gulp. In fact, it is the instantaneous, ever-present quality of nonlocal reality that helps us understand what otherwise would appear to be some fairly bizarre phenomena.

One of the basic facts about nonlocal reality is that we live in it all the time. It's actually not foreign in any way. It's just that, in Western culture, we don't tend to pay attention to it as part of everyday life. Instead, we pass off common nonlocal events as "hunches," "coincidences," "good guesses," "good luck," "an overwhelming need to do something at a particular time," and other explanations that don't require us to ponder the unexpected. We visit nonlocal reality every night when we dream, and most of us spend a good deal of time there when we daydream or fantasize during the day.

In tribal cultures around the world, dreams and fantasies represent *literal* rather than symbolic realities, and are treated as such—they are taken to be as real and tangible as the physical world and the events that occur in everyday life. For the aborigines of Australia, for example, the *dreamtime* is a place as identifiable and familiar as the Outback. Indigenous peoples in the Americas receive guidance and messages from power animals, ancestors, and other kinds of spirit guides. These communications are treated with great respect—as much or more so than information and help received from living leaders, relatives, and friends. For these people, reality extends automatically into the realm of intuition because their worldviews acknowledge and accept as natural non-rational ways of knowing the world.

In fact, intuition is the springboard into nonlocal reality. Historically, intuition was referred to as psychic ability or ESP—extrasensory perception. Now intuition, which encompasses the entire range of nonlocal knowing, is a more useful term. Everyone is intuitive by nature. Some of us don't use our intuition actively and yet we still benefit from it all the time. Others of us apply it directly and have learned to develop intuition as a skill, similar to developing an ear for music, an eye for art, an appreciation of literature. For example, I mentioned that my grandmother called herself a healer and a clairvoyant. In fact, these labels really defined only those aspects of intuition she used most frequently. All her abilities arose from her capacity to be awake to her nonrational faculties—to be *consciously* aware of using them to gather information about herself, others, and her environment.

What my grandmother did is just one example of using intuition actively and effectively. Each of us has particular ways of being intuitive that are natural and effortless to us. Becoming aware of these particular intuitive abilities is no different from identifying any talent or natural ability you may have: a special knack for working with machinery, composing or playing music, doing sports, using words, expressing artistry of some kind, cooking or nutrition, technical wizardry, or any of the innumerable talents that we humans have within our grasp.

Intuition is at work when an answer to a problem suddenly springs to mind "out of the blue". It is there when you hear about a friend and have a nagging sixth-sense feeling that you should contact him. Then you do so only to discover that he was thinking of you as well. It is at work when an image comes to mind that conveys a new understanding, which wasn't available to you in words. It is there when you first meet someone and suddenly an impression or image of a door opening comes to mind, and later the person turns out to be of help to you in some way. Intuition brings those "aha" experiences in which you suddenly see a situation in its larger context or you *know* something you hadn't known a moment before.

There are countless examples of how intuition works in everyday life. Some people report that they have a particular talent for picking the right route for driving to a place they've never been to before, or for choosing the line at a toll bridge that moves the fastest. Others just seem to know how to make choices that work out best for them or have a particular facility for being in the right place at the right time. Still others—and this is an especially useful talent in crowded cities like New York—seem to know just where to go to find the one parking space that's available right when they need it. It is as though there were a special kind of antenna available to scan nonlocal reality and tap into information that isn't yet manifest in time and space and use it for our benefit—if we bother to use the antenna.

This doesn't mean intuition *causes* the parking place to open up or the toll booth lane to move quickly. Remember synchronicity. The underlying mechanism of intuition allows you to tap into relevant information and meaningful coincidences and then use them in a beneficial way. Lots of people could pick up the signal to drive toward a particular area of a parking lot, or down a certain block, but then not listen. Instead, by dismissing an intuitive awareness of where a parking space is available, these drivers continue to search, using only their five physical senses.

Another way intuition weaves its way into daily experience is through the many moments—often barely noticed or ignored altogether—when we seem to have flashes of precognition. For reasons we can't explain, this quality of intuitive awareness comes across as worry. I recall one night when friends were over and I had an inexplicable but strong impression that a glass tabletop in my living room was in danger of falling over. Because there were animals visiting as well, I found myself concerned that one of them might get hurt if this occurred. That was the worry part. My guests were amused by my concern about the tabletop, as it appeared to be solidly in place. Later, when I had gone out of the room. I heard a crash. The tabletop *had* fallen but, fortunately, no one was in harm's way.

This example illustrates one quality of intuitive awareness: it isn't necessarily—or even usually—dramatic. Another quality is that intuition often doesn't make rational sense at the time. My impression about the tabletop was subtle, clear, but utterly inexplicable in rational terms. It didn't come with great feelings of dread or alarm. It was just a realization that floated through my awareness. I caught it because I'm used to paying attention to impressions that drop into my awareness.

Another time I had a powerful and dramatic intuition that an accident was going to occur and that I would be called on to help someone who was injured. I thought it would be a car accident. In an attempt to avoid it, I stayed home for several days. In that time, the accident came to me in the guise of a friend who had been hurt and needed help to manage pain.

I've also heard stories from people who work in sales about having an intuitive sixth sense when they are interacting with potential customers. They describe how they seem to get a flash or a glimpse of the sale being completed even before the discussion begins. With other customers, their intuitive sense is that no door will open no matter how hard they knock.

These kinds of experiences probably don't sound terribly strange or unfamiliar. They happen to most of us some of the time and to others of us a lot of the time. They are common examples of tapping into the nonlocal information field during everyday awareness.

As I mentioned earlier, a characteristic of many intuitive experiences is that they make sense only in hindsight, after time and experience have revealed the meaning of the event within the context of a larger picture. For this reason, it is useful to suspend judgment about your intuitive sense of people and events until you have had time to stand back and review how things worked out. The most important reason for learning to use your intuition more actively is that doing so contributes to a more grounded, masterful life and a greater sense of psychological well-being and wholeness.

MAKE IT REAL
EXPERIMENT #1:
Becoming Conscious of Your Intuition

This experiment comes early in the chapter to invite you to begin to notice when you use your intuitive awareness in your life.

- Give yourself the suggestion that you will begin to be aware of those times when you just seem to know something without knowing how it is that you know it. (Notice how sentences that seek to express nonlocal reality can sometimes be hard to follow!)

- Pay attention to those times when a hunch proves to be correct. Also notice those times when you have a hunch, decide not to follow it, and later discover that your hunch was right. And, remember, we learn how to use intuition as much by our failures to follow it as when we allow it to guide us. The goal is to *notice its operation, whether or not you decided to go with what your intuition told you.* It is also useful to write down what this inner voice tells you so that you can check its accuracy over time.

As you do this experiment, you are likely to discover that the more you pay attention to your intuition, the more reliably present it becomes. It is similar to synchronicity in that, the more you use it, the better it works. For this reason, I recommend writing down your experiences that involve intuition. Writing information down plants it more firmly in consciousness and helps you become increasingly aware of the "feel" or quality that accompanies *accurate* intuitive awareness. Then you can use it purposely with increasing confidence and discover that intuition, used consciously, is a powerful resource.

The Role of Affirmation

Affirmations can be just so many words strung together that we repeat with little or no feeling or conviction, or they can be dynamic extensions of our commitment to living with intention. In the same way creating intentions seems to reach into nonlocal dimensions of reality, tapping into probabilities and synchronicities that support them, affirmations enhance achieving the outcomes we seek. It also may be that the heartfelt repetition of an affirmation becomes a positive self-fulfilling prophecy or a positive self-hypnotic suggestion that encourages us to recognize and respond to otherwise unnoticed opportunities and resources. By repeating an affirmation over time, we create an internal sense of the change or achievement we want to actualize and thereby develop a willingness to let it become part of our lives in the present. It is as though we were developing a new thought, a new internal attitude that is willing and able to accommodate change in a desired direction.

Affirmations are most powerful when they reflect an outcome, a way of being, or an achievement that you want with *your whole being*. The emotional energy behind the goals you seek seems to be a crucial element in activating the nonlocal events that support what the affirmation conveys. For this reason, it is useful to keep in mind that *heartfelt desire is a potent fuel in the process of using affirmations.*

Affirmations lose their power if they reflect an outcome you don't believe is possible to achieve. Using an affirmation as a means of convincing yourself omits an important step: you must first give yourself permission to have your intentions become actual. Then, once you believe in the possibility, an affirmation can nourish your developing belief.

For example, if you were to create an intention to return to school and enhance your career, the first step would be to assess whether you believe you *can* or *should* take this next step. If you discover you have some fears about your capabilities and concerns that going further in school would be a move beyond what your friends or family aspire to, your initial affirmations might look something like this:

- *I give myself permission to explore areas of experience beyond the confines of my familiar world.*

- *Increasingly I discover that my fears and uncertainties are like clouds, disappearing as quickly as they appear.*

- *I allow my deep urge to move forward to help me resolve whatever limiting beliefs or early learnings hold me back.*

Then, as soon as returning to school feels like a viable possibility, you can shift to affirmations that are more directly related to this activity:

- *I engage school with energy and intelligence, and find it is much easier than I expected.*

- *My time at school flows easily and effectively because I discover that I am interested and involved.*

- *I am a success at school and discover that I have plenty of energy to do both school and work tasks effectively.*

Building on small steps is particularly useful when we seek to stretch well beyond our present lifestyle or way of being, and affirmations that relate to *process* are useful in reinforcing these steps. Process affirmations tend to begin with, *I am becoming . . . I am willing . . . I am beginning . . .* or some other statement that conveys the sense of a developing reality that will continue to move us toward our goals over time. For example, when I began to confront my fear of public speaking, I had to use process affirmations because the long-term outcome—affirming that I could speak in public—was simply too terrifying for me to contemplate.

I had to begin with statements such as, *I am willing to begin to learn that it is possible for me to survive speaking in front of people*, and *I am beginning to understand that speaking in public will allow me to share with others ideas I care about deeply*.

As I began to conduct workshops and give presentations, the *fact* of my public speaking became real. The next step was to increase my comfort level. At that point, I moved on to affirmations such as the following: *I surprise myself with the level of comfort I feel when sharing ideas with people . . . I love my audience and recognize that everyone who is present wants me to be successful in my talk . . . increasingly I have fun speaking in public*.

On a more general level my affirmations also took on a new tone: *In my world, I have all the support and resources I need to give effective, powerful talks and workshops . . . I welcome opportunities to share my ideas with others, and I'm grateful for the gifts I receive in the process*.

Not all affirmations deal with achieving specific goals or developments. Some seek to affirm quality-of-life issues or more global awarenesses. I frequently use affirmations that begin with *In my world,* in order to generate synchronicities and probabilities that will enhance particular qualities I want to experience in my daily life. For example, the affirmation, *In my world, events, interactions, and opportunities seem to fall into place to support me in every way possible*, emphasizes becoming increasingly aware of what goes right each day. When you really believe in this possibility drop the *"seem to"* from the affirmation and allow the statement to be an unqualified conviction about the nature of your world.

A general intention to become more mindful might be accompanied by an affirmation that states, *In my world, a mindful attitude pervades every moment, every act*. A desire to live in a world characterized by abundance might find support in the following affirmation: *In my world, I have everything I could possibly need, and there is always enough to share with others*.

MAKE IT REAL EXPERIMENT #2:
Creating Affirmations

For this experiment, take some time to sit down and create an affirmation that either addresses a step you want to take or expresses a more general outcome that will enhance the quality of your life or your sense of wholeness.

- First, write down what it is you seek to accomplish.

- Now, close your eyes for a moment and "shift gears." Become aware of settling into your body, as if you were going to take an inner journey or spend some time meditating, so that you can move into a more intuitive state of mind.

- Make sure you have plenty of paper and begin to write down affirmations that come to mind. Be sure to give yourself permission to "brainstorm" the affirmations—which means writing down *whatever* comes to mind. You can edit later. Write down all the versions of the affirmations that emerge, until no more are available.

- Next, read each affirmation out loud to yourself. Notice which ones have the power to evoke resonance in you, and which ones are flat and without real meaning. Give yourself permission to throw away the ones that have no life in them.

- Do whatever editing is needed to tighten up the wording of each affirmation, if you've created more than one, so that it expresses your intention in a way that is both clear and alive for you.

- Now take a few moments to say each revised affirmation out loud and notice how you respond this time.

- Do you experience any mixed feelings about the affirmation?
- Do you experience a deep desire to achieve what the affirmation suggests?
- Where in your body do you feel a positive impact from the affirmation?

• Use each affirmation daily, or at whatever frequency feels natural, for as long as the affirmation feels alive for you.

EXPERIMENT #3:
Different Ways to Use Your Affirmations

In this experiment, you have the choice of three different ways to use affirmations.

- In my own practice of affirming I find that saying them out loud is very powerful.

- Two other ways are to say them silently to yourself or write them down.

- You can also word your affirmations in first, second, or third person, whichever feels most powerful to you. For example, you could say, *Each day I feel better about* myself . . . *Each day you feel better and better about* yourself . . . *Each day* [your name] *feels better and better about* him- *or* herself.

If you choose to use different forms of addressing yourself, notice the difference in energy or impact you feel with each approach. Then use the one that brings the most resonance to your affirmations.

Intuition and Prayer

You may associate prayer with particular religious approaches but, as I use it here, prayer refers to *any* request or statement made to a spiritual agency perceived to be greater than our individual selves. For example, you might pray to "God", to "Buddha", "Allah", a "higher power", "the Mother", "Our Lord", "the universe", to specific gods and goddesses, to healing angels or nature spirits, to saints or masters, to Life—to whatever reality you grant the power of intercession.

No matter what your religious or philosophical beliefs, your relationship to prayer is likely to be deeply personal and unique to you. As you explore the relationship between intuition and prayer—and how prayer seems to interact with nonlocal reality to affect everyday life—allow yourself to translate what I say into ideas that are consonant with your own belief system.

As a child, I remember reading a prediction in my grandmother's Theosophy books that it would be science that proved the existence of the soul. I doubted that, especially as I went through science classes at school. As it has turned out, though—and much to my surprise—science *does* have a hand in verifying that something more than meets the eye occurs when people pray.

In his book, *Healing Words*, Larry Dossey reviews recent research on the effects of prayer, citing studies in which volunteers agreed to pray for patients in a hospital—people whom the volunteers had never met. In one study, there were two groups: one received prayers, the other didn't. Results showed that the group receiving the volunteer's prayers healed more quickly and felt better than those who didn't. What makes these studies even more convincing is that the participants did not know whether they were in the prayer or non-prayer groups.

Another finding of the studies reinforces the uniqueness of our individual relationship with prayer. While there was a noticeable difference in the success of two different styles of prayer, ultimately *both* worked. Specifically, a more general prayer, such as "Thy will be done," was somewhat more effective than prayers requesting particular outcomes, such as "May this person be healed from cancer." But even with this finding, Dossey points out that certain people prayed more effectively when asking for specific outcomes. Again, our personal relationship to prayer seems to be the most important element in determining its success.

Engaging in prayer requires us to let go of the outcome—to make the request and then "hand it over," as it were. Once formulated, the prayer is like an arrow shot into nonlocal reality. We can have a sense of the direction in which we sent it, but we can't know where it will land—or how it might be intercepted along the way.

My grandmother used to tell me that there were times when asking for healing for someone could mean he or she would die rather than recover. She felt strongly that we needed to be prepared to accept whatever outcomes emerged from spiritual requests for help. For this reason, she took activities involving healing and prayer very seriously. Using today's terms, I would state my grandmother's teaching in this way: *whenever we engage nonlocal aspects of reality, we go beyond the capacities of the conscious mind either to follow or control what happens next.* However, prayer as a form of intention may orient both conscious and unconscious minds toward the most positive probability available and access sources of help from invisible realms of reality in unexpected ways.

There are also forms of prayer that emphasize expressions of gratitude or affirm that the outcome sought has already been received. Such affirmative kinds of prayer invite us to act as if our needs are already met, or that solutions are already on the way.

Whatever particular style of prayer works best for you, notice what happens to the quality of your inner experience when you engage in prayerful communication with something or someone greater than yourself.

MAKE IT REAL
EXPERIMENT #4:
Exploring Your Relationship with Prayer

In this experiment, give yourself permission to explore how you respond to different forms of prayer. If you pray already and have a style of prayer you use regularly, allow yourself to discover your responses when you try something different.

- Begin by finding a place where you can sit undisturbed for a little while. Settle in and identify something about which you want to pray, either for yourself or someone else.

- First, pray in general, asking for "Thy will be done," "the best thing to happen," "that which serves the greatest good," or some similar kind of prayer. When you say the prayer, either mentally or out loud, allow it to be heartfelt. Know that you are asking for something you want and then handing it over to some higher power or energy that will fit what you ask for into the larger context. Notice what happens if you trust that this higher power has your best interests in mind and that you can let go of the need to control the answer to your prayer.

- Next, give yourself permission to experiment with a specific request for yourself or someone else. Describe it and ask for the details to come to pass. Notice any difference in your experience when you request something specific as compared to the more general prayer.

- Finally, notice what you experience when you spend time with affirmative prayer, expressing gratitude for outcomes already achieved, for outcomes that have not yet manifested in your life but that you want to have.

Each of these forms of prayer works for certain people at certain times. Allow yourself to explore them in whatever ways feel most natural and empowered for you. You may discover that there are times when generalized prayer feels more potent and other times when you feel intuitively moved to ask for something specific.

You may also discover that there are times when affirmative prayer feels right and when you feel most comfortable expressing gratitude before you receive what you want or need.

Also, remember that prayers are sometimes answered in unexpected ways that only make sense in hindsight, if ever. Whatever form of prayer you choose, notice what it feels like—each time—to express your prayer and then let it go with a sense of trust that the outcome will emerge in whatever way is best.

Guides, Angels, and Other Sources of Invisible Support

Across cultures and throughout human history, there have been accounts of communication and interaction between people and non-physical beings. As far back as I can remember, my grandmother talked about non-physical beings. In her world there was never any question of whether angels, guides, fairies, nature spirits, ghosts, or other forms of invisible beings existed. They were part and parcel of her daily life, helping with her healing work, inspiring and guiding her. I learned to trust the relationship she had with these beings and to have confidence in the communications and assistance she received from them. I always felt there was a grounded, practical quality to this aspect of my grandmother's work and beliefs and, when I was young, I was surprised that other people didn't have the same view of reality.

Having said all that, I still don't know whether these nonphysical helpers actually exist as separate beings. In my mind, the question remains open as to whether they are representations of aspects of our own consciousness. For example, even as I call on these beings on a regular basis, I still find that I'm not sure if my awareness of them is my own creation—a way of communicating with myself from deeper levels of consciousness—or if they truly exist as entities separate from myself. At other times, I feel quite convinced that they are something separate and individual in their own right.

Because there seems to be no way to ascertain or prove whether these beings are separate entities or if they represent ways we communicate with ourselves on nonlocal levels, I invite you to interpret your experiences in these dimensions in ways that make sense to you at this point in time. Also, if you are a person who doesn't have any particular inclination to believe in the actual existence of nonphysical beings, you might understand what follows as one more way of using the language of symbols to translate intuitive awareness. Viewed as metaphors, these "beings" then become another means by which you can tap into the ever-present information field that is all around us.

For many of us, having dialogues or conversations with non-physical beings can become a regular source of guidance and support. For example, you might have a question that you can't answer in a rational, step-by-step way. If you have developed the metaphor of having a guide—whether human, animal, or some other kind of being—it can be both practical and useful to sit down and literally *ask* the guide for input on your question.

There are any number of ways to register this kind of intuitive experience. For example, sometimes an answer to a question or the solution to a problem will just drop into your head as a complete understanding all at once. At other times, a guide might talk to you in a way that is similar to listening to someone actually giving you an answer. At yet other times, you might find that an image presents itself, and in the experience and interpretation of the image, your answer can be found. For many people, answers often appear in dreams as well.

There is no right or wrong way to communicate with non-physical beings. As unique individuals, our style of communication—and the ways we represent different kinds of guides—will vary. While one person might experience an angelic presence, another might register the same source of inspiration as a human saint or master. Also, as we deepen our awareness of non-physical, nonlocal sources of inspiration and guidance, our ways of representing them to ourselves may change naturally.

In collective terms, a society's relationship with non-physical beings evolves and changes as well. For example, in our culture angels have become accepted in a new, more immediate way. Books teach readers how to communicate with angels and describe all manner of encounters. There has even been a television show about angelic intervention.

Several years ago, I discovered that certain non-physical beings, which my grandmother had honored as teachers, began to appear in recently published books with some noteworthy changes. They were the same beings with the same names, but their origins and the stories told about them had evolved to match emerging cultural beliefs and metaphors. In particular, some whom my grandmother had described as being part of a vast spiritual group of non-physical teachers and guides now appeared as advanced extraterrestrials.

For me, this shift in metaphor demonstrates the freedom and creativity we have available to us for *translating nonlocal awareness into conscious thought and experience*. It doesn't really matter to me how these representations change over the years. What does count is that we continue to access information from nonlocal reality in ways that allow it to be useful in everyday life.

Some people don't want any kind of direct interaction with invisible beings. Instead, they prefer to ask for help from a non-specific, impersonal source, such as the concept of the *universe*, and then stay open to whatever arises in their experience in the form of help, opportunity or information related to their request. What is important to keep in mind is that one metaphor or image is no more powerful or effective than another. Prayer is a deeply individual process. All that is required is that you have a belief system with which you are comfortable and a flexibility that allows you to maneuver in nonlocal reality without constantly being diverted by doubt.

As I mentioned at the beginning of the chapter, when we bring our whole selves along on the journey, we automatically bring along a certain amount of healthy skepticism. As is true with all kinds of intuition, it is important to learn when to trust what drops into awareness and when to recognize that wishful thinking or an investment in a given outcome has gotten in the way of a truly intuitive grasp of the situation. For most of us, practice brings a deepening sense of rightness that develops over time, when we check our intuitive awareness against what actually happened. Here is where hindsight becomes an essential ally along the way. When we compare our intuition about a problem or circumstance with what actually happens, we learn what it feels like when we are accurate as compared to how we feel when we create answers with the conscious mind. It is this special feeling that, in time, brings a greater confidence in what intuition conveys.

It takes practice to learn to trust your intuitive capacities and allow them to become increasingly accurate. Engage conversations with your guide with an open attitude of curiosity and feel free to add a sense of playfulness to the process. There is no need to be deadly serious when developing intuition. In fact, playing with it often supports its blossoming. The more relaxed you are, the more open you will tend to be to a deeper understanding of what you seek to know.

MAKE IT REAL
GUIDED MEDITATION #1:
Communing with Guides, Angels, and other Non-physical Helpers

In this meditation, you have an opportunity to explore your unique style of connecting with invisible helpers. The most important point to keep in mind is that people have different styles of using intuition. For example, some people "hear" intuitive input, while others "see" images and symbols. Still others "sense" or feel intuitively, while others tap into a kind of flavor or quality of experience that is like a "taste" of awareness. One way isn't better than another. In fact, you may find that there are times when you discover that you're especially attuned to internal listening, while at other times you have a felt-sense of awareness without any specific visual or auditory content.

To begin, think of an issue about which you would like some help or input. Choose something that doesn't have too much emotional power. Sometimes, when you seek intuitive awareness about an issue you care a lot about, your emotional investment in the outcome will get in the way of your being able to receive spontaneous, accurate input. It's best to practice initially on less invested issues.

Next, take a moment to settle into a meditative state of mind. You might discover or create a special place where you go to commune with invisible helpers. Over time, you may find that your ability to attune becomes increasingly easy when you simply imagine yourself in this place.

For now, notice the colors, textures, smells, and landscape that characterize your special place. Pay particular attention to those qualities that convey a sense that this is a sacred place where you can easily and comfortably connect with invisible helpers and guides.

Recall your question and focus on your willingness to ask for guidance. Now ask your question, or pose your problem, and allow yourself to sit quietly. Keep your awareness open to receiving whatever information, image, or impression drops in, and tell yourself you can analyze it later.

If you feel yourself starting to struggle to get an answer or becoming anxious or worried about whether you'll receive a response, remind yourself to let go *of your expectations. You can't legislate when your answer will arrive, and right now may not be the right time.*

If something comes, accept it and take a few moments to sit with it, allowing your awareness to deepen. If nothing comes, allow yourself to restate the question or problem and then sit for a few moments simply soaking in the qualities of your special place. Allow yourself to sit in the "creative void," without any demand or tension. Trust that you've done all you need to do by asking and that your own deep wisdom will give you input in the right away at the right time.

Before you come back, be sure to express gratitude for the time you've spent in your special place. If nothing came, express gratitude for the answer or guidance that will emerge for you sometime later—at exactly the right time and in precisely the right way. Assume you will receive an appropriate answer or response eventually.

Take a few moments to write down your experience. Then, later, with the benefit of hindsight, you can look back and check on the accuracy of your intuitive awareness in light of what actually emerges in your life experience.

EXPERIMENT #5:
Remembering to Ask for Help

Hopefully, this experiment will be habit-forming for you. It only requires that you ask for help any time and every time you need it.

- As with the guided meditation outlined above, here you make your request and then let it go without any preconceptions as to when or how you will receive help. What you may be surprised to discover is that the more you ask for input, the more you receive it.

- At first, be sure to keep a record of your requests. Then, when help arrives, note that, too. Over time, you will begin to see a pattern. Eventually, you won't need to keep a record. You will be in the habit of asking for help and you will have developed an internal sense of how the process works best for you.

Connecting with the Beloved

For me, relating to "the Beloved" represents a special category of communing with an enfolding, inspiring, expansive spiritual presence. Nothing is more central to my daily experience that my relationship with the Beloved. In the years since I originally wrote *Sacred Practices*, this statement remains fundamentally true, even as I now include the One, all life, as a representation of my Beloved. This is true for many people, regardless of the name or nature they may assign to this spiritual experience. For some people, the Beloved is Jesus, God, Buddha, Allah, the Ancient Mother, or any of the many gods and goddesses, living or historical.

For others, it is a guru, saint, or other religious figure whose presence and influence is experienced as real, immediate, and alive. For still others, it is the very soul of the earth itself—Gaia in her all-pervasive presence.

Connecting with the Beloved is like being enfolded in the deepest, most accepting love imaginable. It is an experience of being so profoundly connected to love that you are completely and utterly filled with a sense of contentment and well-being. The experience also contains elements relevant to your particular belief system. For example, if you experience the Beloved as not only loving you but also teaching you or expressing through you, you may have a compelling need to serve this spiritual presence. A feeling of wanting to surrender to the Beloved and to accept his or her guidance may also arise.

Someone once said to me that the Beloved was my own spiritual Self. My initial response was to reject the idea. Over the years, though, I've become more open to entertaining the possibility. Within a context of oneness, of collective consciousness, whether I call the Beloved my Higher Self or experience him/her as a separate being doesn't matter. What *does* matter is that I allow myself to feel that I am so deeply loved, guided, and held within and by this presence that I allow the benefits of this experience to nurture my sense of psychological wholeness and the quality of my actions in daily life. Ultimately, because we are all connected anyway, my Beloved and I are one regardless of how I envision "us".

Discovering whether the Beloved actually exists is as problematic as any other question about demonstrating nonlocal reality in tangible form. *A more relevant and practical question is whether having a sense of the presence of the Beloved in life enhances the quality of our experience and the contribution we make to our collective existence.* Even if the Beloved were no more than an unconscious mirror of our own deep love for ourselves, it would be a gift beyond measure. To live each day reflected in that love nourishes a sense of psychological wholeness and well-being regardless of its "true" source.

As you explore your own relationship with the Beloved, allow yourself a flexible mind and an open heart. Give yourself permission to use your intuition to tap into an experience of the Beloved and notice how this connection nourishes your sense of wholeness and enhances the quality of your daily life.

MAKE IT REAL
GUIDED MEDITATION #2:
Connecting with the Beloved

This meditation invites you to connect with the Beloved, in whatever ways make sense to you. You may notice that your relationship with the Beloved evolves over time as your ongoing awareness of this sacred presence in your daily life increases.

To begin, settle in and focus your attention on "home base," at the bottom of the breath. Take a few moments just to be there, inside yourself, in the stillness that exists between exhaling and inhaling.

Allow yourself to imagine a beautiful natural setting somewhere in your inner world. Notice that it is a place that feels sacred to you. Take a few moments to notice the temperature of the air on your skin, the surface beneath your feet, the colors, shapes, and textures around you. You may also notice any sounds or smells that convey the beauty of this place even more vividly.

Become aware of a deep inner pull in a certain direction and allow yourself to follow that pull. Notice that the pull invites you deeper into your sacred landscape, toward a beautiful, private spot. As you approach the sanctuary, notice that you begin to sense a feeling of anticipation, perhaps the sense that an important experience awaits you.

As you enter the private sanctuary that has called you, notice that there is a place where you can sit down and become even more focused on the sacred, safe nature of this place. Take a few moments to sit down and settle in. Become especially aware of opening your heart as you settle in even more.

Now begin to imagine what it would feel like if you could sense the approach of your Beloved. Without any preconceptions, simply notice that you are aware, on some level, that a great being is coming to spend time with you.

Allow yourself, now, to become aware of an impression of your Beloved. There is nothing you need to do, nothing you need to know. Simply allow whatever impression drops into your awareness to be there. You can interpret or analyze it later. Allow your heart and mind to fill with an awareness of the Beloved. Simply be open to whatever comes.

In a way that makes sense to you, give yourself permission to receive the love this being holds for you. If part of you feels that you don't deserve the love of this being, allow that part to become filled with an awareness of the unconditional, complete acceptance the Beloved brings to you. Later, you can work with any part of yourself that wants to push away the experience. For now, just let in the Beloved in whatever ways you are able to do at this time.

Know that your relationship to the Beloved is personal and unique. Take a few moments to commune with this being and simply allow yourself to receive whatever is available to you at this time. You may have a dialogue with the Beloved . . . or you may simply feel yourself filled with the love available to you and need nothing more right now . . . or you may have some other awareness I don't even know how to name.

Just let in whatever is available now.

When you are ready, take a few moments to review your experience and then bring yourself back to an everyday state of consciousness. Be sure to come back slowly and gently, giving yourself plenty of time to shift gears, and bring with you whatever remaining sense of connection to the Beloved you want to carry with you into your daily activities.

There's No Limit . . .

In a multidimensional world, you are never alone. Help is always at hand. Remember to ask and, then, remember to watch and listen. Allow yourself to respond to intuitive promptings that invite you through the very doors that lead to the fulfillment of the outcomes you seek to achieve.

The ideas we have touched on in this chapter barely scratch the surface of how your intuition can help you access the resources, inspiration, and other benefits of nonlocal reality. For example, the oracular realm of accessing nonlocal reality—by using tools such as tarot cards, the *I Ching*, the Runes, and other ways of translating intuitive awareness—offers another useful framework. Living intuitively means using whatever approaches allow you to translate nonlocal dimensions into conscious awareness. It also means learning how to evaluate your level of accuracy and skill in any given approach.

How to learn to use your intuition, trust it, and allow it to pervade day-to-day awareness and activities is an individual undertaking that draws on your deepest sources of creativity and willingness to access nonlocal ways of knowing. Throughout the process, it helps to have others available with whom you can share your experience and get a reality check—people who can support your learning as well as point out when you are on a flight of fancy or indulging in wishful thinking.

In the final chapter, we will weave together the concepts we've explored throughout the book, giving special attention to rituals and other means of fostering a sense of the sacred in everyday life.

Chapter 11

LIVING CONSCIOUSLY

Putting It All Together

*The winds of grace blow all the time. All we have to
do is set our sails.*

—Ramakrishna

Life is an astonishingly creative endeavor. Each moment of every day offers new opportunities to make choices that either enhance or diminish our sense of wholeness and connection. As we have seen, the fluid, shifting world of nonlocal possibilities constantly weaves itself into our seemingly solid world of time and space. Invisible subatomic particles dance and spin, but we see only solid forms. Television and radio waves move unseen through our bodies, even as we see and hear the images and sounds they produce. Probabilities array themselves in patterns of possibility, even as our five senses tell us that reality unfolds in a linear sequence of moments, characterized by fixed laws of cause and effect. Outside our usual conscious awareness, the invisible and visible worlds dynamically interact to create the context within which our thoughts, feelings, actions, and intentions coalesce to shape our personal realities.

In this concluding part of our journey together, we will pay particular attention to ways in which we can honor the interplay of non-physical realities and the material world, and how we can promote and support an experience of the sacred in everything we do. We have explored how to enhance a sense of psychological wholeness by making intention and mindfulness integral parts of everyday living. We now turn to the use of symbols and ritual as a means of honoring the sacred.

The Language of Symbols

You've no doubt heard the saying, "a picture is worth a thousand words." In weaving together an awareness of invisible and visible realities, a symbol speaks volumes. Because symbols carry archetypal *meanings* rather than specific content, they speak to us at deep levels—deeper than the conscious mind can recognize. Some symbols are said to have power and energy inherent in them that can affect our physical state of being. For example, drawing mandalas, which are circles filled with symbols, can provide a profound experience of internal processes. Conversely, gazing at mandalas and the symbols they contain can elicit feelings and other awarenesses that emerge from deep sources of wisdom. The Tibetan symbol for the sacred word *Om*—which resembles an elaborately drawn number three—conveys a centering quality to those who resonate with it. The same is said to be true of the sound of certain sacred words, the *Om* among them.

When I was a child, my grandmother taught me a meditation that focused on symbols grounded in the work of the Swiss psychiatrist, Carl Jung. Once a day for nine months, I visualized three separate symbols for three minutes each: a circle with a dot in the center, a plus sign, and an equilateral triangle pointing up. The symbols themselves were supposed to convey a centering, balancing quality. While I was too young to understand the meaning behind the meditation, I did experience how focusing on the symbols quieted my mind and settled me inside, in spite of the many times I had to struggle to pay attention through the total of nine minutes that seemed to be hours long.

When I did the same nine-month meditation as a young adult, I found that my personal associations to the symbols created the same centered experience. Was it the power of the symbols themselves that created a shift in my internal experience? Was it my belief in the effect my grandmother told me they would have? Or was it the simple fact of settling into a focused meditation? I still don't know. What I *do* know is that I have continued the practice of focusing on sacred symbols as a kind of meditation that brings me into a state of enhanced internal balance and well-being and that I value this form of honoring and celebrating the sacred.

Throughout human history, countless symbols have arisen to express our collective connection to that which is hidden and sacred. Some symbols represent both positive and negative meanings, depending on our personal associations to them or those of our culture. For example, the swastika—a modern symbol of Nazi atrocities—was, at a much earlier time, an ancient, sacred symbol in Buddhism. The image of a coiled snake, its head rising up, symbolizes a source of fear and potential danger for some people; for others, it brings to mind the serpent of wisdom, ready to rise into conscious awareness, or the healing power of the caduceus in medicine.

And so, while symbols may have universal meanings, they also have deeply personal, idiosyncratic messages to convey. I recall a colleague's story of a client who reported a dream in which an old coin played a central role. When my colleague had her client explore the message the coin held for her, an unanticipated awareness emerged. Assuming at first that the coin represented her money worries, she immersed herself in its image and was surprised to see it become a mandala, whose message revealed a deep creative urge in her. By opening herself to the unique meaning of the coin *for her*, she was able to respond by developing an avocation as an artisan working in jewelry.

It is not unusual for symbols to emerge in unexpected ways. A friend lit a candle to honor the passing of a loved one who had struggled long and hard before dying. As the candle burned down, the glass container holding it shattered. To my friend, the shattered container symbolized and affirmed his loved one's release from suffering. This interpretation had deep meaning for him and, in a way only he truly understood, conveyed profound comfort. Another person might have interpreted the experience differently. A close friend gave me a small piece of rose quartz to symbolize our shared interest in the outer reaches of consciousness and in altered states. Whenever I enter an experience that expands or deepens my own consciousness, I hold the stone as a symbol of my friend's continuing presence and support. I also wear a Tibetan healing bracelet as a symbol to remind me of the presence of non-Western influences in my life.

One of my colleagues concentrates regularly on the image of a goddess, a symbol of the empowering presence of the divine feminine in her daily life. By attuning to this symbol each day, she strengthens her sense of connection and well-being and nourishes her experience of psychological wholeness as a centered and confident woman in the world.

As I move through the editing process for this second edition, I'm aware that my emphasis on psychological wholeness in this book has shifted somewhat over the years. At this point, I am more focused on what I can only call "embodied presence", which includes the felt-sense of my physical experience, my embodied state of being, along with a sense of psychological and spiritual well-being. When working with symbols these days, I am most likely to begin with the experience of how the symbol affects my embodied experience—my physical sensations—and then include my more psychologically-oriented responses.

Symbols can come in the form of objects, images, events, people, unexpected moments—anything that translates into tangible meaning and experience for you. Symbols also carry energy. They speak to us outside our conscious awareness and affect the quality of our psychological and physical sense of ourselves. For this reason the kinds of symbols with which we surround ourselves matter. If you look around and your eyes rest upon symbols that lift your spirits, then you are nourishing yourself. If instead you see symbols that carry negative meanings, then you are feeding yourself toxic messages that diminish your sense of well-being. So, it's important to give yourself permission to take symbols seriously and use them to promote a sense of connection and meaning in your daily life.

MAKE IT REAL
EXPERIMENT #1:
Enhancing Your Awareness of Symbols

- In this experiment, find three symbols that convey qualities that make you feel good. You might come across a special stone or leaf that speaks to you in a meaningful way. You may discover music that evokes in you the mystery of life. There might be a small object—a doll, figurine, or some other memento—that brings a smile to your face because it reminds you of something delightful. Perhaps you have a special photograph that portrays a particularly satisfying quality of life. For example, I often look at a photograph of a hot air balloon floating high in an early dawn sky. Each time I see it, I think of possibility and new beginnings and my sense of hope and optimism is nourished.

- As always, there are no right or wrong choices in finding symbols that have meaning for you. Simply look for symbols that convey wholeness and a sense of connection.

- Then experiment with what happens when you pay attention to the symbols, when you look at them frequently and remember they are there. Notice the state of mind they create in you and how your body feels when you focus your attention on them. What kinds of feelings do you experience when you connect with your symbols? Simply become aware of the power the symbols have to shift your mood and point of view. Pay particular attention to those symbols that lift your spirits, for they are resources to which you can turn whenever you need some nourishing psychological and spiritual food.

- If and when a symbol no longer holds meaning for you, let it go and discover a new one.

GUIDED MEDITATION #1:
Sacred Symbols

For this meditation, choose a sacred symbol and hold it in your mind's eye for ten minutes. It can be any symbol you want. The only requirement is that it deepens your internal sense of wholeness, connection, and well-being.

Begin by settling into a place where you can be comfortable, alert, and remain undisturbed for ten minutes. Take a few moments to settle yourself at the bottom of the breath, in the still point between the outbreath and the next in-breath.

Now, bring to mind the symbol you have chosen as the object of your meditation. If you do not visualize easily, simply sense, imagine, pretend, or draw the image in your mind. Ask yourself, If I could visualize this symbol, what would I see?

Whenever you find your mind wandering, simply bring it back to an awareness of the symbol.

After about five minutes become the symbol itself, tap into its qualities and experience them first-hand. Pay particular attention to how your body feels when you connect with the energy inherent in the symbol.

Continue until the ten minutes have elapsed or until you feel a natural end to your meditation. Before you come all the way back, spend a moment or two with the image of the symbol in your mind.

You can return to the symbol as many times as you want and use it as long as it holds energy and interest for you. If and when it feels dull, lifeless, or a chore to visualize, let it go and find a new symbol for your meditation.

Rituals: Honoring the Sacred

Rituals bring life to intention. As with symbols, rituals convey meaning that is beyond words and offer a way for us to make manifest that which exists in invisible realms of consciousness. Engaging in ritual brings a greater awareness to the values, choices, and qualities that shape our daily lives and our relationship to the world around us.

As we explore the role of ritual in acknowledging and celebrating the sacred, and in manifesting our intentions, I want to make a distinction between conscious and unconscious rituals. Ritual pervades our everyday activities. Most of us have a set time we begin the workday and have a ritual for getting ready: this task comes before that one, this shoe goes on first. These are the routinized activities which, if interrupted, create discomfort or bring our habitual rituals into conscious awareness.

The rituals we will explore here are different. They represent conscious, creative actions that symbolically represent or express our intentions, beliefs, and relationship to the sacred. The form of a ritual may be simple or profoundly complex and deep. There are no limits to what rituals can involve, except those imposed by ourselves.

In the meditation group to which I belong, ritual plays a major role. We light candles to begin our gathering, ring bells, share readings, and bring sacred objects to our circle. These activities serve to make more conscious and concrete the mindful nature of our gathering.

In my office, I have a candle especially for rituals acknowledging loss. If a client has suffered a loss and wants to acknowledge it symbolically and ritually, lighting the candle mindfully—often with a heartfelt comment or internal statement—honors who or what has been lost.

When we create rituals to honor the sacred or to celebrate wholeness in any of its expressions, we draw on levels of meaning we sometimes ignore in our more humdrum, everyday routines. A primary quality of engaging in ritual is that it is performed with a full awareness of its meaning—*every time we do it.* That's the power of rituals: they instill vitality to what might otherwise become rote or habitual. For example, when we light candles or incense, part of ritual awareness is to remind ourselves of the *reason* we do so, the *meaning* behind our actions.

Rituals can also serve as reminders of our relationship to oneness, to the life that connects us all. I developed a ritual that utilized a habit intrinsic to my work as a therapist: one of the tasks I must do is keep an eye on the passage of time. Over the years I have trained myself to notice when the clock shows matching numbers, such as 11:11, 2:22, and so on. Whenever I see these kinds of numbers, part of my mind acknowledges my place in the larger scheme of things, that I am a drop of water within a vast ocean. Many times a day, this ritual re-centers me in an experience of wholeness and reminds me that I am part of something much greater than my individual self.

Any activity done routinely and repetitively can become the springboard to a ritual that reconnects you to the sacred as you go through your day. Before meals, for example, you can decide to use the act of preparing to eat as a time when you reflect on and acknowledge your place within a larger whole. Some people pray or use affirmations or ritual mantras before meals to acknowledge their gratitude for the food and for all the people and elements involved in bringing the food to them. Others hold hands around the table before beginning and offer silent thanks for the gift of food.

Rituals can also be used to make significant life passages in a sacred way. For example, a group of friends had to give up a meeting space they had used for years. Before moving out, the group held a ritual, a ceremony of thanks and farewell. Using sage and a candle, they went to all corners of the large room and said goodbye. Each person thanked the space for the experiences it had sheltered and contained, and then reminisced about an important breakthrough or realization that had emerged within those walls. When all were finished, the group sang a song together and then blew out the candle. Extinguishing the candle symbolically represented closing down their relationship with the space—completing their time with it and releasing it with joy to its next occupants.

Rituals can utilize water, plants, soil, sacred objects, flowers, candles, incense, sage—absolutely any material object, substance, or life form that has meaning for you. Recently I visited a small church in New Mexico called *Chimayó*. The church is known as the "Lourdes of the West," because healing miracles have been documented there. Instead of water, the miracles at *Chimayó* come from special soil found in a particular part of the chapel. People come from all over the world to touch the soil, to put some of it on wounds or disabilities, or to bless themselves by putting a dab of soil on their foreheads. The chapel in which the soil is found is filled with candles and holy pictures to which the faithful turn as they enter and leave. All done in silence, the ritual quality of the experience is profound and needs no words to accompany it.

A ritual is its own work of art, whether it involves one person or many, one candle or a whole array of objects. Putting together a ritual is itself a creative act that invites you to consider the meaning behind the actions you want to include. The process of creating rituals becomes a meditation on intention—on symbolically manifesting the essence of that which you seek to express or achieve.

Rituals of Joy

Because my grandmother had a strong Puritan background, she tended to take life, and herself, quite seriously. In my spiritual training with her, one element that was missing was laughter. It took me many years to discover how a sense of psychological wholeness automatically brings with it a sense of humor and delight, and an appreciation of play in both everyday life and the realms of the sacred. I also discovered *ecstasy*, the capacity to become intoxicated with joy in the presence of the sacred.

As you think about creating rituals, keep joy, laughter, and playfulness in mind. Movement, dance, drumming, and singing all provide ways of experiencing delight in an embodied way. In Sufi dancing, the ritual of twirling in dynamic, rhythmic patterns transports the dancer into an altered state in which the presence of the divine is experienced. Drumming while moving in a circle dance offers a ritualized opportunity for communion with the sacred as well as the companions in the dance. Singing sacred songs invites joy to be expressed through sound.

In the exercises that follow, let your imagination guide

you in finding which elements you want to include in creating rituals that nurture your experience of psychological wholeness and support your sense of connection within a larger context of being.

MAKE IT REAL EXPERIMENT #2:
Creating Rituals

This experiment invites you to begin making rituals part of your celebration of the sacred and as a way to manifest your intentions and choices in symbolic form.

- Identify an intention you've made that is important to you at this time. It may be an intention that deals with how you want to be in the world or something you want to accomplish. Write down the intention and keep it nearby.

- Place a votive or tea candle in a glass container and find a place where you can sit quietly, undisturbed, for a few minutes. Gather your awareness and focus on your intention. Notice how much you want this intention to manifest in your life.

- Now light the candle and say your intention out loud. Know that the candle's flame empowers the intention, bringing it to life even more and supporting its eventual realization. Feel the resonating tone of your intention as you gaze softly at the candle. Spend a few minutes being aware of your wish to have the intention become actual.

- When you feel finished, express your gratitude for the power the ritual adds to fulfilling your wish, to bringing about the manifestation of your intention in your everyday life. At this point, you can either blow out the candle or allow it to burn all the way down, symbolically continuing to add power to your intention as it does so.

- As you complete the ritual, become aware of how your actions have added a deeper sense of substance to your way of being in the world.

Over time, expand your use of rituals. Remember, there is no limit to the kinds of rituals you can create. As you make rituals part of your ongoing use of intentions and mindful living, notice how they empower your experience of making choices in the course of everyday living.

EXPERIMENT #3:
Bath Ritual for Birthdays

The following ritual came into my life as a birthday gift from a friend. Since then, I have heard it described in a variety of ways. What follows is an adaptation and compilation of the versions I have been told. The ritual itself is intended to release suffering—either from past experiences or current ones—freeing you to engage your present-day life more fully. This is the long version of the ritual. Feel free to adapt it in any way that makes sense to you.

Before you begin, you will need to gather some items: four flowers of any kind, four new candles of any kind you like—just make sure they will burn for a couple of hours—bubble bath, and a bowl of water in which to float the flowers. Before you begin, the flowers need to be cut from their stems so that you have the blossoms only.

The ritual may be done alone or with a circle of friends. Many people choose to do the beginning and the end of the ritual with clothing on, becoming naked only during the bath itself. Other people prefer to wear a bathing suit in the tub if friends are present and they are uncomfortable being naked together. Still others choose to conduct the entire ritual naked, from start to finish. Do whatever is most comfortable for you. You or someone else needs to run the bath and fill it with bubbles right before you begin the ritual, so that the water will stay warm enough until you get in it.

You will also need to create four wishes, affirmations, and/or intentions that reflect desired goals or developments you seek in the coming year. For example, your list might include the following categories:

- Commitments or intentions for the coming year, or for longer or shorter periods of time;

- Affirmations about your capacity/desire/intention to express more of your whole self in the coming year;

- Wishes for your life path, drawing on the following statement or one you create yourself: *If there were a guarantee of success, and I had no fear about the outcome, I can see my life path unfolding in the following way* [describe here what you would like to happen].

- Request help, guidance, or any other kind of support you would like to receive along the way.

- Begin by cutting the flowers and floating them in a bowl of water. The flowers represent a sacrifice—they will absorb your suffering once you are in the bath. For now, they are honored by floating in the bowl during the beginning of the ritual.

- If friends are present, ask them to gather in a circle with you, the flowers, and the candles at the center.

- Light a candle before reading each of your four commitments, intentions, affirmations, and/or wishes. If you are with a group, take a moment to look at each person present to acknowledge his or her presence as a witness to what you seek in the coming year. If you are alone, gaze at the candle and notice how you feel as you consider the meaning of what you have just read.

- After lighting each candle, either have a friend take it to the bathroom and place it on the side of the tub where it is secure and there is no danger of fire, or do so yourself before you go on to the next step.

- When you feel ready, hold up the bowl of flowers and thank them for the service they are going to provide you. Then take them to the tub and float them on the surface of the bubble bath.

- Next, get undressed, or not, and enter the tub. If you are with a group, have someone read your list of intentions, affirmations, and wishes. If you are alone, do so yourself. Then, as the group meditates outside the bathroom, give your attention to releasing all the suffering you have experienced during your life. Review your life and imagine that all the suffering you have experienced flows spontaneously out of you and is absorbed by the flowers. Stay with the process until you sense that it is finished.

- When you are ready, gather the flowers into the bowl. Either dry and dress yourself or allow your group to help you. Put the candles in the room where you started and, along with the bowl of flowers, gather again in a circle to meditate on your experience. This time sit in the circle itself instead of in the center. If you are alone, sit in front of the candle. Place the bowl of flowers near the candle so you can see them.

- When you feel finished, blow out the candles and bring this phase of the ritual to a close.

The ritual is completed the next day, or later if you

choose, when you take the flowers back to nature and leave them under a tree or some other place where they—and your old suffering—become nourishment for new growth.

The Power of Sacred Objects

A sacred object can be absolutely *anything* that speaks to you of the mystery of life, of meaning and purpose, of the interplay of visible and invisible worlds. Sacred objects can come from nature, in the form of stones, feathers, plants, shells, or wood, and so on, or they can be created by artisans in the form of jewelry, talismans, fetishes. Part of the wonder of discovering objects that encompass a sense of the sacred is the sometimes-unexpected qualities they convey and the strange way they may appear in your life at exactly the right moment, even when you don't realize you are seeking them. It is impossible for me to explain why this happens, though I strongly suspect it has something to do with synchronicity. In my experience, synchronistic coincidences can bring people and objects together in ways that are powerfully alive and meaningful but that may not make sense until later.

I remember a time when I was shopping for a special birthday gift for a friend. My eye fell on a carved, polished stone embedded with crystal and fossils that reminded me of the beautiful interplay of light and shadow. The moment I saw it, I knew it would be just the right gift for my friend. When I took it in my hand, though, everything shifted. I realized that this stone was for me, and I had a vivid impression of it sitting on my writing desk near my computer. In the meantime, I remained open to finding the right gift for my friend. As it happened, another stone captivated my attention and it turned out to be the perfect gift for the special birthday my friend was celebrating that year.

Having learned to listen to the kind of intuitive awareness that let me know the first stone was mine, I accepted the invitation to take it home. Now, as then, whenever my eyes fall on this beautiful, natural work of art, I am inspired anew by an immediate sense of wholeness and appreciation of the interplay of light and shadow. When my writing flows less easily than usual, contemplating the stone centers me and refreshes my intention to keep writing anyway.

Carrying sacred objects with us can be a powerful way to stay connected to a sense of wholeness. I have a friend who travels with a cache of sacred objects. Whenever she arrives at her destination, the first thing she does is set up an altar. Another friend takes a picture of his spiritual teacher wherever he goes, so he can look at it whenever he wants.

Choosing sacred objects involves intention, an open heart, synchronicity, and a willingness to respond when the object appears. It may be more appropriate to say that sacred objects *find us* rather than the other way around. Within this context, we can create an intention that we will discover the sacred objects we seek, and that seek us, at whatever time is right. There can be no demand; instead, our intention *invites* these special objects into our lives.

Because sacred objects find us, they can also sometimes surprise us by letting us know if and when they are ready to move on—for example, when synchronicity intervenes to carry them to the next person who needs them. For this reason, you may find that there will be times when pieces you care a great deal about seem to shout at you to give them to a particular person. If you can't bear to part with the object on a permanent basis, you might see what happens if you release it to the other person on loan. At other times, you may discover, to your initial dismay, that you have lost a sacred object. Whenever this happens to me, I assume that somewhere in the larger scheme of things, it was time for the object to move on—and it did so in spite of my inability to recognize that I needed to release it. This doesn't happen often, but when it does, it is unmistakable and serves to remind us that we don't really "own" anything.

You can also share sacred objects with people you love or for whom you feel a special kinship. You might give each other an object you care about, as a way of honoring the sacred nature of your relationship. A friend of mine has loaned me a beautiful *thanka*—a Tibetan Buddhist wall hanging depicting a sacred theme. I'll keep it until I sense it is time to send it back. Just having it in my space reminds me of the trust and sharing I have enjoyed with this friend over many years. Other friends have certain objects they carry regularly to meditation meetings or gatherings. Over time, these objects become an integral part of the gatherings themselves, their beauty and essence shared with everyone present, and they can become infused with the energy of the group, even though they "belong" to one person in particular.

MAKE IT REAL EXPERIMENT #4:
Carrying the Sacred with You

Choose a small sacred object and carry it with you as often as possible. For example, some people carry small crystals or stones as sacred objects; others carry pictures of spiritual teachers. Still others make sure they have inspirational reading with them wherever they go. If you find yourself in a stressful situation, hold or look at your sacred object and notice what happens. You may find that you can rediscover a sense of connection and ease when you touch your sacred object and the qualities it conveys to you.

GUIDED MEDITATION #2:

Inviting Sacred Objects to Find You

For this meditation, create an intention that you are willing to open yourself to whatever sacred objects exert a pull on you at this time. There is no need to have a specific idea of the kind of sacred object you would like to discover, but if you do have something in mind, that's fine, too.

To begin, take a moment to sit down and settle, focusing your attention on the still point between breaths. Take a few moments simply to be present in the gap between the breaths and allow yourself to enjoy it in whatever way is natural for you right now.

Now focus your attention in the center of your heart. Imagine an eternal flame burning brightly there and that you are seated in front of the flame in the center of your heart. Notice the warmth from the flame and allow it to fill you with a sense of comfort, connection, or any other quality that comes into your awareness.

Create in your heart an intention that you are willing to receive whatever sacred object, or objects will enhance your sense of wholeness and connectedness at this time. In essence, you are sending a message into the larger collective that expresses your willingness to be open to whatever sacred objects find their way to you as a result of your invitation.

Take a few moments to be aware of having sent your intention into the larger collective arena. There is nothing else to do. Now become aware again of where you are, in the center of your heart, in front of the flame. Take whatever time you'd like simply to be present with the flame. Allow it to warm you in a way that emerges spontaneously.

When you feel ready, bring yourself back to your everyday awareness with the full expectation that any sacred objects you are ready to receive will find their way to you at exactly the right time and in precisely the right ways.

Keeping It Grounded: Creating Sacred Spaces

When we live a life characterized by intention and mindfulness, a natural extension of these qualities is the urge to create *sacred space* wherever we find ourselves. The quality of the space we create around ourselves is a material reflection of the attention we give to our presence in the world, and it can greatly affect the quality of daily life.

Sacred space reflects both an attitude and an environment. It may encompass anyplace at all, private or public—home, work, garden, car, bus, restaurant, park, mountains, seashore, desert. *We make a space sacred when we enter it mindfully and treat it with honor and respect.* When we acknowledge that the sacred pervades everything, all the time, then our movements in the physical world provide a moment-by-moment opportunity to affirm that we live, move, and have our being within the constant embrace of the sacred.

One of the most fundamental and familiar expressions of sacred space is found in places of worship. Indoors or out, these spaces *are* sacred. When we enter, we are transported into a state of mind that automatically orients us toward an awareness of the mystery of life. We sense the presence of invisible realms reaching out to touch us lovingly and reverently, and we feel invited to reach out ourselves.

Imagine how it might affect your daily life if these qualities of sacred space were present wherever you found yourself. What would it be like to enter your home and experience a sense of being enfolded in a space that reflects your connection with the larger context that contains you? When your home reflects your conscious attention to what surrounds you, this sacred space becomes not only a safe haven but also an ongoing celebration of living mindfully. Since each of us creates a home that reflects our individuality, the sacred space that emerges around us also reflects our unique relationship to our larger context.

For example, some people prefer clear surfaces that convey spaciousness and simplicity. Others find that surrounding themselves with numerous pleasing objects creates a sense of well-being and comfort. Still others fill their homes with plants and other elements of the natural world as a way of affirming and experiencing their connection with our planet. There is no "right way" to create sacred space. Rather, the material aspects of it emerge as a natural extension of your uniqueness, your relationship with spiritual realities, and your personal understanding of your place within the whole.

Part of creating sacred space is living mindfully. We honor any space in which we find ourselves whenever we allow ourselves to *be* there, consciously and with full awareness. For example, in the simple act of putting our clothes away, we have an opportunity to express gratitude for having clothing. Touching the fabric, folding it or hanging it up, opening a drawer or closet—each action is an opportunity to be present in a meditative moment.

You can also take a moment to feel gratitude for all the people and resources that went into creating the many objects that are part of your life. Everything we have in our lives is present to us because of the efforts and activities of countless people we will never know and countless resources used on our behalf. People who work in the factories that create the objects in our homes; gasoline, electricity, and other resources that make it possible to bring these objects to completion and deliver them to us. Notice your experience when you include all the elements that go into making the conveniences and necessities of your life possible.

The same is true when we use dishes, silverware, pots and pans, scissors, irons and ironing boards, computers and paper: all offer opportunities to take the time to honor the many appliances, gadgets, and other objects that serve us on a daily basis. Putting them back where they belong and making sure they are clean brings a quality of care to our living space that speaks directly to the sacred in life. The attitude we bring to the process is part of what elicits a sense of the sacred. If you come to the task with irritation or resentment, you may be less conscious of your actions, handling objects more roughly than you would like or moving through chores without feeling a sense of connection with how you seek to honor the space in which you live. If you find you feel irritated, take a moment to center yourself. Accept that you are in a bad mood and make a conscious decision to be mindfully present with whatever it is you choose to do. When you bring respect, honor, and gratitude to tasks, you automatically instill in your home the qualities that make it a sacred space.

As I say this, sitting in my home office where I do my writing, I notice the various stacks of papers and "stuff" that peek out from under the desk and around the bookcase. These pockets of messiness within my usually ordered environment remind me of a lesson taught by a spiritual community in Findhorn, Scotland. At Findhorn, there is always a natural space outdoors that remains uncultivated in honor of the nature spirits. It is a space deliberately left untouched by human intervention or intrusion. I experience the piles of papers in my office in the same way. It is the area where my disarray has some expression, where I can let loose and allow my creative self to express some chaos and freedom.

Creating a sacred space isn't just about neatness and mindfulness. For some people, striving for neatness becomes a neurotic way they hold themselves and their world together, and they lose the ease and comfort conveyed by the qualities that pervade sacred space. What matters here is that you create a space that welcomes you, a space within which you are comfortable and feel held, a space that you appreciate and take care to keep in a condition that speaks most directly to you of an experience of mindful awareness.

You don't need a lot of money to create sacred space. All it takes is attention to the small things and a commitment to care for whatever fills your space. For example, giving each item in your home a place where it belongs when not in use goes a long way to creating clear surfaces, a sense of space, a lack of clutter. Finding objects that speak to your own sense of connection to the sacred and placing them around your home gives your eye a meaningful place to rest its gaze. If you can't afford a bouquet of flowers, a single one will do. If you can't afford lot of candles, just one can change the atmosphere and soften it.

For example, I have an altar in my living room in the area where I sit and meditate each morning. At the moment, the altar is a small cardboard box covered with a piece of fabric. While I would prefer a wooden table, I haven't yet found one that speaks to me. As I mentioned earlier, sacred objects are funny that way. They find you, and my altar hasn't found me yet. In the meantime, the box is as important a part of my sacred space as a wooden table may someday be.

As I edit this chapter, these many years later, my eyes fall on the beautiful wooden altar that did, indeed, find its way into my life, as a gift from dear friends. In reading the above paragraphs, I was reminded of the sweet cardboard box that served as my altar for all that time and find myself feeling deep gratitude for the time it played that role in my life.

Extending sacred space beyond your home and places of worship offers an opportunity to carry a mindful attitude and sense of connection with you wherever you go. For example, if you work outside your home, ask yourself what would bring the quality of the sacred into your workspace or work experience. Again, the solution needn't be elaborate. One sacred object, a photograph, or a flower may be all you need to remind yourself that you inhabit sacred space everywhere you are.

Another means to create sacred space in a dynamic, practical, and powerfully positive way is to use Feng Shui—an Asian approach to understanding and maximizing the flow of constructive energy in homes, office buildings, or any other kind of space used for living, working, and worshipping. Through this approach, you can unblock obstacles to your personal and professional development, enhance health and relationships, and generally create an environment that is conducive to a greater sense of wholeness and well-being. You can learn to do Feng Shui yourself or consult with one of the many professionals who offer both intuitive and traditional approaches to creating sacred space.

Sacred space surrounds us at every moment. We cannot *not* be enfolded by its presence. We acknowledge that fact in the ways we relate to our surroundings, in how we hold awareness of the sacred in our minds and hearts. When we enter a space and remember that it is made of both visible and invisible elements, that it is one part of a rich tapestry of wholeness, we honor the sacred inherent in it. When we bring gratitude into a space, we honor its sacred nature. When we remember that the sacred is in everything around us, our recollection honors it automatically.

EXPERIMENT #5:
Creating Your Sacred Space at Home

An important element of this experiment is to create the intention that you will invite a greater sense of the sacred into your living space by becoming more mindful of what you bring into your space and how you treat the things you have. Remember that there is no *right* way to create a sacred space. What counts is the attitude you bring to your space and the quality of experience it evokes in you.

- To begin, take a look around your living space and notice the state of mind, mood, and body created by how you have organized and decorated the space.

- Then, ask yourself what you might do to enhance a sense of the sacred. For example:
    - Do you have an altar on which you can place your sacred objects?
    - Is there a place where flowers would create a calming, inspiring mood?
    - Would a candle enhance the quality of your sacred space?
    - Are there paintings, prints, or objects that would inspire you and add to your sense of the sacred?

- Does each object in your home have a place where it belongs when not in use? How does it feel to you to imagine putting everything in its place?

- Remember to go about this project a little at a time and allow yourself to experiment with different possibilities. Pay special attention to how you feel when you look at your space and see relatively uncluttered surfaces, or how you feel when you consciously create areas where objects are displayed in ways that bring comfort to you.

As with all the experiments, adapt this one to fit your own needs, taste, and sensibilities. There are no right or wrong answers. What is important is whatever allows you to enhance your experience of acknowledging and honoring the sacred in your living space.

EXPERIMENT #6:
Making Your Workplace Sacred

Here, as with your home, explore ways in which you can invite a sense of the sacred more actively into your workspace. Doing so may mean simply having a sacred object within sight or a special plant that represents the sacred in a way that is meaningful to you. Be creative and remember that your relationship with the sacred is utterly personal and unique to *you*.

EXPERIMENT #7:
Acknowledging the Sacred All Around You

Let's expand on the idea of creating sacred space in your home, office, or wherever you spend time. This experiment asks you to create an intention that you will begin to acknowledge more actively the sacred that is around you all the time. For example, when you see an insect or a bird, take a moment to acknowledge the miracle of that life form, of the sacred expressing itself in that way. When you walk under a tree, take a moment to recognize what the tree adds to the sacred space around you—the branches leaves, the trunk and root system, the beauty it offers as one of its gifts. When you walk, acknowledge the presence of gravity, as it allows you to stay connected to the earth and that it is part of the sacred space that enfolds you.

Allow yourself to develop a habit of recognizing and acknowledging the sacred in the space all around you. Notice how gratitude is a constant companion of this recognition. Allow yourself to become aware of other feelings or states of mind and body that arise automatically when you focus on the sacred quality of life.

Honoring the Sacred in Yourself and Others

So far, we've explored how to acknowledge and express the sacred in daily life, at home and at work. Of equal importance is remembering that we—as a bodymind—are also an expression of the sacred, of the mystery of life. Many of us take our bodies for granted, not consciously realizing the tremendous miracle they represent. Being present in your body, tending to it, taking care of its needs are all ways to extend an awareness of the sacred into daily life and to deepen a sense of connection to that which truly is mysterious.

Here the focus is on rituals that honor your body and its relation to the sacred. When you begin your day, for instance, what are the rituals and activities that you engage in to take care of your body and prepare yourself for the activities that await you? Do you take time to really notice and acknowledge your body, to thank it for the miracle it represents? Bathing or showering are times when ritual and mindful awareness can focus especially on your body and your relationship to it. Brushing your teeth, combing your hair, shaving, or putting on makeup can all be carried out as a ritual that allows you to give your body your full attention and respect. Exercise, stretching, and yoga add to the ways you can honor your body and acknowledge its irreplaceable contribution to your life and well-being.

Another powerful expression of the sacred in your body is your sexuality. How you honor and engage this dynamic aspect of your being *matters*. Some traditions teach tantric practices, which involve engaging in sexual activity as a form of meditation. Being mindful during sex or masturbation—being present in your genitals or anyplace else in your body that arouses sensuality or sexual pleasure—allows you to bring intention, choice, and awareness into your experience. Enhancing your level of comfort with your own sexuality offers yet another means of celebrating your body and the sacred life expressing in and through it.

As important as how you honor yourself is how you honor others, body and soul. If you have children, pay attention to the awareness you bring to the daily chores of caring for them. Focus on the ways your hands touch their bodies, paying special attention to the quality of your touch. Do you reach out softly and gently with reassurance, or do you grab, yank, poke, or barely make contact? In other words, are you mindfully present when you touch your children?

With a lover, there are many opportunities to honor the sacred in the other. The body your lover brings to you is no less a miracle than your own. To engage lovemaking with tenderness and respect extends your awareness of the sacred in both of you. Developing rituals of shared pleasuring can give each of you a chance to deepen a sense of connection and intimacy.

MAKE IT REAL EXPERIMENT #8:
Experiencing Your Body as Sacred

- This experiment invites you to become increasingly aware of the fact that your body is nothing short of a miracle, a true mystery. For this ritual, you will need a mirror—preferably a full-length one, but any large size will do—and a candle. Choose any kind of candle that evokes in you a sense of the sacred.

- With lights on, take a few moments to look at yourself in the mirror, with your clothes on. Notice how you are dressed and how you experience yourself as you look at your body from all sides. Be sure to allow any mixed feelings, and simply be aware of what you observe and feel in response to taking this time to really look at yourself.

- Next, take off your clothes and look at your naked body. For some people, this is an uncomfortable experience, so notice if this is true for you. If you are embarrassed to look at yourself naked, ask yourself where you learned to feel this way about your body. There is nothing else to do here. Just look at your body and bring to mind the incredible miracle it represents. It knows how to heal itself, keep you breathing, pump your heart, keep all your organs functioning, and to do countless other activities—most of which you never bring to conscious awareness.

- Now put on a loose, comfortable garment, turn off any lights, and sit down in front of the mirror. Light the candle with an awareness that, as you do so, you are honoring your body and the miracle it represents. Begin at the top of your head and allow your consciousness to move down through your body. Pay attention to every aspect of your physical being, including those parts that please you as well as those that cause you discomfort or difficulty. If you have any physical disabilities that give you mixed feelings, or areas of chronic pain that burden you, send energy to these areas from your open heart—whatever love you can feel, whatever compassion emerges naturally. Be sure to allow mixed feelings, as well. Invite a lived experience of wholeness into your body.

- Close your eyes and take a few moments to allow your awareness to move from the top of your head to the tips of your toes, acknowledging all parts of your body. At each point along the way, give thanks for the service your body gives you.

- Just before you blow out the candle, repeat your intention to become increasingly aware of the sacred nature of your body and your willingness to honor it during daily rituals of self-care. Your intention might look something like this: *It is my intention to become increasingly aware of the miraculous and mysterious nature of my body, and to be mindfully present during my daily rituals of self-care.*

EXPERIMENT #9:
Getting Dressed Mindfully

Getting dressed for the day becomes yet another opportunity to honor your body and to recall the contribution of the many life forms that made it possible for you to clothe yourself. Whether your clothes are new or old, dressy or casual, isn't the issue. What matters is that you care for them mindfully.

- As you choose your clothes and put them on, notice how you do so. Are you gentle and patient with buttons, zippers, sleeves, and pant legs, or are your movements jerky and impatient?

- Do you experience your presence in your hands and fingers as you handle your clothing and put it on your body? Being present in your hands and fingers allows you to connect with your body more directly and deeply.

- How do the clothes feel on your body? Do they fit comfortably and feel good on your skin? Do they smell good and evoke a pleasant feeling in you? Does what you are wearing make you feel good about yourself?

- Next, bring to mind the resources involved in creating the fabric that touches your skin right now. Vegetables, animals, and minerals gave their lives. People extended their efforts to gather the resources and make the fabrics, and to shape them into clothing. Others were involved in shipping and selling the clothes that now are yours.

- Look at yourself in the mirror and spend a few minutes being aware of the opportunity you have each day to honor yourself and others in the mundane but potentially sacred act of getting dressed.

EXPERIMENT #10:
Honoring the Sacred in Others

In the rush and crunch of everyday life, the familiarity of interacting with people we know well, and the impersonality of moving through a sea of strangers, it is easy to forget that *everyone* is a manifest expression of one life—of the sacred in physical form. This experiment invites you to keep this basic premise in mind.

- As you interact with people today, remain aware of how you treat them. In particular, notice how you interact with them physically. Notice the quality of your touch and the ways in which you move your body during these interactions with others. Are your movements smooth and comfortable? Hesitant? Aggressive? Just notice.

- Next, create an intention to become more mindful of the ways in which you interact with others. Choose to increase or reinforce those actions and attitudes that enhance your capacity to honor the sacred in everyone you meet.

Stretching the Envelope

In the deluge of demands and unexpected crises of daily life, it is easy to forget how important it is to nourish your sense of wholeness and your connection to the sacred. For this reason, putting some time aside each day for reading inspirational writing, listening to sacred music, doing yoga or meditation, sitting quietly contemplating a flower, candle, or some other beautiful object is a helpful addition to whatever else you may do to take care of yourself.

At this point, you might protest, "I just can't add one more thing to my day!" I can relate to the feeling. What I think you'll discover is that nourishing your sense of wholeness through inspirational means is so self-reinforcing that it becomes one of the elements in your day you wouldn't think of going without.

Over time, as you weave an awareness of the sacred into your day-to-day activities, your tendency to experience gratitude, connection, meaning, delight, humor, and a deepening feeling of psychological wholeness expands. You find your place in the world and actively affirm and honor it. The choice to be more mindful, to live with intention, is constantly present as part of an ongoing celebration of the sacred—an expression of your full self.

We humans are meaning-making creatures. There is no way around it. Our minds create stories, explanations, fantasies, and dreams. As we have seen, scientific research is beginning to suggest that these internal activities may actually affect the external world, bringing about synchronicities and self-fulfilling prophecies. If this is the case, we might as well focus on that which nourishes us most profoundly. To do this, you need only remember that you are a participant in a world of mystery and magic that is the result of a dynamic interplay between visible and invisible realms, linear and quantum realities.

Within this fluid context of probabilities and limitless potential, we have the opportunity to allow ourselves to receive the fullness that life holds for each of us, the passion and richness of our unique expressions. Within it all, we journey alone, together, and we do so within a multidimensional environment of immediate and available support.

Recommended Readings

Since *Sacred Practices for Conscious Living* was first written, there has been the explosion of the Internet and all the resources that it offers. Because the recommended readings listed here were compiled in the mid-to-late 1990's, I encourage you to look on the Internet for additional resources related to the subjects covered in each chapter of the book. In the years since *Sacred Practices* was first published, there have been countless new books put on the market, as well as many informative youtube clips uploaded, along with the wonder of Google. All of these have emerged as previously unimaginable resources.

I have compiled a list of recommended readings for each chapter. The temptation was to list every book I've read that has nourished my own journey; then I got hold of myself. What I decided to do was include books that are mostly up to date, that address the specific topic of each chapter, or that in some way seem to me particularly relevant and useful. I'm sure I have omitted some excellent books that have shaped my thinking and I apologize in advance for that. Also, many of the books could well have been listed in more than one chapter. For this reason, I recommend that you go to a bookstore and look at the table of contents of any of the books that seem to call out to you. What touches you most might be material unrelated to the chapter in which you find the book listed.

Following is a list of resources that are more general in nature, that contain articles and information relevant to *Sacred Practices* on a continuing basis.

I've had to revise this list because, here in 2015, none of the resources initially offered still exist. Here are some of the resources I currently use regularly for inspiration:

Spirituality and Health Magazine
www.spiritualityandhealth.com
866-485-2026

www.conscious.tv
This is a British on-line interview show that offers conversations about many aspects of spirituality, as well as bringing the sacred into everyday life.

www.batgap.com
Buddha at the Gas Pump is another on-line interview show. Many of the interviews deal with non-duality experiences people have had.

www.youtube.com
Visiting youtube and searching for any subject you may wish to explore more deeply can provide a rich and surprisingly useful source of deepening and learning.

There are many other resources available these days. I encourage you to search on the Internet for those that nourish your particular spiritual orientation and practice. Also, I haven't added a recommended reading list for the new Chapter 1, so I encourage you to look on-line for resources that will offer further support to whatever interests you in that chapter.

INTRODUCTION

Chopra, D. (1995). *The way of the wizard: Twenty spiritual lessons for creating the life you want.* New York: Harmony Books.

Feldman, C., & Kornfield, J. (Eds.) (1991). *Stories of the spirit, stories of the heart: Parables of the spiritual path from around the world.* New York: HarperSanFrancisco.

Keen, S. (1994). *Hymns to an unknown god: Awakening the spirit in everyday life.* New York: Bantam.

Muller, W. (1996). *How, then, shall we live? Four simple questions that reveal the beauty and meaning of our lives.* New York: Bantam.

Wakefield, D. (1996). *Creating from spirit: Living each day as a creative act.* New York: Ballantine.

2. THE SHADOW:
An Invitation to Dynamic Wholeness

Bates, C. (1991). *Pigs eat wolves: Going into partnership with your dark side.* St. Paul, MN: Yes International Publishing.

Bly, R. (1988). *A little book on the human shadow.* San Francisco: Harper.

Dallett, J. O. (1991). *Saturday's child: Encounters with the dark gods.* Toronto: Inner City Books.

Galland, C. (1990). *Longing for Darkness: Tara and the Black Madonna.* New York: Penguin.

Grof, C., & Grof, S. (1990). *The stormy search for the self.* Los Angeles: Tarcher.

Johnson, R. A. (1991). *Owning your own shadow: Understanding the dark side of the psyche.* New York: HarperSanFrancisco.

Joy, B. (1991). *Avalanche: Heretical reflections on the dark and light.* New York: Ballantine.

Keen, S. (1988). *Faces of the enemy: Reflections of the hostile imagination.* New York: Harper & Row.

Markova, D. (1994). *No enemies within.* Emeryville, CA: Conari Press.

Miller, W. A. (1989). *Your golden shadow: Discovering and fulfilling your undeveloped self.* New York: Harper & Row.

Moore, T. (1992). *Care of the soul: A guide for cultivating depth and sacredness in everyday life.* New York: HarperCollins.

O'Kane, F. (1994). *Sacred chaos: Reflections on God's shadow and the dark self.* Toronto: Inner City Books.

Sanford, J. (1981). *Evil: The shadow side of reality.* New York: Crossroads.

Staub, E. (1989). *The roots of evil: The origins of genocide and other group violence.* New York: Cambridge University Press.

Vaughn, F. (1995). *Shadows of the sacred: Seeing through spiritual illusions.* Wheaton, IL: Quest.

3. COMPASSION AND LOVINGKINDNESS:
Living With An Open Heart

Badiner, A. H. (Ed.) (1990). *Dharma Gaia: A harvest of essays in Buddhism and ecology.* Berkeley, CA: Parallax Press.

Borysenko, J. (1990). *Guilt is the teacher, love is the lesson.* New York: Warner.

Borysenko, J. (1993). *Fire in the soul: A new spiritual optimism.* New York: Warner.

Chodron, P. (1994). *Start where you are: A guide to compassionate action.* Boston: Shambhala.

Dalai Lama (1984). *Kindness, clarity, and insight.* Ithaca, NY: Snow Lion Productions.

Dalai Lama (1992). *Worlds in harmony: Dialogues on compassionate action.* Berkeley, CA: Parallax Press.

Easwaran, E. (1989). *The compassionate universe: The power of the individual to heal the environment.* Petaluma, CA: Nilgiri Press.

Eppsteiner, F. (Ed.) (1988). *The path of compassion: Writings on socially engaged Buddhism.* Berkeley, CA: Parallax Press.

Ingram, C. (1990). *In the footsteps of Gandhi.* Berkeley, CA: Parallax Press.

Mitchell, S. (Ed.) (1989). *The enlightened heart: An anthology of sacred poetry.* New York: HarperPerennial.

Parry, D. (1991). *Warriors of the heart.* Cooperstown, NY: Sunstone. (This book is about dynamic conflict resolution, living with an open heart, and becoming a "positive changemaker".)

Salzberg, S. (1995). *Lovingkindness: The revolutionary art of happiness.* Boston: Shambhala.

Shatideva. (1979). *A guide to the bodhisattva's way of life.* Dharamsala, India: Library of Tibetan Works and Archives.

Young-Eisendrath, P. (1996). *The gifts of suffering: Finding insight, compassion and renewal.* Reading, MA: Addison-Wesley.

4. GETTING GROUNDED:
Nurturing Yourself as Bodymind

Anand, M. (1989). *The art of sexual ecstasy: The path of sacred sexuality for Western lovers.* New York: Tarcher/Putnam.

Anand, M. (1995). *The art of sexual magic.* New York: Tarcher/Putnam.

Bonheim, J. (1992). *The serpent and the wave: A guide to movement meditation.* Berkeley, CA: Celestial Arts.

Camphausen, R. C. (1996). *The yoni: Sacred symbol of female creative power.* Rochester, VT: Inner Traditions International.

Carter, M. (1994). *Body reflexology: Healing at your fingertips.* West Nyack, NY: Parker Publishing.

Claire, T. (1995). *Bodywork.* New York: Morrow.

Ellis, G. (1993). *The breath of life: Mastering the breathing techniques of pranayama and qi gong.* North Hollywood, CA: Newcastle.

Hendricks, G. (1995). *Conscious breathing: Breathwork for health, stress reduction, and personal mastery.* New York: Bantam.

Monroe, R. (1971). *Journeys out of the body.* New York: Doubleday.

Nash, B. (1996). *From acupressure to zen: An encyclopedia of natural therapies.* Alameda, CA: Hunter House.

Steinberg, D. (Ed.) (1992). *The erotic impulse: Honoring the sensual self.* Los Angeles: Tarcher.

Sky, M. (1990). *Breathing: Expanding your power and energy.* Santa Fe, NM: Bear Publishing.

Weil, A. (1995). *Spontaneous healing: How to discover and enhance your body's natural ability to maintain and heal itself.* New York: Knopf.

5. PRACTICING MINDFULNESS:
Living Consciously

Findhorn Community. (1975). *The Findhorn garden: Pioneering a new vision of man and nature in cooperation.* New York: Harper.

Goldstein, J., & Kornfield, J. (1987). *Seeking the heart of wisdom: The path of insight meditation.* Boston: Shambhala.

Goleman, D. (1990). *The meditative mind.* New York: Tarcher/Putnam.

Kabat-Zinn, J. (1990). *Full catastrophe living.* New York: Delta.

Kabat-Zinn, J. (1994). *Wherever you go, there you are.* New York: Warner.

Kornfield, J. (1993). *A path with heart: A guide through the perils and promises of spiritual life.* New York: Bantam.

Kornfield, J. & Breiter, P. (1985). *A still forest pool: The insight meditation of Achaan Chah.* Wheaton, IL: The Theosophical Publishing House.

Nhat Hanh, T. (1990). *Present moment, wonderful moment.* Berkeley, CA: Parallax Press.

Nhat Hanh, T. (1991). *Peace is every step.* New York: Bantam.

Nhat Hanh, T. (1975). *The miracle of mindfulness: A manual on meditation.* Boston: Beacon Press.

Redfield, J. (1994). *The Celestine prophecy.* New York: Warner.

Tart, C. T. (1994). *Living the mindful life.* Boston: Shambhala.

6. GRATITUDE AND GENEROSITY:
Engaging A Prosperous Life

Chopra, D. (1993). *Creating affluence: Wealth consciousness in the field of all possibilities.* San Rafael, CA: New World Library.

Chopra, D. (1994). *The seven spiritual laws of success.* San Rafael, CA: Conari Press.

Conari Press Editors. (1993). *Random acts of kindness.* Berkeley, CA: Conari Press.

Conari Press Editors. (1994). *More random acts of kindness.* Berkeley, CA: Conari Press.

Dore, C. (1995). *The powervision manuscript: An emergency handbook for getting money fast.* Newport Beach, CA: PowerVision Publishing.

Fox, M., & Sheldrake, R. (1996). *Natural grace: Dialogues on creation, darkness, and the soul in spirituality and science.* New York: Doubleday.

Harvey, A. (1994). *The way of passion: A celebration of Rumi.* Berkeley, CA: Frog Ltd.

Mandel, B. (1994). *Wake up to wealth.* Berkeley, CA: Celestial Arts.

McCarty, M. & McCarty, N. (1994). *Acts of kindness: How to create a kindness revolution.* Deerfield Beach, FL: Health Communications.

Roman, S., & Packer, D. (1988). *Creating money.* Tiburon, CA: Kramer.

Roman, S. (1986). *Living with joy.* Tiburon, CA: Kramer.

Ryan, M. J. (Ed.) (1994). *A grateful heart: Daily blessings for the evening meal from Buddha to the Beatles.* Berkeley, CA: Conari Press.

7. ONENESS AND INTERCONNECTION:
The Interplay of Collective Consciousness

Gold, P. (1994). *Navajo & Tibetan sacred wisdom: The circle of the spirit.* Rochester, VT: Inner Traditions International.

Harvey, A. (1996). *The essential mystics: The soul's journey into truth.* New York: HarperCollins.

Roberts, B. (1993). *The experience of no-self: A contemplative journey.* New York: State University of New York Press.

Sheldrake, R. (1991). *The rebirth of nature: The greening of science and God.* New York: Bantam.

Sheldrake, R. (1988). *The presence of the past: Morphic resonance and the habits of nature.* New York: Vintage.

Spretnak, C. (1991). *States of grace: The recovery of meaning in the post-modern age.* San Francisco: Harper.

Weber, R. (1986). *Dialogues with scientists and sages: The search for unity.* London: Routledge and Kegan Paul.

Wolf, F. A. (1994). *The dreaming universe: A mind-expanding journey into the realm where psyche and physics meet.* New York: Simon & Schuster.

Wolinsky, S. (1993). *Quantum consciousness: The guide to experiencing quantum psychology.* Norfolk, CT: Bramble Books.

Wright, M. S. (1983). *Behaving as if the God in all life mattered.* Jeffersonton, VA: Perelandra.

Zohar, D. (1990). *The quantum self: Human nature and consciousness defined by new physics.* New York: Morrow.

8. CREATING POSSIBILITY:
The Dance of Intention and Synchronicity

Boyd, C. (1974). *Rolling Thunder.* New York: Delta/Random House.

Combs, A., & Holland, M. (1996). *Synchronicity: Science, myth and the trickster.* (2nd Ed.). New York: Marlowe.

Davies, P., & Gribbin, J. (1992). *The matter myth: Dramatic discoveries that challenge our understanding of physical reality.* New York: Simon & Schuster.

Dossey, L. (1989). *Recovering the soul: A scientific and spiritual search.* New York: Bantam.

Gawain, S. (1983). *Creative visualization.* New York: Bantam.

Goswami, A. (1993). *The self-aware universe: How consciousness creates the material world.* New York: Tarcher/Putnam.

Kaku, M. (1994). *Hyperspace: A scientific odyssey through parallel universes, time warps, and the tenth dimension.* New York: Oxford University Press.

Miller, T. E. (1991). *Fools Crow wisdom and power.* Tulsa, OK: Council Oak Books.

Murphy, M. (1991. *The future of the body: Exploration into the further evolution of human nature.* Los Angeles: Tarcher.

Peat, F. D. (1987). *Synchronicity: The bridge between matter and mind.* New York: Bantam.

Seligman, M. (1990). *Learned optimism: How to change your mind and your life.* New York: Pocket Books.

Storr, A. (1983). *The essential Jung.* Princeton, NJ: Princeton University Press.

Talbot, M. (1986). *Beyond the quantum.* New York: Bantam.

Talbot, M. (1991). *The holographic universe.* New York: HarperCollins.

Vaughn, A. (1979). *Incredible coincidence: The baffling world of synchronicity.* New York: Ballantine.

Wolf, F. A. (1988). *Parallel universes.* New York: Touchstone.

9. OPENING TO YOUR OPTIMAL FUTURE:
Saying Yes to All You Can Be

James, T. (1989). *The secret of creating your future.* Honolulu: Advanced NeuroDynamics.

Kabbalah Learning Center. "The Kabbalah Beginner Course." Audiocassette series. Available from: The Kabbalah Learning Center, 83-84 615th Street, Richmond Hills, New York 11418, 718-805-9122.

Lazaris. "The Future Self." Two-tape audiocassette presentation. Available from Concept Synergy, Post Office Box 3285, Palm Beach, FL 33480, 1-800-678-2356.

Napier, N. J. (1986). "Envisioning Your Future," "Your Optimal Life Path." Guided Meditations on CD. New York: Nancy J. Napier, www.nancynapier.com.

Napier, N. J. (1990). *Recreating Your Self: Increasing self-esteem through imaging and self-hypnosis.* New York: Norton.

Napier, N. J. (1990). "Your Future Self." Guided Meditation on CD. New York: Nancy J. Napier, www.nancynapier.com.

Napier, N. J. (1993). *Getting through the day*. New York: Norton.

Roberts, J. (1974). *The nature of personal reality*. Englewood Cliffs, NJ: Prentice-Hall.

Roman, S. (1989). *Spiritual growth: Being your higher self*. Tiburon, CA: Kramer.

Zdenek, M. (1987). *Inventing the future*. New York: McGraw-Hill.

10. INTUITION AND WELL-BEING:
Affirmation, Prayer, Guides, and Other Nonlocal Phenomena

Anderson, J. W. (1994). *An angel to watch over me*. New York: Ballantine.

Anderson, J. W. (1992). *Where angels walk: True stories of heavenly visitors*. New York: Ballantine.

Burnham, S. (1990). *A book of angels*. New York: Ballantine.

Burnham, S. (1991). *Angel letters*. New York: Ballantine.

Burns, L. (1985). *Develop your psychic abilities: And get them to work for you in your daily life*. New York: Pocket Books.

Doore, G. (Ed.). (1987) *Shaman's path: Healing, personal growth and empowerment*. Boston: Shambhala.

Dossey, L. (1993). *Healing words: The power of prayer and the practice of medicine*. New York: HarperCollins.

Durckheim, K. G. (1989). *The call for the master: The meaning of spiritual guidance on the way to the self.* New York: Dutton.

Easwaran, E. (1987). *The constant companion.* Petaluma, CA: Nilgiri Press.

Einstein, P. (1992). "Uncommon sense total intuition system." Six-tape audiocassette series, including workbook. Available from: Uncommon Communications, Inc., 561 Hudson Street, Box 57, New York, NY 10014.

Halifax, J. (1991) *Shamanic voices: A survey of visionary narratives.* New York: Viking Penguin.

Harner, M. (1990). *The way of the shaman.* New York: HarperSanFrancisco.

Houston, J. (1987). *The search for the beloved: Journeys in mythology and sacred psychology.* New York: Putnam.

Jovanovic, P. (1995). *An inquiry into the existence of guardian angels.* New York: M. Evans & Company.

Keating, T. (1994). *Intimacy with God.* New York: Crossroads.

Lazaris. "The Unseen Friends." Audiocassette. Available from: Concept Synergy, Post Office Box 3285, Palm Beach, FL 33480, 1-800-678-2356.

Matthews, J. (Ed.). (1992) *Paths to peace: A collection of prayers, ceremonies, and chants from many traditions.* Boston: Charles E. Tuttle.

Miller, C. (1995). *Creating miracles: Understanding the experience of divine intervention.* Tiburon, CA: Kramer.

Roads, M. (1987). *Talking with nature.* Tiburon, CA: Kramer.

Roads, M. (1990). *Journey into nature.* Tiburon, CA: Kramer.

Roman, S. (1986). *Personal power through awareness*. Tiburon, CA: Kramer.

Targ, R., & Harary, K. (1984). *The mind race: Understanding and using psychic abilities*. New York: Villard.

Vaughn, F. (1979). *Awakening intuition*. New York: Anchor Books.

Whitaker, K. (1991). *The reluctant shaman: A woman's first encounter with the unseen spirits of the earth*. New York: HarperSanFrancisco.

11. PRACTICING WHOLENESS:
Putting It All Together

Anderson, S., & Hopkins, P. (1992). *The feminine face of God: The unfolding of the sacred in women*. New York: Bantam.

Cameron, J. (1992). *The artist's way: A spiritual path to higher creativity*. New York: Putnam.

Feinstein, D., & Mayo, P. (1990). *Rituals for living and dying*. San Francisco: Harper.

Fox, M. (1994). *The reinvention of work: A new vision of livelihood for our time*. New York: HarperCollins.

Lagatree, K. (1996). *Feng Shui: Arranging your home to change your life*. New York: Villard.

Levine, S. (1991). *Guided meditations, explorations and healings*. New York: Anchor.

Linn, D. (1995). *Sacred space: Clearing and enhancing the energy of your home*. New York: Ballantine.

Rossback, S. (1991). *Feng Shui: The Chinese art of placement*. New York: Penguin Arkana.

Scott, G. (1991). *Shamanism and personal mastery: Using symbols, rituals, and talismans to activate the powers within you.* New York: Paragon House.

Spear, W. (1995). *Feng shui made easy: Designing your life with the ancient art of placement.* New York: HarperSanFrancisco.

Swan, J. (Ed.). (1991). *The power of place: Sacred ground in natural and human environments.* Wheaton, IL: Quest.

Venolia, C. (1988). *Healing environments: Your guide to indoor well-being.* Berkeley, CA: Celestial Arts.

www.ingramcontent.com/pod-product-compliance
Lightning Source LLC
Chambersburg PA
CBHW021800220426
43662CB00006B/130